RITALIN
NATION

RITALIN
NATION

*Rapid-fire Culture and the Transformation
of Human Consciousness*

Richard DeGrandpre

W. W. NORTON & COMPANY

NEW YORK · LONDON

For information about permission to reproduce selections from this book,
write to Permissions, W. W. Norton & Company, Inc., 500 Fifth Avenue,
New York, NY 10110.

The text of this book is composed in Electra
with the display set in Humanist 777.
Desktop composition by Justine Burkat Trubey
Manufacturing by Quebecor Printing, Fairfield, Inc.
Book design by Jo Anne Metsch

Library of Congress Cataloging-in-Publication Data
DeGrandpre, Richard J.
Ritalin nation : rapid fire culture and the transformation of human
consciousness / Richard J. DeGrandpre.
p.   cm.
Includes bibliographical references and index.
ISBN 0-393-04685-0
1. Attention-deficit hyperactivity disorder—Social aspects—United States.
2. Methylphenidate hydrochloride. 3. United States—Civilization 1945–
4. Diagnostic errors. I. Title.
RJ506.H9D476   1999
618.92'8589—dc21   98-20687
CIP

W. W. Norton & Company, Inc., 500 Fifth Avenue, New York, N.Y. 10110
http://www.wwnorton.com
W. W. Norton & Company Ltd., 10 Coptic Street, London WC1A 1PU

1 2 3 4 5 6 7 8 9 0

Contents

In the '90s, ADD has emerged as a symbol of American life.

EDWARD HALLOWELL, coauthor, *Driven to Distraction*

Preface

RITALIN is a drug, a stimulant drug, used in the psychiatric treatment of millions of children in the United States. These children are said to suffer from attention deficit disorder (ADD), which Ritalin treats by calming them down. *Ritalin Nation* is the story of the fastest culture on earth—American culture—and how this culture of speed has transformed human consciousness and, in doing so, created a nation hooked on speed and the stimulant drugs that simulate speed's mind-altering effects. For most of us, our dependence on pharmacological versions of speed begin and end with caffeine. For millions of others, however, the pharmacological solution to the growing need for speed extends far beyond the occasional can of Coke or cup of coffee. These solutions include powerful stimulants like cocaine, methamphetamine, and Ritalin, all of which have very similar pharmacological properties.

The "ADD" child is of course the perfect example of the need for constant sensory consumption. Studies have documented, for example, how hyperactive, attention deficit children turn into everyday normal children under sensory-rich conditions. They have shown how these children begin to fall apart when the sensory stream begins to fade. They have also shown how, under suboptimal sensory conditions, children are calmed by the backdrop of stimulation that Ritalin so elegantly provides (a pharmacological effect that also happens to occur in most children). Thus, for the millions of children who are currently lining up for Ritalin, and for the many thousands of adults who have also begun to use it, the problem has less to do with an innate brain dysfunction, for which there still remains no scientific evidence, and more to do with how the rise of rapid-fire culture this century has transformed human consciousness.

In this book I have tried to clarify the relationships among rapid-fire culture, consciousness, and our growing reliance on stimulant drugs. From the start, my goal has been a simple one: to tear down the mythology that enshrouds ADD and its Ritalin solution and replace it with a clear and sensible account of what is happening to all of us as a result of our hectic, hurried lives.

All this began for me several years ago with an episode of *60 Minutes*. Listening to their report on the rising popularity of Ritalin, I was surprised and troubled by the absurd explanations so-called experts gave for how Ritalin affects the behavior of the "ADD" child. I was equally struck by the fact that millions of American children were now being diagnosed with ADD and given Ritalin, a practice that accounts for about 80 percent of all Ritalin consumption in the world. Both these findings persuaded me that I should do something, partly because, as someone with special training in both pharmacology and psychological science, I knew that the popular understanding was riddled with misinformation. Ritalin is not a special medication for children that corrects some brain abnormality. Indeed, its history of street abuse as a run-of-the-mill psychostimulant is at least as long as its history as a drug of choice for children. Nor is ADD an established medical disorder. Aside from a small percentage of children who have had an identifiable injury or illness that led to hyperactivity, there is no evidence whatsoever that the problems defined as ADD have a clear-cut biological origin. In fact, longitudinal studies have shown that these problems, and a whole host of other childhood problems, are developing more and more frequently in our society. This rise in prevalence of these problems can be explained only in terms of the changes that have been taking place in the fabric of daily American life.

WHEN one reads this book, it may be useful to keep in mind its organization. The first chapter provides an introduction to rapid-fire culture and its transformation of human consciousness. Chapters 2 and 3 take a step back from the present moment to provide a history of how we arrived at where we are today. Specifically, Chapter 2 examines the nature and history of time and how changes in ways of living (and thinking) have transformed the rhythm of people's lives and their experience of time. Chapter 3 puts this into the context of the twentieth century, when all that was slow began to accelerate, from modes of transportation to modes of communication, ending in present-day America with rapid-fire culture in full swing. This sets the stage for Chapters 4 and 5, which explore the nature of the problems defined as "ADD" (Chapter 4) and the nature of the solution defined as Ritalin (Chapter 5). (Readers who have an immediate concern with these two themes might first read these two chapters and then return to Chapters 2 and 3 afterward.) The book ends with Chapter 6 with some practical suggestions about how to bring greater sanity to our hectic lives. I propose that we can do this by doing two things: first, by developing a greater understanding of the societal forces that alter us psychologically and push our lives in directions we would not consciously choose and second, by learning to live more deliberately, so that what happens to us and our children is something that we plan according to specific priorities and choices rather than something we fall into by accident.

IN the writing of this book, a number of individuals proved to be of considerable help, both editorially and emotionally. My good friend Terry Racich served as the "first reader" of the book, and to her I owe a great many thanks. My editor at Norton, Angela von der Lippe, who had the courage and, I think, wisdom to take on a topic as controversial and divisive as this one, also deserves special appreciation. Angela's assistant at Norton, Ashley Barnes, generously provided detailed and insightful editorial assistance, which was enormously helpful. Also of editorial assistance was Lou Haag, who carefully read and commented on early versions of the manuscript and provided early encouragement. I also want to thank my friends Paul, Debra, and Bruce for their help and support, a number of students who assisted me in the research and writing of this book, including Laura Smack, Amy LaFreniere, JoAnn Hurst, Dan Triggs, and Craig Farnum, and colleagues Sharon Lamb and Richard Kujawa. Thanks to you all.

THIS book is dedicated to my mother, Leona F. DeGrandpre.

RITALIN
NATION

The Hurried Society and
Its Experience

Please let me tell you about boredom, let me go on about the exquisite varieties of boredom I have known and attempt to describe the range of my indifference. I promise to make it absorbing—indeed the very prospect of doing so opens before me such an ocean of boredom, such a dismal, flat, immensity in which to pull you in after me that I'd better not try it because it probably won't work. The failure of boredom is that it is never gripping.

KEN JACOBS,
"The Day the Moon Gave Up the Ghost"

IN the 1950s we envisioned a promised land of halcyon days and pacific nights. Life, we thought, was on the verge of blossoming into an endless seascape of rest and relaxation. Books were even sold about how to cope with the impending "crisis" of having too much free time. Now, only a few decades later, this hypnotic vision of a golden age has mysteriously washed away into a never-ending stream of rapid-fire days and jetlag nights. We're either in a rush, recovering from the rush, or rushing to rush some more. As a cover of an *Utne Reader* magazine headlined in 1994, "TOO BUSY Even to Read this Magazine? Then Read this Magazine!"[1] Of course we don't remember the national referendum to abandon our hopes and dreams for a tranquil future, because no such referendum ever happened. Far from being a choice, the *hurried society* is a curious and seemingly chronic cultural affliction. We know not from where it came; we're only certain that it's got to go. . . . And go it does.

How is it that we have become a nation strung out on excitement? Or, as the existential novelist Milan Kundera has asked, "Why have the pleasures of slowness disappeared?"[2] Leisure, slowness, idleness, relaxation, simplicity—these all have become past-times of American culture, replaced by an almost singular obsession with speed. Even a British lord visiting over one hundred years ago took notice of the urgency that animates everyday American life, prompting him to ask: "Gentlemen, why in heaven's name this haste?" Another British lord, philosopher Bertrand Russell, wrote the essay "In Praise of Idleness," published in 1932 in *Harper's* magazine. He voiced a similar concern: "Hitherto we have continued to be as energetic as we were before there were machines. In this we have been foolish, but there is no reason to go on being foolish forever."[3]

For reasons we shall explore in this book, both leisure and slowness have been overthrown in a conquest for excitement and speed. This raises provocative questions: Is attention deficit disorder (ADD; or as it is now called, attention deficit hyperactivity disorder, or ADHD) really a newly discovered medical disease, or is it a culture-induced brain dysfunction that results from our growing addiction to speed? Might the craze over stimulants like cocaine, crack, methamphetamine, and ecstasy in the 1980s and 1990s have a deep cultural connection to our speeding-up society? And might the rush for speed also be connected with the rise of coffee/caffeine culture and the Ritalin solution?

That we have become a Ritalin Nation is obvious when we look at the brief history of this stimulant drug. ADD has become the most commonly diagnosed child psychiatric disorder in the United States. Ritalin, prescribed as treatment for ADD in about 90 percent of all cases, is a powerful psychostimulant that, when taken via the same route of administration, has pharmacological and psychological effects that are almost indistinguishable from those of cocaine.[4] Prior to the 1960s hyperactivity and attention deficits were rarely noticed and rarely treated as medical problems. Then, in 1961, the Food and Drug Administration (FDA) approved Ritalin for use in children with behavior problems. By 1975, 150,000 children in the United States were being prescribed drugs to reduce

Culture-Induced ADD?

Edward Hallowell, coauthor of the bestseller *Driven to Distraction* (1994), has been a leading voice in the ADD/Ritalin movement. Unfortunately his book, published one year after Peter Kramer's *Listening to Prozac*, offers its readers much the same playful sensibility about how we should tinker with our physiology (via drugs) and try to have more fun with what these authors see as our hard-wired, inherited pathologies. This attitude of succumbing to our inner sickness was especially clear in a 1997 article by Hallowell in *Psychology Today* on "ADD: Why I'm Glad I Have It." But even Ted Hallowell agrees that culture plays a clear role in "ADD," as is suggested in his writings on "A Culture Driven to Distraction:"[7] He writes:

—*America today suffers from culturally induced attention deficit disorder, or what I call "pseudo-ADD." That's one reason ADD has captured the imagination of so many people, and why the diagnosis has become so seductive that it sometimes seems more like a designer label on a piece of clothing than a real, potentially disabling disorder.*

—*Pseudo-ADD has many of the same core symptoms as true ADD—a high level of impulsivity, an ongoing search for high stimulation, a tendency to restless behavior and impatience, and a very active, fleeting attention span.*

—*It's easy to see how our culture can induce an ADD-like state. When I was a little boy, growing up in the 1950's, television had only recently come into every American's living room, and dial telephones had not yet appeared in my small town. Now we all have access to everyone else, any time, anywhere, always. A colleague of mine recently received 40,000 pieces of e-mail in a week. Computers, cell and car phones, satellite technology, fax, copy and answering machines, VCRs, cable TV, the Internet, video conferences—all these are now commonplace. We are, as the cliché has it, wired—stimulated and speeded up day and night, constantly sending and receiving messages. . . .*

While these remarks are certainly appropriate, one problem remains. A common criticism of the ADD label has been that physicians cannot reliably tell the difference between normal children and those who at times appear to have ADD. In the above, Hallowell brings to the table a third category, asking us to distinguish among the healthy child, the child with biologically based ADD, and the child with culture-based ADD. Nobody doubts that a small number of children are born with or, because of disease or head trauma, develop the symptoms of ADD. What inquiring minds want to know is, What percentage is ultimately determined by biology and what percentage by culture?

their hyperactivity, prompting Peter Schrag and Diane Divoky to write *The Myth of the Hyperactive Child*. By the late 1980s Ritalin was in regular use in about 1 million American children, and in 1988 there were twenty-nine chapters of the new support group, CH.A.D.D. (Children and Adults with Attention Deficit Disorder). In 1989 child advocate Alfie Kohn raised further doubts about the legitimacy of the "ADD" disorder in an *Atlantic Monthly* essay titled "Suffer the Restless Children." Since then Ritalin has grown in use to more than 2 million children (and increasing numbers of adults), with an almost fivefold increase in its consumption in as many years. In fact, the United States consumes a whopping 80 to 90 percent of the total Ritalin consumption in the world. Meanwhile, with the huge financial boost from Ritalin's manufacturer, Novartis (previously CIBA Pharmaceuticals), more than five hundred new chapters of the CH.A.D.D. support group have sprung up, welcoming more than 32,000 members.[5] The U.S. Drug Enforcement Administration estimates that by the year 2000, 15 percent of all school-age children (8 million) will go on to use Ritalin.[6] Welcome to Ritalin Nation.

THE RUSH OF RAPID-FIRE CULTURE

QUESTIONS about speed are gaining greater relevance in these times, as the pace of American life continues to accelerate; this century even the acceleration of culture itself has been accelerating.[8] As a consequence of speedup, the overall pace of our lives, day in and day out, now far exceeds that of any other nation. To give an example of the rush in American culture today, a study found in 1971 that *one in five* adults surveyed said they felt "always" rushed. By 1992 this number had jumped to more than *one in three*.[9] The lives of children have undergone a similar acceleration. As David Elkind writes in *The Hurried Child*, "Today's child has become the unwilling, unintended victim of overwhelming stress—the stress borne of rapid, bewildering social change and constantly rising expectations."[10] No wonder more and more Americans have begun questioning the virtues of our national obsession with speed, in which all things are to happen quicker, sooner, faster.

Now whether or not you see your life, or your children's lives, as sped up, chances are you're underestimating the changes that have taken place. One reason is that the speeding up of society has been gradual enough over the years that the current pace of life is often experienced as normal or ordinary. As society goes faster, so do the rhythms of our own consciousness. This is especially true for children, who grow up in concert with the latest speed. As an eighth-grade teacher complains, "The reason our children don't follow directions is that they're tuned out. These children don't listen. They have so much stimulation—they're used to the TV blaring, the stereo, the household commotion. I'm not sure so many are ADHD; they're just restless because they don't have anything inside. They're so used to being entertained."[11] As this passage suggests, by our adapting to speedup, the transformation of human consciousness actually has the unanticipated effect of neutralizing its intended rewards. We pursue newness and change yet quickly come to experience these changes as no more stimulating than before. Hence, it's not until we compare our lives with the generation before us, or the generation before it, that we really see the hurried society taking shape.

When Sean Connery returned as James Bond in the 1983 production *Never Say Never Again*, the newest in high-tech gadgetry was, as usual, put at his disposal. When you watch this film today, however, you notice something peculiar: In a crowded casino setting, where various games of chance are available for play, many are shown playing Atari video games, as if they were some exotic activity. In one scene Bond actually finds himself in the middle of one of these games, playing for high stakes against his antagonist. What these scenes make clear, at least in hindsight, is how quickly the "state-of-the-art" technology can become just a silly old game. The mind neutralizes our gains by adapting to our attempts to rev it up.

Two other simple but revealing examples are the old rotary phones and the old-fashioned bathroom sinks with their separate hot and cold faucets. With the technological advances of Touch-Tone dialing and the single-tap faucet, these devices have not only been simplified but have also been sped up. They give us exactly what they always did, but they do it faster. Just how sped up we have become in return is apparent whenever we stumble upon these antiquated devices today. Have you ever stood there fretting, tapping your foot, waiting impatiently for the rotary dial to unwind itself, one number at a time? Have you ever scalded your hands with hot water because you refused to take the time to fill the basin with both hot and cold? If either of these actions applies to you or those around you, then you know, at least historically, that life is speeding up. Remember, these devices were not a source of frustration for earlier generations. The only reason this old, once very useful technology seems out-of-date today is that it has fallen behind the pace of contemporary consciousness. Indeed, these very same tools of daily existence were once "this year's model," and they too sped up the life that existed before them. Hence, it's not the advance of technology per se but rather its impact on our attention, awareness, desires, and frustrations that is important.

The rush of American life that has emerged as a consequence of this impact often gives outsiders the impression that some urgent task has been undertaken to save the nation. While there can be no doubt that the hurried society today has a connection to our energetic national temperament and the extraordinary technological revolutions of our time, the quickening of American life also seems to have much to do with individualist themes. When we hear liberal cries for revitalizing our communities or conservative cries for more traditional values—both of which are heard often enough—

what we're really hearing is a concern people share about American life becoming too isolated, too hedonistic, and too short on civility. As we come to rely less on others and have fewer others to rely on ourselves, we lose the obvious virtues of social organization. If something needs fixing, we know no one who can (or is willing to) fix it; if grandma lives eight hundred miles away, she cannot take care of the kids; if an adolescent cannot stand the lack of privacy at home, she or he moves out.

None of these problems will be solved by our supposed technological interconnectedness. Technology always serves to mediate our experience, coming between one and another; thus it fits in best where human connections are already broken. Electronic mail and "chat rooms" are good examples since they represent how social interactions mediated by technology lack much or all of the emotionality and intimacy that we, as social animals, ultimately need and desire. Meanwhile, everyone knows the result: With everyone having to fend for himself or herself, we have become a societal puzzle made up of millions of distinct pieces, with individuals and families all scrambling in different directions trying to satisfy their own isolated wants and needs. Naturally, children are the ones who suffer most here, since these individualized priorities are not tailored by or even for them.

Consequently, because of the rush, the bottom line in American life has become—as the very phrase "bottom line" suggests—*numerical.* The world has become a more one-dimensional place, where all is evaluated quantitatively or economically. This quantitative worldview can be seen, for example, in the debate over assisted suicide, in which we're struggling to come to grips with the difficult fact that life is not only about quantity (how long we live) but also about quality (how well we live). The problem is that the first of these, quantity, seems so easy to formulate, whereas the second, quality, seems almost impossible. The numerical bottom line is also summed up in the prevailing assumption that "the person with the most toys wins," the ethos of shop-until-you-drop materialism. Today the acquisition of material goods as a way to infuse one's life with meaning has become an all too easy and all too common— *and all too unsuccessful*—solution. A 1997 study that tried to quantify this love of the inanimate object, for example, reported that 57 percent of women and 42 percent of men said they were more excited by the idea of an unlimited shopping spree than the idea of sex.[12] And with the quantity question eclipsing the question of quality, we're seeing the soothing and solid replaced more and more by the fast and cheap. Typically this goes unnoticed, however, since the opportunity to consume more is afforded by the fact that things wear out faster or are thrown away rather than fixed. Sadly, this often includes even our own personal relationships.

As we find ourselves wanting to do more of A, B, and C, at the same time having to do more of X, Y, and Z, it's no surprise, then, that our lives are more hurried than ever before. Moreover, as our lives assume this shape, there's a growing need for each of us to connect the hurried society to our own conscious experience of it. In the end it's not just that we and our children *are* more hurried; we also *feel* more hurried. This feeling should be taken as a warning that we have fallen into attitudes and habits toward living that are not in fact leading to the promised land, for neither ourselves nor our children.

CONSCIOUSNESS UNDER FIRE

LIFE in rapid-fire culture means first and foremost a life in constant motion, an end to slowness. In these times of rush, either we are in motion or something's in motion around us. Within this hurried sphere of motion, both the pace of life and the intensity of the stimulus world around us continue to intensify, largely because of ongoing transformations taking place in the modes of human experience. Whether it's electricity, division of labor, industrial automation, the telephone, the cinema, the automobile, the television, the jet airliner, the computer, the fax machine, or the virtual worlds of cyberspace, the hard structures of daily life continue to cast and recast the nature of interpersonal relationships, from social and romantic relationships to relationships between parents and their children. As they do, they're also radically transforming time, space, and the fabric of human consciousness. Rapid-fire culture gives rise to a rapid-fire consciousness, an unsettling temporal disturbance of the self that then motivates an escape from *slowness*, thus keeping us forever in the grip of the hurried society.

The first step in drawing this connection between consciousness and the hurried society is to realize that we live in a culture that is absolutely saturated with stimuli. We all are in the world, and it is spinning around us faster and faster. Have you noticed how, wherever you go these days and whether you like it or not, there is always some sight, some sound, or some smell fighting for your attention? There's "Attention, shoppers!" at the market. There are bigger and brighter signs and billboards lining the stores, the streets and highways, and even whole buses. There's the blaring music (and TV!) when we fill up at the pumping station. There's the pounding bass that reverberates out of the rap mobiles and muscle cars cruising with their thirty-inch woofers turned up and their windows rolled down. There's the uninvited "entertainment" sent through the phone as we're put on hold, and there're the annoying, random phone calls we receive from our "friend" the telesalesperson. There's the constant begging for our money that shows up each day in our junk mail. There's the sensorium of watch alarms, car alarms, and ringing cell phones. Of course there's also the endless Muzak that fills every office, elevator, coffeehouse, or restaurant. Everywhere we go it seems something has to be playing.

When I sit in my office at the college where I teach, I can hear the dull roar of traffic from outside. I cannot see the traffic from my window, and I cannot hear the contribution of any one car, but I nevertheless work with a constant blanket of noise filling the background. It's not that this noise is distracting or irritating, however; there's every evidence to suggest that if we work or live around some constant sound or smell, even sounds and smells that newcomers find unpleasant, we're apt to grow accustomed to and perhaps even become dependent on them. We all know those smells that give farmers their sense of home and security. Yet when we drive by their farms, we say, "Oh, how can they live with this smell?" Another, more extreme example is the veteran soldier who finds him or herself missing in some strange way the intensity of the combat experience. As Vietnam vets proved, we cannot necessarily expect someone just to switch overnight from living a violent and varied experience to living a calm and quiet one, a discovery that also has implications for how we are going to recover from our growing sensory addictions.

Again we see that the intrusion of unsolicited stimuli into our lives does not need to feel obtrusive in order for it to have a real effect on the rhythm of our consciousness. As though we have stepped off a carnival ride and still feel the world spinning, there's a tendency to incorporate the sensory world into our own expectations about the speed at which the world should turn. Even if we do not find disturbing the bombardment of buzzes and whistles from the outside world, we are likely still to develop a psychological tolerance to them. Taken as a whole, then, this means that our sense of what is a "normal" sensory experience can, and for most of us does, far exceed that which was considered normal and acceptable by earlier generations. The negative consequence is that with uninvited stimuli constantly hitting us from all directions, we are developing an unconscious need for increased stimulation. *We're not just moving through our lives faster; we're also acquiring a heightened need for speed.*

This notion of tolerance takes on even greater importance as we consider a second and more powerful realm of stimulation in our lives; that ever-widening ocean of stimuli that both adults and children voluntarily bring to the shores of their own consciousness. If we return to my office for a moment, we can hear a murmur of traffic in the background that did not exist, say, twenty years ago. In the foreground, however, within the confines of my small office, there is a whole other dimension of buzzes and whistles that I myself can turn off and on. Even if I put up a note saying "Do not disturb," close my door, and open up a good book to read, there still remain several sensory worlds that can pop open at any time, gobbling up or short-circuiting my already shrunken attention span. From a single position in my small office, even if I exclude all those wonderful forms of stimulation that require no electricity (such as enjoying the view out the window), I can still print in any of several locations, write on either of two computers, send E-mail anywhere in the world, read E-mail, listen to phone mail, make a call, take a call, search the library shelves, wander around any number of databases, do some walking or talking on the Web, listen to my mini hi-fi stereo, or do any possible combination of the above. Thus, despite my sincere attempt to work in a rather isolated environment, it sometimes seems as if I am operating some kind of hotel switchboard, running the lives of dozens of people, all of whom go by the name me.

When looking at this sensorium of stimuli hovering around us, at all that is needed to make us feel alive in the moment, we have to wonder what this is doing to us in the long run. If we plug into potent sources of stimulation more and more, and stay plugged in for longer periods, what are the chances that at least some of us will develop restless minds and impulsive personalities? For children, this is an even greater concern, for they have more stimulus choices, less of an acquired taste for slow activities (such as chess or reading), and less self-control to manage these choices in a manner that produces a harmonious inner experience. Indeed, isn't it possible that over time we and our children are learning to indulge, rather than resist, our feelings of boredom by constantly switching our attention from one thing to something that is, at least for the moment, more immediately stimulating? Isn't it also possible that this switching strategy will make it gradually more difficult for us to take comfort in the quiet and the slow?

Of course not everyone has the kind of office switchboard available to him or her that I have. But it is a mistake to think you really need one. From the chemical shock wave of junk food to the bizarre, pseudoreality of phone sex, our society has gone to great lengths to ensure that there is plenty of stimulation to go around—twenty-four hours, seven days a week. In fact, when we do an anatomy of leisure time, it appears as though the single least expensive source of stimulation accounts for more than all the rest, especially for children: television.

Even if we ignore the overwhelming content problem that exists for television, there's still no doubting that TV fits the high-wired, impulsive lifestyle. How often do you turn on the TV "just to see what's on" and then find it difficult to turn it off? I've heard this confession dozens of times from friends and students, just as I have seen it described in studies of television addiction.[13] That so many people drift into TV world without thinking, or find they cannot separate from it once it's on, tells us how easy it is to forfeit self-control and succumb to the never-ending providers of effortless stimulation. In the case of children, this takes its greatest toll, for we know that they are much less likely to develop other ways of occupying themselves—other habits, other skills—as long as the television sits on its throne, staring down at them.

Like a cartoon I once saw of a man lounging in front of a television, saying to himself, "To think people are watching this," the popularity of television tells us that the stimuli in our environment do not have to be earth-shattering to seize upon our conscious minds. Even most children diagnosed with ADD have no problem attending to self-chosen television programs. As soap operas and repetitive computer video games prove time and time again, a steady flow of passive stimulation appears to be just as powerful as an overpowering explosion of sights and sounds, all of which have the same effect of raising our need for constant sensory consumption. Indeed, the history of television itself shows how much our visual technology alters our conscious perceptions.

Soon after television arrived on the scene, it became an impressive, sometimes even dazzling experience to watch, one that quickly put radio in the shadows. Now, many years later, we have become accustomed to larger higher-resolution color screens, remote controls and cable programming. Indeed, we are now waiting for the next leap forward in television technology: digital television (DTV). Unfortunately our own short-lived history with TV tells us that DTV will likely do to people's appreciation of color TV what color TV did to their appreciation of black and white. After all, do we really enjoy our larger than life TVs that much more than did earlier viewers growing up on black and white? When is the last time you heard someone say, "Isn't this color picture just stunning?" or "Isn't this remote control just the handiest thing you ever saw?" As we know but refuse to accept, excitement has a habit of wearing off; that's why we keep trading in our old sets for new ones. True, amazing improvements have been made in television, from picture quality to programming to video and remote control. But have these technological innovations really resulted in a change in quality of life? Most of us simply take them for granted, wanting more.

The mind's perpetual tolerance to the latest in technology also means that we are caught in the middle of an escalating competition for our attention. This in turn means that more and more powerful stimuli are being pointed at our senses, ultimately leading to greater sensory needs and a greater likelihood of withdrawal. Just compare television advertisements and television programming from the 1960s or even 1970s with those from the 1990s (even a comparison of the earliest and latest music videos shown on MTV provides a striking example). While the former sends Generation X children bouncing off the walls, the rapid and relentless succession of highly complex sounds and images that come from much of the latter gives older generations a splitting headache. Another example is spectator sports. To meet the growing needs of the sport spectator, there have been a number of attempts in recent years to speed up baseball; for example, much like the shot clock in basketball, in professional baseball there is a new twelve-second limit, within which the pitcher is obligated to throw the ball.[14] Similar attempts at speeding up sports include shorter time-outs and the elimination of jump balls in basketball, and the use of more powerful rackets in professional tennis. As these examples ultimately suggest, we are not going to understand why we as a nation have abandoned slowness—and why we suffer terribly as a consequence—until we realize that it is not just the hectic pace of life that makes the American experience unique. The speedup of culture means we experience more stimulus events each day, but the nature of these events also has undergone a dramatic transformation. This is why, to understand fully the nature and impact of rapid-fire culture, we must look at the intensity of the high-energy stimulus worlds that we, our friends, our children, and our fellow citizens all have been inhabiting since birth.

Why is it, though, that we are always turning up the stimulus? An obvious reason is that more intense stimuli do a better job of reaching our shortened attention spans; they may even keep us from making grave mistakes. Ultimately, though, the seduction of speed lies in the fact that once we develop expectations of a life of constant newness and change, the latest in speed becomes perpetually attractive. That is, once we engage in this inflationary logic, there is no escaping the consequence, which is that stimuli will have to be constantly intensified if we wish to recover the desired short-term rewards that can come from stimulus amplification. The history of the automobile demonstrates this inflationary practice. Many of the changes we interpret as mere aesthetic or technological improvements also represent changes in the intensity of the stimulus. Perhaps the best example is the change from the tiny taillights we see on wide-bodied cars from the 1950s and 1960s to the relatively giant taillights we find on many of today's economy cars. The fact that taillights have existed all along shows us that designers knew they were important. But why did they grow larger and brighter? It wasn't just speed, since many of the older cars drove at speeds similar to those of today. Rather, the answer seems to lie with the fact that the old lights no longer affect us as they once did. A related example is the brake lights that blind us from the rear window of the car in front. Again, why is it that we're having to add more light gradually to produce the same effect? A third example is the dashboard and interior lights. Anyone who drives a vintage car knows not only that today's instruments have been greatly expanded in size, but that their intensity has also been turned up several notches. Initially these changes probably enhanced the safety of driving. The real question, though, is whether these so-called improvements are lasting or simply producing a mode of consciousness that can now be reached only by the most intense stimuli.

This brings us to our third and final point regarding rapid-fire culture. With there being so many sources for obtaining effortless stimulation, and with these stimuli intensifying, we have to wonder not only about what we are spending our time doing but also about what we are doing no longer. While there is a rich complexity in the unplugged world, from working on a farm to building a table to reading a book, this nonelectrified mode of experience tends to be lost to the senses as we turn ourselves over to rapid-fire culture. Moving in and out of high-intensity environments is something done in many cultures around the world, from the fast, urban life of Japan to the autobahn of Germany. What keeps these accelerated moments in check are the *pockets of slowness* inserted between them. The French and Italians may drive like absolute lunatics (with their stereos blasting and their cell phones ringing), but they also may spend an hour or two each evening relaxing at the dinner

The Perpetual Lure of Speed

The changes that have taken place in processing speeds of computers in the past two decades have been dramatic. Our adaptation to these changes in speed has also been dramatic; hence, we are always wanting faster and faster machines. To see the changes in speed that have taken place, compare them with what would be comparable improvements in the automobile.[15] This story begins in 1981 with the Intel 8086 computer, which had an average speed of 4.77 megahertz and an average price of $5,000; in 1985 we had the Intel 80286 computer, with 10 MHz at $5,000; in 1992, the Intel 80486 computer, with 66 MHz at $4,000; in 1996, the Pentium computer, with 100 MHz at $3,000; and in 1998, the Pentium II computer, with 300 MHz, also at $3,000. Now if the same changes had taken place for, say, a 1981 BMW that cost $14,000, that earns 17 mpg, and that has a maximum cruising speed of 100 mph, we get the following results:

—The 1985 BMW should go 1,000 mph, get 170 mpg, and cost $14,000.
—The 1992 BMW should go 15,000 mph, get 550 mpg, and cost $11,200.
—The 1996 BMW should go over 100,000 mph, get 5,000 mpg, and cost under $8,400.
—The 1998 BMW should go more than 500,000 mph and cost the same $8,400.

In other words, if we drove our cars today at the same speed as we drive our computers, we could fill the tank and travel for 75,000 miles at 500,000 miles per hour. Imagine, then, how impressive it would be if each time we cranked up our little supercomputers, we continued to experience the same dramatic, cumulative difference between their pressing speeds and the sluggish machines of fifteen years ago. What actually happens may be disappointing, but it is also revealing: Each time we give in to the lure of speed and buy a faster computer (or for that matter any piece of "timesaving" technology), we reap the immediate rewards of making things go faster. But this typically turns out to be no more than a honeymoon experience. Like tolerance of drugs, after the latest speed has substituted itself as the new standard for our normative (expected) experience, we lose the joy of speed and are left instead with the residual, heightened expectations that make us yearn for even more. This means that those who go out of their way to purchase and use the fastest, newest machines also come to expect and require an almost instantaneous result. Consequently, unlike computer users of a decade ago, computer users today need be left in the lurch only for a few seconds before they begin to experience a growing sense of restlessness. If we substitute video game technology in place of computer technology, this finding applies equally well to children. They too have become adapted to increasingly sophisticated machines.

table. On the other hand, we in the United States were the first to lose the checks and balances afforded by downtime.

To appreciate this loss of downtime, you might stop reading and consider all the activities of a typical week for you and your children; then examine the number of activities that could be considered relatively high in intensity (watching TV or a video, munching on snacks, switching from activity to activity), those that would be considered active and of low intensity (gardening, reading a book, talking with a neighbor, meditating), and those that should be low intensity but are not because they're done in a rush (interacting with your children and vice versa, making or eating meals, or doing housework or homework). If as children or as adults we are always on the run, from when we get up in the morning until we go to bed, little opportunity is left for us to push the reset button and return us (and our minds) back to a rhythm of comfort and slowness.

EACH day we are the target of a flood of unsolicited stimuli, we are scheduling a constant and widening stream of activities into our daily lives, and in the meantime, we are gradually giving up the slow activities that could unwind us. The same holds true for kids. They too are bombarded by a flood of unsolicited stimuli, they are scheduled into the herky-jerky pace of daily life, and they never slow down enough to learn ways to live within slowness that could unwind them. These three points about consciousness under fire have, I think, a number of important psychological and social implications. Put in a nutshell, the problem of living in the hurried society lies in the utter impossibility of sustaining—minute by minute—the heightened sensory needs that result from chronic involvement in high-intensity lifestyles.

Everybody knows that each generation moves a little faster than the one before, but the pace of change this century, with its revolutionized modes of experience, has moved us into whole new dimensions of electronic reality and sensory drama. In fact, with the rise of the information age and the ubiquity of computers at home and work, we are splitting off into multiple selves. On the one hand, there is the *technological self*, in which the interface with technology synchronizes our conscious minds to the rhythm of the microchip and gives us increasingly realistic virtual worlds in which to live and dream; implants of microchips into the human brain (now under study in animals) may be the next step in our interfacing with the machine. There is, on the other hand, the *social self*, which moves within human relationships that operate at relatively slower speeds and with old-fashioned rules of engagement. It thus seems that until the former personality, the technological self, takes over the latter personality, the social self—a time when we will live only among virtual beings of our own design—the divided self will continue to be deeply conflicted. In other words, we will continue to suffer from wanting the best of two contradictory worlds: a technological, materialist world full of excitement and adventure and a social world full of security and tranquillity.

SENSORY ADDICTIONS: CULTURAL PROBLEMS HAVE A WAY OF BECOMING PSYCHOLOGICAL ONES

SENSORY addictions, whether in the child or adult, refer to a disturbance of conscious experience in which the person suffers from an inability to cope with *slowness*. As rapid-fire culture gives rise to a rapid-fire consciousness—and, for children, an inability to regulate their own behavior—sensory addictions develop, motivating us to engage in more stimulus-seeking behaviors. At the heart of this developmental problem lies the emergence of a phenomenological experience of unsettledness, characterized by feelings of restlessness, anxiety, and impulsivity. Hyperactivity and the inability to attend to mundane activities exemplify the type of escape behavior that the "sensory addicted" child or adult uses in order to maintain his or her needed stream of stimulation. This is why, for instance, when classroom activities are in fact engaging, the "ADD" child suddenly vanishes.[16] Of course the "solution" of having teachers and classrooms be more exciting, stimulating, or entertaining will not work because it will only perpetuate children's sensory addictions in the long run.

Our inability to cope with slow down has, in consequence, the destructive effect of keeping us from engaging in important but unstimulating activities, such as paying attention to classroom instruction, reading books, or stopping for a traffic light that's turning red. Indeed, the principal method of soothing our sensory addictions has been to make sure the needed flow of stimulation goes uninterrupted, a solution that has led to the use of powerful stimulant drugs like Ritalin. The success of Ritalin thus lies in the fact that it provides a potent backdrop of stimulation, freeing the individual of the need to engage in the sensation-seeking behaviors that define the ADD diagnosis. Consider the case of Eddie:

> Eddie, age nine, was referred to a child psychiatrist at the request of his school, because of the difficulties he creates in his class. . . . His teacher complains that he is so restless that the rest of the class is unable to concentrate. He is hardly ever in his seat, but roams around the class, talking to other children while they are working. He never seems to know what he is going to do next, and may suddenly do something quite outrageous. His most recent suspension was for swinging from the fluorescent light fitting over the blackboard, where he had climbed in the transition from one class to the next, and since he was unable to climb down again, the class was in an uproar. . . .When he was taking

[Ritalin] he was much easier to manage at school in that he was less restless and possibly more attentive, even though other aspects of his behavior were unsatisfactory.[17]

While stimulants were only partly effective in Eddie's case, because they have little effect on his problems with defiance and misconduct, it is nevertheless easy to see how Ritalin has its "calming" effects by providing him with a relatively intense, behaviorally independent source of stimulation. As long as Eddie has Ritalin, he no longer needs to leave his seat to produce his needed levels of stimulation.[18] In this sense, Ritalin has a prosthetic function much like that of the drug methadone: It does not eliminate the addiction but rather maintains it in a less destructive fashion. In the end, sensory addictions have the characteristic effect that all addictions have, which is to keep us from the activities that would unwind us, while motivating us to consume more of what has already made us addicted.

One reason why we fail to anticipate the possibility of sensory addictions has to do with the common but false belief that human consciousness has a fixed structure and rhythm that stand outside the assault of stimulus bombardment. In truth, consciousness is *adaptive*, meaning that one's current experience of space and time is *relative* to one's experiences. This confusion about the dynamic nature of consciousness helps explain why people rarely consider whether a lifetime in rapid-fire culture can actually radically change them, both inside—physiologically—and outside—behaviorally. I think my earliest introduction to the limits of the "untouchable" view of human consciousness was when I was a teenager taking driver's education. This was a lesson passed on to us future road warriors about the dangerous transition from highway to city speed. (This was Montana after all, with its wide open spaces and liberal speed limits.) You must realize, the instructor would say, that when you merge back into city traffic (dropping out of warp), you're apt to underestimate your own speed and drive too fast. The conclusion was immediately obvious to me as a budding psychologist: The mind adapts to higher speeds almost instantly, and then it unconsciously motivates us to conform to these elevated speeds, taking us with them into an accelerated future.

A second reason we fail to see how sensory addictions develop has to do with another false assumption, which is that speed, excitement, and consumption are the surest way, perhaps the only way, to maximize personal contentment. This way of thinking leads us to believe that a faster, more intense lifestyle cannot help translating into greater happiness or, inversely, that a life of slowness will mean we are letting life pass us by, that we are not living life "to the fullest." Even those who say they reject the material pursuit of happiness still have a tendency to live lives that suggest otherwise. In fact, this contradiction between one's actions, habits, and practices and one's thoughts and values reveals the powerful influence the hurried society has on us and our everyday lives.

Keeping in mind the idea, then, that human consciousness has a natural ability to absorb and adapt to intense stimulus experiences, we can consider why it might seem odd to suggest that our strung-out, pill-popping culture is addicted to excitement. As any thoughtful drug addict would freely remind us, life in the fast lane rarely delivers all that it promises. If each of us possesses a highly adapted consciousness that conforms to our surrounding levels of stimulation, it should be no surprise that it is next to impossible—at both a physiological and a psychological level—to sustain a continual sense of excitement. As Diane Ackerman tells us in A Natural History of the Senses (1990), we have long known that tolerance to stimulation is a basic process of our human nature: "Our senses crave novelty. Any change alerts them, and they send a signal to the brain. If there's no change, no novelty, they doze and register little or nothing. The sweetest pleasure loses its thrill if it continues too long. A constant state—even of excitement—in time becomes tedious, fades into the background, because our senses have evolved to report [only] changes. . . ."[19]

To see the real danger in this vicious cycle of speedup, though, we must also consider that the mind's elevated need for speed has a tendency to carry over and pollute other areas of living. Like many motorists who get stuck in traffic day after day yet never learn to relax, we find our overall sense of speed and urgency keeps us from adjusting to the slow spots that remain and that will always remain. We have to realize, after all, that much of what we do has not been and cannot be sped up. Sitting in traffic, waiting for the elevator, reading a book (forget speed reading), teaching your child to draw, and building a lasting, intimate relationship all are activities for which electronic appliances need not apply. Indeed, too many important activities in life today are being squeezed out of existence by the haste and impatience that are bubbling out of our heightened expectations about how fast the world must go. Adding to this is one of the ironies of the hurried society: As society speeds up, we want things to happen faster and faster, yet we increasingly lack the skills (and the time) to do anything ourselves. Whether it is changing the oil in our car, fixing the dishwasher, mending a torn pocket, recovering from illness, or resolving marital disputes, we have an increasing dependence on the services of others, for which we are increasingly made to wait!

As it turns out, then, rather than end up with a joyride of high excitement, or even a middle-of-the-road case of idle pleasure, what we are finding is that rapid-fire culture yields an insatiable, frustrated demand for constant stimulation. This is why you may find the claim that we are hooked on speed and excitement to be inconsistent with your own experience, since the adaptation to speed quickly nullifies the rush that initially comes from speeding up. Ask yourself, Do you fear an empty hour? When the jet stream of stimulation slows down, as it inevitably does, do you suffer a sense of unease, discomfort, restlessness, or anxiety? Can you sit still, and if so, can you do it comfortably and regularly? When you are brushing your teeth, for example, do you just stand there, or must you move around, pacing? When you're reading a book or listening to a slow or boring speaker, do you feel the impulse to get up and do something else? When your body is not racing but your mind still is, do you need a sleeping potion to knock you out? As these problems suggest, the hazard of plugging into high-intensity worlds is that they do not easily let go.

Realizing that sensory addictions do in fact exist, we can see why we, like Eddie in the example above, are unconsciously driven to avoid or escape any and all situations that lead to such unsettling sensations, as we do by engaging in more of the activities that can maintain a satisfactory level of stimulation. (We can also see why when we return from slow vacations in slow-paced cultures, like

Mexico, it may suddenly seem as though American culture were spinning out of control.) For adults as well as for kids, today's escape behaviors include a continuous stream of activities like watching television, playing computer games or having adventures in cyberspace, or talking on the phone, but they also encompass more subtle sources of self-stimulation, such as fidgeting, chronic use of caffeine, snacking on foods, smoking cigarettes, or simply living the lifestyle of keeping busy, always rushing from one activity to another. While some of these activities are intense and some are not, it is the overall volume of them one after another that ultimately yields a heightened need for speed.

Feeding the beast of our sensory addictions is not the only drawback of rapid-fire culture, however. We also have to consider the hazards of living in a society filled with people all trying to satisfy them. Even if we sidestep high-intensity worlds, as many from older generations have, we will nevertheless suffer as long as we live around those who haven't. Consider the elderly couple who unveil their vintage '66 Bonneville for a pleasant Sunday drive. They pull out of their garage and merge smoothly into traffic, traveling at exactly the same speed as everyone else . . . well, at least psychologically. The problem is that their sense of "cruising" has gradually fallen twenty years behind the inflationary pace of harried American life. They go at a speed that is comfortable to them, but this is not a comfortable speed for the rest of us. What we have here is a collision of two different temporal worlds. In order for these innocent bystanders of speedup to drive at the same objective speed as everyone else, they would have to go at a speed that for them would be both uncomfortable and potentially dangerous. Indeed, because many seniors have not succumbed to societal speedup, they are finding the world to be moving increasingly at the "wrong" speed. Even those of us with the appropriately shrunken attention spans are apt to draw the same conclusion: that the civility of public life is going out with a rush.[20]

ADDING INSULT TO INJURY: THE RITALIN SOLUTION

IN our zeal to build a world of action and adventure, we are undermining the very contentment we seek. Moreover, this consequence of rapid-fire culture has become especially difficult for children. Saturated in chronic stimulation from birth, more and more children are showing the signs of sensory addictions. Are children growing up at their own, natural pace, we might ask, or are they being sucked into the stream of hyperculture, where they too are developing heightened sensory expectations and at even earlier ages? Consider a study that compared the development of problem-solving styles in first graders who were taught by either slow-paced or fast-paced teachers. In their report—"The Effects of Teacher Tempo on the Child"—researchers concluded that while the first group of children learned to approach problems in a slow and careful manner, the second was markedly more impulsive.[21] This illustrates nicely how children readily incorporate the external rhythms of their surroundings.

This generational effect reminds me of an observation a close friend shared with me. Raising a son, he mentioned how he often found himself having to curb the urge to impose his own sense of time and speed on his toddler son, rather than let him determine his own pace. My friend, whom I would consider a rather patient person, noted how he would be ready to move on to another activity, but only because he himself had become bored. His son was still very much interested in what they were doing and was probably less than pleased, at least at first, with the sudden change to something new. Indeed, studies have shown that such overintrusiveness during the child's infant years actually predicts distractibility, which is an early precursor of later hyperactivity.[22] As one study describes, "the mother disrupts the baby's ongoing activity rather than adapting the timing and quality of her interactions and initiations to the baby's state, mood, and current interests." [23] Here again we have a case of two temporal worlds colliding.

Tragically the problems of sensory addictions in children have been obscured by the notion that millions of American children (and adults) are suffering from a ubiquitous biological disorder called ADD. Because many readers will undoubtedly have a particular interest in this topic, let us consider briefly some of the problems with this approach and then return to them in more detail in Chapter 4.

The American Psychiatric Association (APA) describes its recommendations for diagnosing and treating psychological problems in the *Diagnostic and Statistical Manual of Mental Disorders,* now it its fourth edition (*DMS IV,* 1994)[24]. Since the publication of the first *DSM,* the APA has repeatedly changed its mind about the nature of this problem. In *DSM I* (1952) the disorder was nonexistent; in *DSM II* (1968) it was defined as Hyperactive Reaction of Childhood; in *DSM III* (1989) it was defined as Attention Deficit Disorder; and in *DSM IV* it was defined as Attention Deficit Hyperactivity Disorder. What the APA would like us to believe is that this revisionism represents the mark of scientific progress. Medical science has defined the problem more precisely in recent times, psychiatrists would say, because modern tools and techniques have led to a better understanding of the etiology—the underlying causes—of ADD. However, when we examine the many labels that have been used to define the problem, we find that these shifts were never the result of any medical or scientific discovery. In fact, it is hard to imagine what kinds of discoveries would lead psychiatrists to change the diagnosis from a problem of behavior (hyperactivity) to one of attention (ADD) and then to problems with both behavior and attention (ADHD). If experimental or clinical research showed that the problem was really with attention rather than hyperactivity, why was hyperactivity reestablished as part of the diagnosis?

Numerous mental health professionals have remarked on the persistent bias in psychiatry toward a biological explanation of these problems.[25] Irwin Jay Knopf sums this up using an earlier label for ADD (minimal brain dysfunction, or MBD), writing that "it is difficult to understand how and why the concept of MBD and of its neurological basis has been so extensively accepted and perpetuated by many American writers in the absence of definitive corroborative evidence. In contrast, the idea of MBD is generally rejected by leading English writers as unsound and unsubstantiated."[26] So what is the basis for saying there is a brain disorder affecting millions of children, making them hyperactive or inattentive? Does ADD even exist? To answer these questions, we must make a crucial distinction between ADD as the *name* for a collection of symptoms, the causes of which are unknown, and ADD as a *cause* and *explanation* of these symptoms. While the former idea is undeniable, the latter is not.

More than anything else, ADD represents a growing prejudice in our culture—led in large part by the powerful influence of psychiatry professionals and pharmaceutical companies—which is that personality and behavioral traits are inborn and biological. This genetic viewpoint overshadows a view that is still dominant in psychology, however: the *developmental* view. This is the idea that over relatively long periods of time (years or decades), life events inculcate in children durable psychological traits that can be highly resistant to change. This enculturation process produces everyday, normal traits, like personality, language learning, social norms, and motor skills. But it can also produce unusual traits, such as psychopathology, genius, and criminal deviance. The advantage of developmental models lies in their ability to explain, for example, the ongoing changes we are currently observing in the societal prevalence of certain psychosocial problems, such as crime, drug abuse, child abuse, and suicide. Such changes cannot be explained away as biological disorders since this would mean that our overall genetic constitution (the human genome) has changed significantly in a very short period of time.

Indeed, despite the highly successful efforts by the APA to define ADD as a well-established disorder of the brain, three decades of medical science have yet to produce any substantive evidence to support such a claim. The current fashion is to link ADD to a chemical imbalance in the brain, or to abnormalities in the size of certain brain structures, or to a disorder of the brain's frontal lobes, where glucose utilization is thought to be abnormally low. In the 1970s psychiatrists argued similarly that hyperactivity resulted from a brain dysfunction, although the fashion then was to blame other brain structures, such as the reticular activating system (RAS) or the caudate nucleus (a nucleus of the brain responsible for inhibitory control of movement). No problems in any of these areas were ever established. Moreover, all this hints of pseudoscience, since scientists have failed to make the prima facie case that even if these were valid findings, they would represent anything more than the underlying physiological correlates of behavior, both of which could be the result of any number of developmental factors.

In medical terms, this way of thinking represents the failure to distinguish between physiological phenomena as *correlates* of behavior versus *causes* of behavior. The physiological process that corresponds with the behavior of, say, hyperactivity may in fact be caused by the same experiences that led to the hyperactivity itself. After all, behavior always has physiological strings attached, no matter what the ultimate causes of that behavior may be. For example, when two people behave in two different ways, such as when one scratches his head while another does not, we know that there are at the same time different brain processes going on inside their heads (i.e., the brain processes that govern intentional motor movements like head scratching). Realizing this obvious fact, we avoid the blunder made in biological psychiatry, in which it is assumed that such differences in brain processes must be the causes of the observed behaviors. To the contrary, the man scratches his head because it itches.

Because psychiatrists have not demonstrated any underlying biological causes of ADD, they are often asked to explain how they differentiate between the biological disorder of ADD and the normal behavioral fluctuations we see in children every day. When faced with this question, psychiatrists freely concede that there is no biomedical test for ADD. Instead, psychiatrists, general practitioners, and pediatricians all rely exclusively on observation and case histories in making their medical diagnoses. This means that if a child has some persistent problem with attention or hyperactivity, either at school or at home, he or she becomes, by virtue of this evidence alone, a candidate for the diagnosis. By interpreting any durable or enduring behavioral trait as the product of some singular, inner biological cause, however, physicians overlook the possibility of a developmental problem. In doing this, psychiatrists are jettisoning what was once a core tenet of theirs: that family, social, and cultural problems often manifest themselves as psychological ones.

Unlike the biologically reductionistic explanation of ADD, the possibility that ADD is really a culture-based, developmental syndrome allows for the changes we've seen taking place with regard to its prevalence. "When I was teaching 10 years ago, I hadn't even heard of Ritalin or attention deficit disorder."[27] This remark by a high school principal makes a very important point. Concern about widespread use and recreational abuse of Ritalin often raises the specter of overdiagnosis or the overprescribing of Ritalin. Yet this statement clearly suggests something else—namely, that problems of attention and hyperactivity have increased dramatically over the past few decades. If this were merely a case of labeling, then parents and teachers must have suddenly become very hostile to behaviors that have long existed, both at home and at school. In fact, the evidence points strongly in the other direction: Teachers today are faced more than ever with behaviorally, cognitively, and emotionally challenged kids.

For example, many teachers and school administrators are reporting an increase in psychological disturbances in childhood. Research also supports this conclusion. One study, examining children and adolescents over a thirteen-year period, reported significant increases in problems at school with attention, sociability, anxiety, delinquency, and aggression.[28] Also of importance are gender and cross-cultural findings. Psychiatrists and the AMA have yet to explain, for example, why boys should run more than three to five times the risk of diagnosis as girls (nor have they explained why this gender gap is suddenly closing). Neither have they explained why the diagnosis of ADD occurs much more frequently in the United States than it does, for example, in Western Europe.

As this brief summary of ADD suggests, although there may be a growing awareness about the hazards of the hurried society, this awareness has yet to have an impact on the popular (and medical) understanding of how children are affected by intense sensory consumption. Consider a 1997 article in *Newsweek* that describes the impact of hurried lifestyles on children's behavior.[29] Although this piece actually has a figure entitled "Attention Deficit," referring to how little time certain parents now spend with their children, there is no mention of ADD anywhere in the entire article. Just suggesting that today's culture of work and hurried lifestyles might be connected to the increase of this diagnosis seems somehow forbidden.

When discovering the biological bias in psychiatry and the evidence that ADD is really a developmental problem, many wonder why psychiatrists are so persistent in their drive toward a biological explanation. There is a relatively simple answer: Psychiatrists, like other physicians, are trained only to search for the immediate physical basis of a problem. Indeed, partly because of the rise of managed care, the greatest single activity engaged in by psychiatrists today is the prescribing and monitoring of the use of psychoactive drugs, a treatment that emphasizes immediate, short-term "solutions" but ignores all possible ultimate developmental and cultural causes. Again, this is not to say that the symptoms of ADD do not exist or that biology has no role to play. Rather, the point is that there can be no understanding of what's going on in children's psychological worlds without first considering the powerful cultural forces acting upon children's development. Even if biology were to be linked directly to developmental problems like ADD—although it has not been—concluding from this that the problem is "caused" by biology would still be highly questionable. Whatever biological influences exist, we must realize that it is the dramatic cultural changes in our lifestyle, not changes in human biology, that correlate with the rise of ADD.

Meanwhile, the most common claim in defense of ADD comes from the idea that the effects of Ritalin in children diagnosed with ADD are unique or "paradoxical." That is, we assume that the effects of the drug prove the existence of a biological disorder because we believe that a "stimulant" drug would not normally decrease hyperactivity or increase attention. Psychiatrists like Edward Hallowell, who argue that ADD is wholly biological, rely heavily on this very logic: "The evidence that ADD has a biological basis has mounted over the last 20 years. First, and most moving, there is the clinical evidence from records of millions of patients who have met the diagnostic criteria and who have benefited spectacularly from *standard treatment*. . . . The fact that *certain medications* predictably relieve target symptoms of ADD means that these symptoms have roots in the physical world."[30] By "standard treatment" and "certain medications" Hallowell means of course Ritalin, the effects of which, he says, prove the biological basis of ADD. If this is the "most moving" evidence in favor of ADD, there is indeed a big problem. In the first place, psychiatrists know that studies have long shown Ritalin and other stimulants to have these same effects on most non-ADD children. As Michael Rutter, a noted specialist in child disorders from the University of London, writes, "Stimulants . . . tend to improve attention and reduce activity in all people, children and adults, irrespective of whether or not they are hyperactive."[31]

Since most children "benefited spectacularly" from taking Ritalin, does this mean that most of them also have ADD? Of course not. The fact that Ritalin has powerful behavioral effects in children diagnosed with ADD proves nothing about the existence of any brain disorder. Indeed, as we shall see in Chapter 5, not only do studies fail to suggest that Ritalin's effects are unique, they also show that its effects are by no means a guarantee for long-term improvement in either academic performance or prosocial behavior.

A related problem with using Ritalin as a diagnostic tool for assessing ADD as a biological disorder concerns a logical fallacy that plagues much of psychiatry today. Because of the widespread use of medications in the "management" of psychological problems—from psychosis to depression to anxiety to ADD—there has been a strong tendency in psychiatry to argue that the effects of these drugs prove these problems to have a biological basis. Medical scholars have often criticized this kind of reasoning as *ex juvantibus* logic, which means that the reasoning is conveniently going backward from the effects of the drug to the cause of the problem.[32] The concern here is that because drugs do not have a single or precise site of action, their effects cannot in any way indicate the source of the problem. Professor of psychiatry Alvin Pam makes this clear, writing: "The efficacy of a drug does not prove that a particular mental disturbance is biochemically determined. For example, aspirin relieves headaches but no one contends that headache is brought about by 'aspirin deficiency.'"[33]

As all this suggests, many psychiatrists and pediatricians seem to have little idea how Ritalin, a stimulant, slows kids down. Indeed, as someone trained in psychopharmacology I'm often struck by the faniciful explanations I hear professionals give to this question. The fact of the matter is that the *effects* of a drug, whether taken for "therapeutic" or "recreational" reasons, have an enormous psychological component. For instance, there is considerable evidence showing that the "trip," "high," or "euphoria" produced by a drug varies from person to person and can be radically altered by the psychology of the drug user, including the reason why the drug is taken and what he or she expects from the drug. Some of these findings were reported in a *Scientific American* article describing how regular cocaine users could not tell the difference between cocaine and caffeine under blind conditions, a finding that helps explain how Ritalin can be pharmacologically very similar to cocaine (and the amphetamines) and still not produce an addiction in its users. What this means in terms of Ritalin's use for ADD is that the effects of the drug are not at all surprising or paradoxical: A stimulant drug such as Ritalin may decrease behavior and a depressant drug such as alcohol may increase behavior; it all depends upon the psychological and environmental contexts in which the drug is taken.

A CULTURE OF NEGLECT

IN 1990 the noted child expert and family scholar Urie Bronfenbrenner wrote: "Recent studies reveal that a major disruptive factor in the lives of families and their children is the *increasing instability, inconsistency, and hectic character of daily family life.* . . . In the absence of good support systems, external stresses have become so great that even strong families are falling apart."[34] These changes, both in the nature of the family and in the developing lives of children, represent what is defined here as an emerging *culture of neglect*. This is a culture in which the demands and expectations of society have given rise to a dramatic overall increase in work and stress, a conflicted sense of life priorities, and a cynical view of what is possible for ourselves, our families, and society as a whole. In this climate, where millions of children are "needing" to be drugged with a powerful stimulant (Ritalin), parents and teachers are increasingly facing off against each other, either placing blame or attempting to escape it. What the notion of a culture of neglect tells us, however, is that neither of these important institutions can be singled out and blamed for what is happening in the lives of children, just as neither will by themselves resolve the problems that children are experiencing. Today, as throughout all American history, these institutions have been shaped by larger cultural forces, and it is these cultural forces that must be reckoned with if we wish to deal effectively with the psychological and social problems of our time, including the problems associated with the diagnosis of ADD and the use of drugs with children.

Because it is the very center of where things happen, the family has often been blamed for children's problems. This is one of the reasons why parents are so quick to accept biological explanations of what is wrong with their children—since they think that if they are blamed, they will be left alone to solve a problem they already believe is out of control. Thus, although the family is certainly caught in the middle as the medium of exchange, the crisis of the child in the family is really only part of the larger crisis of the family in society.

In his book *Ties That Stress: The New Family Imbalance*, David Elkind describes the revolutionary changes taking place in the social institution of the family.[35] He begins with the nuclear family, which has served for more than a century as a safe haven from the growing stresses of the outside world. Professor Elkind goes on to show, however, that the family is shifting away from this "modern" formulation to one that he calls postmodern. This new structure, the *permeable* family, represents the loss of homelife as a "refuge and retreat from a demanding world," replaced by a diffusion of the family into other social institutions, which lie beyond the boundaries of the traditional household.[36] The broad implications of these changes in the family were summarized in a 1989 conference of family scholars at Stanford University, "What Do Families Do?" In the published volume that followed from the conference, *Rebuilding the Nest*, three principal conclusions were drawn:

- As a social institution, the family in America is increasingly less able to carry out its basic functions.
- The quality of life for America's children is declining.

- Our family dilemma is not simply one of public policy or economics but is also one of cultural values and social institutions.[37]

In *The Ties That Stress*, Elkind explains these trends, stressing that while the imbalance of the *nuclear* family was in favor of the child and thus protective of the child, the new imbalance of the *permeable* family has shifted in favor of the parents. Hence the solution of giving our kids only "quality time," which has not been a tenable solution because it has only shifted the problem, rather than solved it. While millions of new moms are filing into the full-time work force, the situation for fathers has not changed a bit, thus leaving children behind in someone else's care. A consequence of this shift is that many of the psychological stressors that plagued motherhood now plague childhood. For example, mothers whose psychological needs were not met by vacuous homelives suffered psychological and emotional problems that often led to such things as depression and drug abuse. Now it is children whose psychological needs are unmet that suffer from emotional and behavioral problems.

Elkind does not place blame for the negative effects of the "permeable family" on parents, however. Rather, he interprets these changes as part of the larger changes taking place in American society. He writes, "It is simply that the demands of postmodern life are different from those that obtained in the modern world. Like passengers on a jetliner whose cabin has suddenly depressurized in midair, postmodern parents know they have to put their own oxygen mask on first, before they can attend to the safekeeping of their children."[38]

If we look closer at these "ties that stress," we will find that the hurried society contains a set of interlocking cultural contingencies and consequences that bode poorly for the child. The first has to do with the fact that instead of children learning to stimulate their own minds and organize their own behavior, they have been swept up and into their parents' race with time. An advertisement I received in the mail for a JCPenney catalog sums up the child's place in Mom's hectic schedule: "Traffic jams. Kids to school. Work. Meetings. Deadlines. Rush hour. Soccer practice. Groceries. Cooking. Dishes. Laundry. Homework. Bathtime. Pay bills. Call mom. All this and you still need to try to squeeze in a little bit of time to go shopping! Life is busy enough. . . . let us help!"

The hectic pace of life has led to such chaotic and dysfunctional homelives that some have even confessed to treating work as the place of refuge, because it is the only place they can find some peace of mind.[39] As documented in Juliet Schor's *The Overworked American: The Unexpected Decline of Leisure*, the demands of the workplace and the demands of prosperity have made it more and more difficult for parents to preserve and protect the developmental world of the child.[40] Again, Elkind sums this up nicely: "Many of today's parents . . . no longer regard themselves as solely responsible for meeting the emotional needs of their offspring. Many of them do not think of children and youth as requiring a full helping of security, protection, firm limits, and clear values, and many of those who still believe in the goodness of those things no longer have faith in their ability as parents to provide them in today's complex world."[41]

The hurried society also means that parents as a whole have become conflicted about where raising children stands in their overall sense of priorities. Parents often show a clear idea of how much time they *should* spend with their children, but as expressed in ideas like quality time, they also have an idea that much of this time can be loaned out to other activities (such as work), assuming that these activities will pay off for the family in the long run. While some families are forced to be two-career families (or working single-parent families), many others are lured into the culture of work by a variety of social mechanisms, including the diminished value we place on the role of "housewife" and the romanticized image we increasingly have of the "aspiring" careerist. One such father notes about his daughter: "I think she's doing OK. If it were up to me, I'd spend more time with her. I wish I were able to stay at home. But that's just not possible." Another father says of his children: "I've curtailed my business to be with them more, but I hope as they grow older and our lives slow down a little I'll get to spend more time at the office."[42]

These commentaries show both these forces in action. In the first we find a parent who has a clear sense of what he should be doing but falls short because of economic concerns. In the second we find a parent who has been able to compromise his work schedule somewhat but who really would like to get back to his office. Sometimes it is because we have to, and sometimes it is because we want to. In either case, though, as a product of our culture of neglect, this trickle-down theory of child rearing doesn't seem to be working. Instead, we find more and more cases like the following: "For the New York Lawyer, it all hit home in the grocery store. She had stopped in with her 6-year-old to pick up a few things, but since the babysitter normally did the shopping, she was unprepared for what was about to happen. Suddenly there was her son, whooping and tearing around the store, skidding the length of the aisles on his knees. 'This *can't* be my child,' she thought in horror. Then the cashier gave a final twist to the knife. 'Oh,' she remarked. 'So *you're* the mother.' That was the moment when the lawyer was forced to admit that spending 'quality time' with the kids didn't seem to be working."[43]

The culture of neglect and the failure of its quality time solution ultimately bring us back to our question of how the hurried, unstructured lives children are living today connects to the rise of sensory addictions. This begins with the loss of family structure. The absence of a predictable, consistent (and slow!) state of affairs at home leads to a failure of the child to develop an internal structure of self-organization and self-control. But "structure" does not only mean routine and ritual; it also means being there, patiently, when the child is in need of attention. When children begin showing signs of trouble, they need more than just rewards and punishers from day care workers, teachers, baby-sitters, or nannies. We all know that healthy child development stems from an emotional bond between the child and his or her parents, something that can fail to occur properly (or fail to continue) when parents have shifted much of their parental responsibilities elsewhere.

Meanwhile, many of the things keeping kids occupied in the absence of a close-knit family structure are high-intensity activities. Thus the culture of neglect also means that more time will be spent in passive, light entertainment and that less time will be spent each day reclaiming the benefits of the calm and quiet. Not only does this apply to the kinds of activities kids engage in, such as watching TV versus reading a book, but it also has to do with the frenzied lifestyle of constantly being shuttled between different caregivers and different activities. These varied activities often give rise to a hatred of structure and an even greater need for stimulation, both of which can lead to the child's being completely "unmanageable" under conditions of slowness—at school, at the dinner table, when it's time for bed, when housework or homework needs to be done, or when the child is told no. A nursery school teacher summarizes: "Nowadays when parents bring these kids in the morning, we have to spend at least half an hour either waking them up or calming them down. They come from houses where the TV is going all the time, ride in cars with the music blaring—it's no wonder some have blocked it out and others are bouncing off the walls. We used to be able to start out activities as soon as the children arrived, but now we must always begin with a nice long transition period to get them tuned in."[44] In other words, rather than develop the skills of self-control that we all need, and that most all people used to develop, stimulation becomes a substitute structure for the child, and when it goes, so does the child. The last straw occurs when, as the child begins to show the clear signs of too little structure and too much impulsivity, there is no one consistently there to monitor and smooth out the rough edges before they begin to threaten the child's well-being. The eventual consequence: Either the parent or the school decides something drastic has to be done to match the drastic nature of the problem. Unfortunately the only drastic solution tried thus far has been the Ritalin solution.

IN conclusion, then, it seems clear that the impact of the hurried society is both direct and indirect. Involvement in high-intensity worlds can turn us into sensory addicts, and for many it already has. This transformation of human consciousness represents a *direct* effect of exposure to rapid-fire culture. However, the hurried society also eats away at many of the core structures of family and community life that provide children with stability and security, which is an *indirect* effect of rapid-fire culture. This "effect" of rapid-fire culture, in having its own deleterious effects on patience, attention, and self-control, then becomes a further cause of our psychological disturbances. Thus rapid-fire culture also has the effect of altering conscious experience and behavior *indirectly* by altering family and community structures.

Great Misadventures in Time

There is no time. There is only life.

LUC BESSON
The Fifth Element

WHEN we think about our lives and the world in which we live, we cannot help wondering about how things might have been different or if there is still time for things to change. We wonder why we do the things we do and feel the way we feel. We wonder about humanity and its potential for greatness and its seemingly equal potential to fall into destructiveness. Because we can look back upon the past and also toward the future—*because we are temporal beings*—we want to know the sources of the self, of how we become who we are. From where does the great diversity of the human experience arise, including our likes and dislikes, our hopes, expectations, emotions, and our satisfactions and dissatisfactions? Are these filled in by cumulative life experiences in a complex, diverse, and changing world, from our biological inheritance, or are they the product of some freestanding inner will? Which is ultimately greater, nature (human biology) or nurture (human experience)?

My own areas of study, psychology and psychopharmacology, are only two among many disciplines caught up in the debate over nature versus nurture. As it turns out, the most promising approach to nature/nurture questions in recent times has been not to approach them at all. Rather, as the science of human nature moves forward, there is a growing interest in the biobehavioral sciences in redefining these questions by stressing that the concepts of nature and nurture are really just abstractions. The psychological and social phenomena that we observe, according to this view, cannot be divvied up into neat little piles labeled "biology," "experience," and "human will." The emphasis of this alternative approach lies instead on the repeated coming together of nature and nurture, day in and day out, and how this gives rise to an emergent whole—the *self*—that is greater and more complex than the sum of the parts. One reason why the idea of an emergent self may be difficult to imagine is that it develops under the cover of darkness, concealed behind the mask of time.[1]

The support for an alternative, emergent view of the self comes from a diverse array of neuroscientific, genetic, psychosocial, and historical research. What this research has been finding—often with surprise and sometimes reluctantly—is that there exists a highly complex, interwoven relationship between the forces of nature and nurture. As one journalist sums it up, "Experts now agree that a baby does not come into the world as a genetically preprogrammed automaton or a blank slate at the mercy of the environment, but arrives as something much more interesting. For this reason the debate that engaged countless generations of philosophers—whether nature or nurture calls the shots—no longer interests most scientists."[2] Like the child who looks at the earth's soil with his magnifying glass and discovers another living universe, the advancement of more precise scientific instruments in the behavioral sciences has led to discoveries of previously unknown levels of complexity. As the Nobel laureate Gerald Edelman writes in *Bright Air, Brilliant Fire: On the Matter of the Mind* (1992), "putting the mind back into nature has precipitated a series of scientific crises, for the data on the brain, mind, and behavior don't correspond to the pictures we have been using to explain them."[3]

The emergent view of the self, which stresses the ongoing interaction between nature and nurture, suggests that we will never have an understanding that will enable us to sift through the developmental process and weigh the separate influences of biology and experience. In one scientific study, for example, researchers examined the contribution of genetic and developmental history in adults who suffered from depression. Although both these variables scored as significant factors in predicting depression, it was the interaction between them that scored the highest.[4] In other words, the influence of each factor was dependent on the other, such that the effects of both were magnified when combined together, creating a multiplicative rather than additive effect.

Even at a theoretical level, there may be no satisfying our urge to quantify the influence of nature versus nurture. This can be illustrated with a simple example. Say we compare two communities. In one community the members share very similar life experiences with one another, whereas in the other, the personal, social, and cultural experiences vary dramatically. What we will find as a consequence is that the psychological diversity that exists in the first community will have much more to do with biological factors than in the second. This contingency in our biology can be seen in the example of intelligence: If the amount and quality of nurturing and education do not vary, the differences in people's intelligence should track, albeit imperfectly, genetic differences; if, on the other hand, there are great differences in the amount and quality of schooling and homelife, individual genetic differences are likely to be washed away. As every geneticist knows, the contributions of nature and nurture are not static (even the fingerprints of identical twins are not the same), but rather vary from time to time and culture to culture. Noted cultural anthropologist Clifford Geertz sums this up nicely:

> . . . there is no such thing as a human nature independent of culture. Men without culture would not be the clever savages of Golding's *Lord of the Flies* thrown back upon the cruel wisdom of their animal instincts; nor would they be the nature's noblemen of Enlightenment primitivism or even, as classical anthropological theory would imply, intrinsically talented apes who had somehow failed to find themselves. They would be unworkable monstrosities with very few useful instincts, fewer recognizable sentiments, and no intellect: mental basket cases. As our central nervous system . . . grew up in great part in interaction with culture, it is incapable of directing our behavior or organizing our experience without the guidance provided by systems of significant symbols.[5]

As Geertz tells us, genes are like the letters of the alphabet: They are crucial to telling a story, but from them alone we have no idea what the story is going to say. Only within our history, viewed from the context of our highly structured social institutions and our social norms, can we gain any sense of how we have become who we are.

THE NATURE AND NURTURE OF RITALIN NATION

IN our exploration of Ritalin Nation, looking upon the relationship between culture and human consciousness, we will find this alternative, emergent view of the self to be quite helpful. This is because *sensory addictions* and the culture that produces them are each the cumulative "emergent" products of history. It is for this reason that we cannot understand these phenomena by working solely within the "parts are parts" philosophy that characterizes the old nature versus nurture approach.

To give an example, in the first chapter I outlined how many Americans growing up today are experiencing a very similar array of societal conditions—rapid-fire culture—that yield a particular set of psychological experiences—the transformation of human consciousness. This idea, that a dramatic transformation in human society can produce in turn a dramatic transformation in human consciousness, is not, however, a claim about the powerful influence of nurture *over* nature. To the contrary, emphasizing that the human brain is highly adaptable points to the amazing powers of the human mind in keeping up with, and participating in, the ongoing, rapid changes taking place in human culture. Indeed, it is because we have overlooked our own natural, biologically based capacity to assimilate changes in the sensory world that we have fundamentally misunderstood the psychological consequences of living in a hurried society.

Now if all this seems wrongheaded, it may be because you're holding on to the idea that because we have a complex nervous system, we must also have a rigidly defined and organized brain. But this is not so. Complexity does not mean that every facet of human nature is preordained for some "domain-specific" purpose (such as the oft-hypothesized role of biology in male domination and mate selection). If it did, the design and neural layout of the brain, which happens to be thousands of years old, would not be at all suited for today's unique challenges, from driving in high-speed traffic to learning the ins and outs of computers. This can be seen, for instance, at the very place where neurons come together to produce consciousness. As research in neuroscience has shown, the cerebral cortex alone has about one million billion neural connections (yes, that's one million billion connections), a number that far exceeds what our genes could possibly organize on their own (indeed, as we shall see in Chapter 4, it's experience that does most of the organizing).[6] This can also be seen when we compare simple and complex organisms, from bacteria to baboons. As any student of biology knows, such a comparison shows that the evolution of a complex nervous system is almost always in a direction toward enhancing the species' adaptive plasticity. This is why the most complex organisms are also those that can and must learn to cope in the unique and changing ecological conditions into which they are born.

This brings us to an important distinction for thinking about attention deficit disorder, which has to do with a confusion between "natural" facts and "historical" ones. The melding of modern mind and modern culture represents a long-standing mutual interaction. Neither is imaginable without the other. The products of this interaction reflect in turn the forces of nature, including our own human nature. Despite this fact, the *particular* cultural practices and psychological characteristics that emerge as a consequence represent historical facts, not natural ones. This is why the study of the origins of nature goes by the name natural history. Thus, the fact that American society has a unique pace of life does not mean that it had to turn out this way, nor does it mean that our hurried society is merely a symptom of some underlying, fixed human nature. Complexity comes about only because nature and nurture play second fiddle to history—that is, the dynamic interaction over time between nature and nurture.[7]

This distinction between nature and history raises the possibility of ADD being a "historical" rather than a "biological" problem. To assume there exists a single biological, psychological, or cultural explanation for all those diagnosed with ADD, or to assume that

Ritalin "works" because the problem is a biological one, is again to take an overly simplistic, nature versus nurture approach to the problem. It may indeed be that a small percentage of children are either born with or develop an early tendency toward the restlessness that many see as the classic sign of ADD. This early trajectory may even yeild a child who is completely out of control. The real tragedy lies, however, in the very real possibility that had a child lived a slower, more structured life, he or she might have just as easily become a vital member of society. Only history will tell us the long-term consequences of letting this uniqueness be twisted into something so unwanted that we end up eliminating it with a powerful, mind-altering drug.

Examples of such an oversimplified understanding can be found in almost any textbook or magazine article that describes ADD. For instance, in the very first sentence of an article in a nursing magazine entitled "Attention Deficit/ Hyperactivity Disorder: A Guide to Diagnosis and Treatment," we read the following: "ADHD is a biological condition and is not caused by psychogenic factors."[8] One thing to notice about this statement is how only two factors are considered: The problem has only one cause, and it's either biological or psychological. The possibility of a more general influence—society, culture, history—is left out of the equation altogether, not to mention the possibility that there may be different combinations of factors that together produce roughly the same behavioral outcomes (a process known as the *law of equifinality*).[9] The second thing to notice is how, in typical nature/nurture fashion, the two choices are presented as mutually exclusive of each other: One factor has everything to do with ADD; the other has nothing to do with it. Despite the confidence with which this statement is asserted, we know it to be false. Even for medical problems like cancer and especially for psychological ones, problems that develop during one's life are rarely, if ever, found to be wholly biological. Even the identical twin of a brother or sister who has something like schizophrenia—perhaps the most heritable of all psychological problems—has less than betting odds of ever developing schizophrenia (the chances are actually less than one in three[10]). The same is true for ADD. If ADD were solely biological, then both identical twins would have it or neither would have it; in reality, the odds of both having it are even less than that for schizophrenia.

In contrast with the nature versus nurture approach to understanding hyperactivity and inattention, the emergent view of the self looks at ADD in the first instance as neither biological nor cultural. Like the proverbial chicken and the egg, the realms of nature and nurture are so inexorably intertwined in children's lives that each acts as both a cause and an effect of the problem. We know, for example, that if the problems of ADD had only to do with biology, then their incidence should not change over relatively short periods of time, but of course they have, and dramatically. As was noted in a standard textbook of abnormal psychology, "genetic factors may play a role in ADD's etiology, but they account for problems in only a small percentage of children with it."[11] Nor should the problems vary across cultures, as they also do, and again dramatically. The same holds true for culture. If culture were solely responsible for the symptoms of ADD, then we should see the same ADD symptoms in most individuals growing up in rapid-fire culture, and of course we don't.

As with all psychological and medical problems, the same exposure to damaging environments does not result in exactly the same problem or the same intensity of the problem (even in the case of HIV and AIDS, some individuals with repeated exposure have never actually become HIV-positive). Of course many of the key factors underlying these individual responses are biological ones, including basic genetic differences that can make us more or less likely to *develop* such problems. This is not to say, however, that so-called predispositions for hyperactivity and inattention are problems in and of themselves. To the contrary, the very same genetic influences that may put someone at risk may also, under other circumstances, be very healthy for both the individual and society (e.g., high-energy, extroverted).

One concrete example of this "genetic uncertainty" can be seen in the case of sickle-cell anemia, a problem most commonly found in people of African descent. Sickle-cell anemia, a heritable blood disease that can be painful and debilitating, occurs when individuals receive the problem gene (the allele) from both parents.[12] What is interesting is the fact that inheriting only one copy of this recessive gene actually confers upon the person a resistance to malaria, and without giving the person sickle-cell anemia. Hence, even if we could eliminate this so-called risk from the human genome, we would not want to, for this would only put many more people at risk for something potentially worse.[13]

A metaphorical example may also be helpful in thinking about the role of inheritance in ADD. Say an arsonist pours gasoline on ten neighboring buildings and sets them afire. Afterward we find that five buildings, all of them made of stone, were saved; the five made of wood burned to the ground. In this metaphorical example, think of the arsonist as representing the hazards of culture (nurture) and the building materials as the individual's genetic makeup (nature). What do we conclude from this outcome? Should we conclude that the building materials were the "cause" of the fire? Of course not. In fact, we may still see building with wood to be a virtuous thing, especially if it has some attributes more useful than building with stone (such as availability, cost, and aesthetics). Obviously, if we want to save our buildings, what is most important is that we keep people from lighting them afire.

Unfortunately this is not the logic we find when we look at how growing numbers of psychiatrists (and behavioral geneticists) are talking about human genetics and behavioral problems. They see the construction of the buildings (genetics) rather than the fire starter (culture) as the cause. Indeed, despite the fact that it is clearly the latter that is new (or changing) and despite the fact that it is the latter that ultimately determines why and when the "buildings will burn," even much of the public has come to view the biology of the self as more important than what is happening to it. Why do we do this? We do it in part because blaming the child's genetic material locates the problem solely within the nature of the individual (versus the nature of society), thus simplifying the problem and setting the stage for individualized, marketplace solutions like Ritalin.

THE PSYCHOLOGY OF TEMPORAL MECHANICS

HAVING just sketched some of the reasons for taking a broader, more historical and developmental approach to Ritalin Nation, we can now begin a careful study of its history. This will be our task here and in Chapter 3. As the title of this chapter—"Great Misadventures in Time"—suggests, this begins with an investigation of ourselves as temporal beings.

Although this focus on the psychological dimensions of time may seem like a departure from our main topic, understanding it is actually crucial for our eventual grasping of the nature of sensory addictions—of how life in rapid-fire culture gives rise to a compressed sense of time, which shortens our attention spans, makes us impatient, and encourages impulsivity and the pursuit of constant sensory consumption.

Because we are temporal beings, changes in the pace of life can have profound effects on our experience of time, just as our experience of time can have a profound effect on our pace of life. Again, like the chicken and the egg, these causes are also effects, creating an interlocking series of changes in the tempo of our surroundings and the rhythm of our consciousness. As medieval historian Aron Gurevich remarks, "Few factors in a culture express the essential nature of its world picture so clearly as its way of reckoning time: for this has a determining influence on the way people behave, the way they think, the rhythm of their lives and the relationships between them and things."[14]

In the first chapter I presented what is one of the central themes of this study—namely, that the nature of human consciousness is unavoidably shaped by the workings of the world around us. Rather than a single "static," "correct," or "true" human consciousness, there appears to be a mutual transformation going on between the culture we live in and our conscious experience of it. This means that markedly different, durable states of human consciousness have existed and continue to exist around the world. As Julian Jaynes argues in his classic work *The Origin of Consciousness in the Breakdown of the Bicameral Mind* (1976), even consciousness itself may be a relatively recent, culturally inspired phenomenon.

Of course, unlike cultural anthropologists, who live side by side with people of very different psychological and cultural practices, most of us have little or no firsthand knowledge that different *mentalités* even exist. Hence, we should not be surprised that the pluralistic view of consciousness contrasts sharply with conventional thinking. In areas of cognitive psychology and neuroscience, for example, we find that consciousness is viewed in simple terms as something that inevitably results from basic neurophysiological processes that are unique to humans. These processes are thought not only to bring conscious experience to life but also to animate conscious experience in basically the same way for all people, for all time. By contrast, when we consider the possibility of human consciousness's being transformed by the world around us, this turns the question of consciousness into a historical one. What, in other words, is the social history of conscious experience? What is the cultural context of our developing minds, and how does it impact on the way we come to experience our lives? As we examine these questions in terms of the changing nature of consciousness, however, we encounter a unique set of complications that have to be considered first, which concern the nature of time.

If one were to take the time to read all the newspaper stories, magazine articles, and books that explore the growing social and psychological hazards of our fast-paced culture, one would discover a common, underlying theme: a race against time. This theme has to do with a change that is taking place in the temporal structure of our society and, ultimately, in ourselves. Somehow, despite all our affluence and all our achievements in timesaving technology, we find ourselves in a peculiar position: We are, or at least we feel as if we are, always on the move, always behind, always rushed, and always out of time. As a study of New Yorkers concluded, they *"know exactly what time it is . . . and they're running late."* And when they were asked how often they were rushed, the usual answer was "most of the time."[15]

This "there's-never-enough-time" existentialism raises general questions that have yet to be explored from a broad, historical point of view.[16] What is our relationship to time, and how does this affect our experience of it? How does this relationship shape in turn our experience of ourselves and the world around us? The question we must first ask, though, is what exactly do we mean by "time?" As with Stephen Hawking's huge best-seller *A Brief History of Time*, we hear a lot of fancy, abstract ideas about time and its connections to the universe at large, but what is time for those of us who do not plan to travel near the speed of light? As it turns out, even the time we read off the clock is not exactly what we might think.

Interestingly, just as we typically underestimate the changeable nature of human consciousness, seeing it instead as having a universal, fixed structure, we also treat time in much the same way, assuming that it too has a universal, fixed structure. We assume that time exists outside our bodies as a measurable, physical entity, much like weight or distance. It is not uncommon, for instance, for me to find students in my courses who believe that clocks respond to some external, flowing substance called time, which is of course absurd. Although we talk about time as if it were something out there, waiting to be captured—like "time in a bottle"—clocks and watches do not in fact measure a physical substance that acts upon them, at least not in the manner in which a scale reacts to the gravitational force of some external object or the way in which a light meter measures the intensity of electromagnetic radiation. Instruments of time simply offer a display of periodic cycles that correlate, more or less reliably, with the movement of the planetary orbs and, perhaps most important, other clocks. As the great mathematician Gottfried Wilhelm von Leibniz wrote three centuries ago, "space and time are orders of things, and not things," by which he meant that space and time exist only as concepts we use to make sense of our experience of ourselves and the universe around us.[17]

At least for us earthlings, then, time is not a substance with objective properties. Instead of living our lives relative to time, or "within" time, what we actually do is live our lives relative to one another, relative to our built environments, and relative to our ecological surroundings. The relationships we have to these surroundings determine our experience of life's unfolding, which is then described using the concept of time. As Michael Ende writes in his novel *Momo*, "Calendars and clocks exist to measure time, but that signifies little because we all know that an hour can seem like an eternity or pass in a flash, depending on how we spend it. Time is life itself. . . ."[18] Thus it's not that the concept of time is unimportant, but rather that its significance lies in its capacity to describe the nature of our relationships to the social and physical world and the phenomenological experience that these relationships then produce. Such a temporal experience can be seen easily enough in expressions like "Time flies when we're having fun." This shows both that the experience of time is transformed by our relationship to the world and that time is a useful, albeit imperfect, description of this relationship.

The traditional view of time as a flowing, external substance has had three consequences: First, it has tricked us into believing that time can be measured and quantified; second, it has led us to believe that the psychological experience of time, including the passage of time, is at best an untrustworthy distortion of reality; and third, it has kept us from noticing what is most important about time, which is that we can change the nature of it, and do, by changing the ways in which we live. Such temporal distortions can be seen in how we prioritize an *objective* notion of time (as defined by clocks and calendars) over a *subjective* notion of time (as defined by phenomenological experience). Expressions like "I lost track of time" illustrate this, in that subjective time is viewed as a flimsy distortion of something that exists independent of us. As geographer David Harvey remarked about "clock time," "even when we do not conform to it, we know very well what is being rebelled against."[19]

I once saw an amusing example of how objective time plays big brother to subjective time in one of those "hurry and order now" television advertisements. This was an ad for a wristwatch, but it was no ordinary wristwatch. According to the ad, what made the watch unique was its ability to abolish jet lag by gradually running a little fast or a little slow as one flew from east to west, or vice versa. If you were traveling east from Hawaii to California, for instance, you would simply program the watch for the new, later time zone, and when you arrived, your new watch would display the correct hour. Of course you have to look occasionally at the watch while in flight; otherwise your "nervous" system is going to be just as shocked by the time change as it would have been without the watch. Herein lies the rub: You must continuously overrule your own subjective perception of time—which is not likely to correspond with the strangely accelerated or slowed-down time—by looking at the gradually shifting objective time shown on your wrist. If subjective time is running ahead, as when one flies east, the objective time shown on the watch pulls it back down; if subjective time is running slow, as when one flies west, objective time pulls it ahead. As the watchmaker seems well aware, turning ourselves over to the authority of objective time easily overrules our free-spirited subjective time.

Keeping subjective and objective time in mind, we are now in a position to give a more precise account of the nature of time. In short, time does not exist so much as do the events that produce it. According to this view, objective time has to do only with orderly periodic movements (clock time) and how these movements have become organizers of social behavior. These movements can come from the night and day cycle, a sundial, a Rolex, or a cesium atomic clock. Subjective time, on the other hand, refers to the actual experience of events, which gives rise to the conscious awareness of what we call temporality. For example, if we crawl into a cave for six months or even lie in a sensory deprivation tank for a few hours, time gets lost. The absence of events (or at least the absence of familiar events) creates an absence of time—a temporal black hole, if you will. Meanwhile the objective time of the clock keeps rolling on. Hence, a watched pot never boils simply because there's not much going on here in the way of events. By contrast, a continuous stream of relatively intense stimulus events—as is found in the hurried society—speeds time up. Because events are what carry consciousness along, experiencing more of them in the same temporal period means "time will fly."

Of course, as the example of the wristwatch shows, clock time can rope in and crush subjective time at any moment, as it does under either of two conditions. First, if we "keep our eye on the time," as we often do, subjective time becomes subordinated to clock time. Now you know why we call a watch a watch. The second condition occurs when the experience of events is already familiar to us and thus are already coded in clock time. For example, if you look at the clock after each drive to work, eventually you will be able to judge accurately the (objective) time without even consulting the clock. In the study of New Yorkers mentioned above, for instance, researchers found that people could guess the time to within a few minutes, and people who did not wear watches were even more accurate. This is despite the fact that these respondents represent a somewhat biased sample since they were the ones who were willing to stop and answer the researchers' questions about the time. Others, when promised by the researchers that it would only take a minute, responded, "I don't have a minute." Apparently they knew *exactly* what time it was.

A BRIEF HISTORY OF TIME

IF we want to know more about the virtues of objective and subjective time, we can go one step further and ask which one of these two temporal attitudes has history on its side. What, in other words, is the history of time? Interestingly, when we look back upon the time before the industrial age, when clocks didn't matter, we discover that of these two ideas, neither objective nor subjective time adequately fits with the relationship people had with time.

As it turns out, the dichotomies of objective and subjective—like other psychological dichotomies, such as inner and outer or self and other—are really only appropriate for our *modern* understanding of the world. By this I mean that the self that emerged in premodern times was constructed differently, and this means in turn that the nature and experience of time were also different. The self that existed in the Middle Ages, for example, was one in which the individual was more evenly woven into the fabric of family and community practices; thus he or she lacked the isolated and well-defined boundaries of individualism that we view today as normal and healthy. Consequently, people did not see themselves as lone subjects in an objective world, and that is why it makes little sense to speak of an objective or a subjective time. Certainly we can describe this early experience of time as highly subjective, but this is misleading; it is more accurate to state that for them, time as an external substance simply did not exist.

In going back to the times when clocks didn't matter, what we're really talking about is going back in time before the birth of that "awe-inspiring symbol of fleeting time," the mechanical clock.[20] This device was invented late in the thirteenth century and was in many places quick to revolutionize the nature of social relations.

According to historian Aron Gurevich, by the fourteenth and fifteenth centuries, clocks were making their way into public display, largely because of their placement on the face of town halls in many European cities. Prior to this change, the meaning of time was connected intimately to the church, where the ringing of the church bells symbolized the church's orchestration of social actions and its control over the temporal structure of daily life. Time's meaning was incorporated within religious practices, which were still very central to people's lives. The clock that was later displayed on the town hall, on the other hand, much like the existence of the town itself, stole time away from the church. As seen today, time eventually lost its place as something incorporated within religious life, secularized by its association with the banal, daily affairs of town living. As Gurevich writes, "the town community made itself master of its own time, with its own special rhythm."[21]

Historians are also quick to remind us, however, that the impact of the mechanical clock on the evolution of culture is far from straightforward. Because our experience of time does indeed have a deep connection to the way in which we live, and vice versa, the history of clocks has been almost as diverse as civilization itself. Of course today, with the ubiquity of precise, inexpensive clocks and watches, we are easily swayed by the idea that clocks, once invented and made reasonably accurate, were of such obvious utility that everyone and every society quickly put them to use. This is consistent with the idea that time is something outside us, waiting to be discovered and then measured, and it is just as misleading. The truth of the matter is that the usefulness of clocks depends in the first place on whether social relations and social events are in need of the organizing force and external authority that clocks bring.

The essential feature of life that makes clocks useful has to do with the number of events occurring in daily life. If you're engaged in activities squeezed between a whole host of other activities, many of which involve people who are also engaged in their own tight network of activities, then of course you need to "keep your eye on the time." Living in the age of time management, as we do, we're all aware that losing track of time can mean embarrassment, a loss of opportunities (or even a job or a friend), or a great inconvenience, as when you miss a doctor's appointment scheduled six weeks earlier. Writing in 1881 that "a delay of a few moments might destroy the hopes of a lifetime," physician George M. Beard had anticipated the psychological hazard of a world on time.[22]

If, on the other hand, we engage in activities that are open-ended, that pose no risk of bleeding into time already dedicated to other responsibilities, then we do not have a need for rationed time. As Jeremy Rifkin notes in *Time Wars*, "The more complex the social environment, the greater the need to reserve pieces of the future ahead of time."[23] According to this equation, we can obtain an estimate of the hurriedness of a society by examining the prevailing reliance on standardized time. Hence, it's no surprise to find that people of "primitive" cultures often thrive without clocks and, when introduced to them, find them incomprehensible.[24]

In fact, the history of the clock as a powerful influence on the evolution of culture bears an interesting resemblance to the history of the wheel. The invention of the wheel, along with fire (much earlier) and the clock (much later), stands out as a cultural icon of innovation, progress, and civilization. Despite our assumption that the wheel and the clock were inherently useful tools put to immediate use, history tells us that both had a very mixed introduction into the workings of society. As historian of technology George Basalla points out about the wheel, there is a popular idea that it was the centerpiece of transportation and that transportation was the centerpiece of civilization: "[T]o be without the wheel altogether is sufficient to set a culture apart from the civilized world."[25] The problem with this view, much like the popular view of the clock, is that it is at best only partly true.

It is true that the wheel had an important function in ancient European times, for religious ceremonies, military operations, and the transportation of goods. However, in other parts of the world, such as Southeast Asia and North and South America, cultures often prospered without the use of the wheel. In fact, there is evidence that at least some of these cultures actually had this technology but never put it to "functional" use or abandoned it for something else. Basalla notes, for example, that in the Near East the wheel was abandoned for the camel for more than one thousand years—until the time when European imperialism forced its rein-troduction. There were also other groups that appeared to employ wheels only for use in making "nonfunctional" things, such as toy-like figurines.[26] This compares well with the attitude toward the mechanical clock, as is described in this passage by Aron Gurevich: "On arrival in China, the Europeans, as is well known, took over many ancient Chinese inventions, and in turn acquainted the Chi-nese with some of their own. And although medieval China culti-vated a cavalier disdain of everything foreign, the Chinese emperors were captivated by the mechanical clock—not as an instrument for the precise measurement of time, however, but as a toy!"[27]

Temporal relativism is as true for ancient cultures as it is for so-called primitive societies today. For example, I once read an account concerning members of a contemporary Amazonian tribe, some of whom adored wearing and examining wristwatches. The funny thing was, they had no interest whatsoever in the watch as a timepiece, as was evident from the fact that the watches either did-n't work or were set to the "wrong" time. Another example comes from contemporary anthropologists reporting on the difficulties of teaching schoolchildren in nonindustrialized cultures an objective sense of the concept of temporal duration. Whereas we take for granted our ability to perceive accurately ten "clock" minutes or one "clock" hour, these children, who otherwise were intellectually quite capable, repeatedly failed this task. Frustrating their Western mentors, children might report the duration of something like a two-hour bus ride as taking a few minutes, whereas others were con-vinced it took several hours.[28] The problem here is that these indi-viduals lack one of our central, culturally conditioned concepts of time, which is that it is linear and thus fixed: An hour is an hour, and a day is a day. Indeed, this example stands in stark contrast with American children, who at an early age are introduced to clocks and watches as meaningful instruments for capturing time. Because the schoolchildren in nonindustrialized nations may have no notion of linear time, they provide a perfect example of what hap-pens when one's raw experience of time has not been corrupted by the dominance of the clock.[29]

Perhaps most striking is the fact that a soft attitude toward time has appeared for brief moments even in industrialized nations. For more than a dozen years after the French Revolution of 1789, France divided the month into ten-day weeks and the week into ten-hour days. Similarly, Stalin's Soviet Union had at first five- and then six-day weeks. In American history time has also gone through some dramatic changes. As recently as the late nineteenth century American towns still set their own time, so that one town might be twenty minutes or a half hour behind a neighboring one. However, because this was also the time of the powerful railroads, the federal government was persuaded in 1883 to establish the national time zones we use today.[30] It seems that in order for the trains to run on time, there had to be some agreement about just what time it was. Stephen Kern, in *The Culture of Time and Space, 1880–1918*, summarizes this transition toward a synchronized time: "There were many . . . who reacted adversely to the introduction of standard time, but the modern age embraced universal time and punctuality because these served its larger needs. . . . The passion in the debate about homogeneous versus heterogeneous time was generated rather by those novelists, psychologists, physicists, and sociologists who examined the way individuals create as many different times as there are life styles, reference systems, and social forms."[31]

THE TEMPTATIONS OF TIME

As the history of time suggests, and as Kern's distinction between homogeneous and heterogeneous time suggests, time is fundamental to both cultural practices and conscious experience. It is also deeply tied up in these practices and experiences. That is, our sense of time not only moves us to act but also motivates actions that then engender our sense of time. This dialectical understanding of time, although complex, has the virtue of allowing us the freedom to say that time and its associated technology have had an enormous impact on human society, as well as to say that for certain times and places, the time we moderns know and adhere to simply did not exist.

Both these points have an important role to play in our understanding of Ritalin Nation. We want first of all to appreciate how our ongoing relationship to time structures the underlying rhythms, thoughts, and actions of our daily lives. We also want to appreciate the idea that this is a historical fact rather than a natural one. If the latter were true, if time were the universal substance it's often thought to be, the great diversity in time and human consciousness that still exists today, even in our own communities and in our own lives, would cease to exist. This is the reason why, in our study of Ritalin Nation, time must be investigated phenomenologically—in terms of actions, events, and experiences—rather than physically—in terms of the mechanical movements of a clock.

A good place to begin this phenomenological study is with the realization that despite the hegemony of the clock, there remain powerful psychosocial influences on our experience of time. This is true both in terms of the immediate present—such as the experience of time while sitting through classroom instruction—and in terms of the passage of time during one's overall lifetime. By failing to appreciate the relationship between how and under what conditions we live our lives and how we experience time, we have fallen prey to a dangerous trap: *Just as our assumptions about a fixed consciousness have kept us from recognizing that conscious experience is undergoing a radical transformation, assumptions about a fixed time have kept us from realizing that cultural life is transforming the temporality and rhythm of modern experience.* Regarding both consciousness and time as fixed structures in the world actually obscures the reasons why, despite all our timesaving technology, time seems to be the one thing we don't have.

In the first chapter I described in broad strokes how a hurried life can create sensory addictions. We saw how the speedup of culture has a direct impact on our conscious experience, which it does by changing our underlying expectations about how fast things should go and how intense they should feel. By creating a conscious experience in which slowness is experienced as unpleasant, sensory addictions have a tendency to instill in us a forward-directed temporal stance, an escape from the present. After all, is it not a chief function of our busy, sensory-laden culture to distract us from the present or, more precisely, to make the present something so fleeting that it hardly even exists? In doing this, rapid-fire culture has its most devastating effect: It alienates us from the only temporal location within which we can truly experience the world, the present.

What does it mean, though, to give one's full sensory attention— one's full body and soul—to living appropriately in the moment? Imagine the following: "How long did Adam and Eve stay in the Garden of Eden? Seven hours is the answer. So man's innocence lasted a few hours of one day! But these were hours spent in paradise, and to them the Christian mind ascribed a content that would fill earthly years."[32]

Although I doubt a full appreciation of the present could succeed so well as to stretch the moment into what seems like hours, weeks, or even years, there's no doubt that life in Eden means a slower pace of events, with one's undivided senses directed upon them. When this way of being is achieved, a positive, altered state of consciousness is reawakened. For example, a friend once reported to me about his leisurely, summer travels that when he woke each day with no fixed plans and no crucial destination, his days stretched out into what, during his nonsummer months, would have been the equivalent of weeks. As he gradually turned his senses back to a time of slowness, days of smooth, sensual calm emerged, proving that less from an absolute point of view can become considerably more from a psychological one. The physical and the psychological invert themselves, so that to waste time is to save it and to save time is to waste it.

Walking home one day, I overheard a girl from the neighborhood, about eight years old or so, say something to a friend. It was a beautiful Vermont afternoon in April, and the sun was busy melting the snow. Swinging from behind the screen door of her front porch, the young girl said to her friend as she was leaving, "I can't wait until summer." To this her friend replied, in a fading voice, "Me neither . . . see you later." Now these are not unusual remarks, I agree; in fact, their familiarity is part of what I want to stress, for I think these remarks illustrate an important tendency in our culture, apparent even in very young children, to downplay or disregard the present, cultivating instead an anxious anticipation of the future. In the case of the girl, she retreats into her home from one of the most pleasant afternoons of the year, and what most occupies her are future plans about a summer still several weeks away.

Now for all I know, this young girl might have just finished a long treatise with her friend on the joys of spring, but somehow I doubt it. This kind of future-directed—"TGIF"—consciousness has become this century a ubiquitous feature of American life.[33] As the existentialist philosopher Soren Kierkegaard had already observed a century ago, "Most men pursue pleasure with such breathless haste that they hurry past it." (Imagine what Kierkegaard would think of rapid-fire culture today!) Looking upon my own childhood, I know from firsthand experience how a never-ending yearning for future events can undermine one's ability to appreciate the moment and, ultimately, life as a whole. *There really is no time like the present.*

Because it's obvious that at least physically we can exist only in the present, what does it mean to suggest that what we actually do is live in the future? When we ruminate about and plan things to come, when we study and work toward some anticipated eventuality, and when we imagine and harbor certain expectations about what the future could, should, or will be like, what we are often doing, albeit unintentionally, is redirecting our consciousness away from the present and into the future. When we do this, there is a tendency, again unintentional, of undervaluing our sense of the present. For instance, these days it seems as though people have given up experiencing the moment to such a degree that when traveling, they knowingly substitute in place of firsthand experience cameras or video cameras. The logic seems to be that if you've lost the ability to relax and appreciate the moment, you might as well record it for a time when perhaps you can. This reminds me of a quote I once heard, although I have since forgotten the author: "Happiness is not something you experience; it's something you remember." To the extent this is true, it would certainly be less so if we quit rushing through the present, hurrying on to an idealized future. At a minimum, keeping our senses on the present would at least ensure a memory of the past that would be more vivid and worth remembering.

The notion of "killing time" is of course the classic expression of this modern, future-directed consciousness. Once I was placed on hold and the radio station coming over the phone announced, "Here's another thirty minutes of continuous light rock to make your workday go faster." We have all been there. Housewives bored out of their minds; employees working long hours, alienated from their two jobs; kids bored to death by school: These are people living under conditions where the weekdays become sentences of suffering, where living solely for the weekend becomes a mental preoccupation. We can also find future directedness in our own imaginings of the more distant future, in how we constantly set our sights on some distant goal, only to set them on yet another one once that goal has been reached (or abandoned). Because the pursuit of happiness tends to direct our attention away from the present, it can actually have the negative effect of diminishing our experience. As psychologist Donald Campbell once said, "The direct pursuit of happiness is a recipe for an unhappy life."[34]

As with the example above of the girl's anticipation of summer's arrival, children also show clear signs of this future directedness. Every parent knows the story: Children want to hurry and grow up so that they can do what their older brothers and sisters can do. Then once they grow into these shoes, they want to do adult things, like own a car or exercise more independence. As adults they want still other things: new cars, jobs, money, houses, or new spouses. (Some even come to the end of this road and begin yearning for earlier times, when life was less complicated.) All this is not to say, however, that planning for the future is by any means an inherently destructive activity or that looking to the future and appreciating the moment are mutually exclusive activities. Heaven help those who in these times of rapid transition do not think of the future. The point is that our obsession with the future becomes futile when the future we wait for never arrives or arrives with repeated disappointment because it lacks the romantic trimmings with which we have imbued it.

The hurried society, by encouraging a future-directed relationship to time, also has the effect of *accelerating* time. By "accelerate" I mean simply that time is experienced as moving faster through people's lives. This happens not only because the events of daily life have been underexperienced and thus undervalued but also because they have become compressed. First, because the moment passes with less awareness, like the adolescent who is in such a hurry he doesn't chew his food, events of the day represent less of an experience and thus also less of a memorable event. If time is marked off by experience of events, but that experience of events never breaks the surface of consciousness, it's no wonder that time flies. Meanwhile, the pacing or unfolding of events has become compressed. With our sights set on a better future, we constantly pursue methods for making that future happen sooner rather than later. The birth of the credit card is just one example of how we have shattered the temporal distance between wanting something and getting it. By reeling in the future at faster speeds, however, we cannot help tampering with the stream of consciousness, which ends up only further accelerating the experience of time. For better or worse, you simply cannot accelerate the motion of your life without also accelerating the experience of it.

Furthermore, as the hurried society speeds up the passage of time, we have a tendency to react by trying to "save time." This then creates a vicious cycle, in that now the need one feels to "save time" leads us to hurry all the more, thus further accelerating time. John Whitelegg, a professor of geography, sums up this paradox nicely, using another example from Michael Ende's novel, *Momo*:

> Michael Ende's novel *Momo* describes the changes which took place in the daily lives of a small community when "time thieves" persuaded the residents to save time rather than "waste" it on idle conversation, caring for the elderly and similar social activities. The effects were dramatic: as the traditional café was converted into a fast-food outlet and other changes took place, people were too busy saving time to find any time for each other. The village barber found that: "he was becoming increasingly restless and irritable. The odd thing was that, no matter how much time he saved, he never had any to spare; in some mysterious way, it simply vanished. Imperceptibly at first, but then quite unmistakenly, his days grew shorter and shorter. Almost before he knew it, another week had gone by, another month, and another year, and another and another.' "[35]

At this point there is a need for a clarification. Earlier, in Chapter 1, I described how exposure to rapid-fire culture can create situations in which time seems almost to come to a standstill. This may seem to suggest the opposite conclusion from above, that exposure to fast-moving, high-intensity worlds causes time to slow down rather than speed up. If ten seconds can seem like an hour, shouldn't a day seem like an eternity?

While it is true that because of sensory adaptations, time slows down when the sensorium around us slows down, our discomfort with slowness results in our embracing faster-paced lifestyles. The hurried society sells us an escape from the unsettling experience of slowness, but in doing so, it also produces an acceleration of time (and a continued need to escape slowness). Indeed, because the passage of time is connected deeply to the degree to which we are chronically engaged in high-sensory lifestyles—full of activities in which "time flies"—the greater one's sensory addiction, the greater the overall acceleration of time. *It is thus an ironic twist of our modern fate that the more we keep our days, and our children's days, busy and hectic, perhaps even with activities we truly enjoy, the more we actually shorten the duration of our lives.* As with the barber in Michael Ende's *Momo*, the result of this compression is that weeks, months, years, and even whole decades begin to slip out from under us.

Herein lies the dangerous trap mentioned earlier. Wanting to drink deeply from the cup of life, we feel as though we must fill the cup as full as possible. But as we cram more and more into each day and more into each year, hoping to make life more meaningful, we find ourselves suddenly looking back upon time, wondering how it all passed by so quickly. Your travel agent or your accountant may assure you that you've lived a full life, but a printout of expenses won't change the fact that you know something's gone awry. If, however, we reorient our relationship to time, prioritizing the subjective, nonlinear reality of time over its objective, linear absolute, we will start to see how different lifestyles can actually stretch, fold, or compress time, thus altering the temporal structure of our lives. If effective time management means living a full life, it also means wasting time by living slowly, rather than saving it, by hurrying.

STUCK IN TIME

JOHN Stuart Mill once wrote that "no great improvements in the lot of mankind are possible until a great change takes place in the fundamental constitution of their modes of thought." If Mill's formulation is correct, might it not also be possible that a change in our psychological constitution, brought about by a new relationship between time and human society, could do the opposite and put a kink in the foundation of human society? As we look into this possibility, that Ritalin Nation represents a temporal disturbance in human consciousness, the history of premodern times is an illuminating place to begin. The basic idea is this: If the hurried society has a deep connection to human consciousness and its experience of time, we should find in earlier historical periods both a different mode of consciousness and a different experience of time.

In a basic sense, we can say that medieval times are the most recent period wherein we can still locate signs, however faint, of an attitude toward time that is radically different from ours. "Time for medieval society was a slow-moving, leisurely and protracted affair," writes Aron Gurevich. Communities at this time were predominantly rural and agrarian, governed by the feudal system. As dramatized in the film *The Return of Martin Guerre*, the psychological self in premodern times was deeply enmeshed with and subordinate to a larger family and community structure, including what we might now call the extended family. As the French historian Jacques Gélis writes, "Dependent on the family, the individual alone was nothing. The bearing of children established a link between past and future, between humanity that was and humanity yet to come. To break the chain was unthinkable."[36]

What makes the life story of Martin Guerre so interesting is its tale of one man taking up the social roles of another, both men becoming indistinguishable as a consequence. Although the wife of Martin Guerre, Bertrande de Rols, knows (and is grateful) that the man returning several years later, Arnaud du Tilh, is not truly her husband, other family members and members of the village fail to discern the physical and psychological differences and thus join her in welcoming him back. This story paints a striking contrast with modern times, when one's social roles are more isolated and less defining and when individualism, personality, and physical appearance are paramount. Indeed, it's impossible for us to imagine someone impersonating us simply because he or she bears some crude similarity and because he or she can successfully take up our social roles.

Stories like *The Return of Martin Guerre* remind us that in premodern times the individual self simply did not exist in the world in the way that we understand it today. In modern times children are raised in a social setting that constantly stresses the need to break from the family in order to start independent lives. Individuals in ancient and medieval times, on the other hand, held on to deep psychological connections that developed within a larger family whole. This was not necessarily a conscious choice, of course. Individuals relied on one another largely because they had to and because there were often severe social sanctions for breaking from the ranks. Nevertheless, these social contingencies laid the foundation for keeping families and communities together. Indeed, one might say that the same still holds true. Healthy communities stay intact, or come about, only when people have a true dependence upon one other. We see this today, for example, when there are emergency situations, such as floods, fires, or earthquakes, when people come together, re-creating a true community, if only temporarily.

The tightly interwoven family of medieval times often thrived under this necessity, which meant in turn that the extended family cultivated a sense of self that lacked the hard-and-fast boundaries between one person and another that we take for granted today. As Jacques Gélis suggests, back then "the individual alone was nothing." Indeed, because one's identity was so enmeshed with family and community, we might conclude that the individual would have lost his or her own identity if these connections had been severed. By contrast, the dependence on the extended family in premodern times—which created a secure, whole psychological self—would be seen today in just the opposite light, as putting individual identity and selfhood at risk. Consider, for example, how suspiciously we view traditional tight-knit cultures, such as the old orders of Amish, Quakers, and Mennonites. Because we typically associate the freedoms of individualism as a prerequisite of human contentment, we look at this devotion to the larger community—the sacrifice of the individual for the common good—and wonder how the individual could possibly find happiness. In truth, these cultures actually suffer from significantly fewer problems of depression, suicide, and the like than groups with the same ethnicity living in urban conditions.[37]

We can also find something akin to these differences in the nature of the "emergent self" when looking at the disparity between eastern and western notions of identity. As anthropologist Clifford Geertz writes, "The Western conception of the person as a bounded, unique, more or less integrated motivational and cognitive universe, a dynamic center of awareness, emotion, judgment, and action organized into a distinctive whole and set contrastively both against other such wholes and against its social and natural background, is, however incorrigible it may seem to us, a rather peculiar idea within the context of the world's cultures."[38] What the difference between Eastern and Western selves tells us is that while the Western world gradually shifted from a collectively defined self to one defined much more in terms of the individual, other cultures preserved, whether by conscious intention or not, a deeper reliance on social interdependence.

Because the self in premodern times had such a different relationship to itself and other selves from what we see today, it also had a fundamentally different relationship to time. Agrarian life and the extended family, especially in the early Middle Ages and before, cultivated a *cyclical* temporal experience. Life was rooted in the daily and seasonal cycles of one's immediate experience, and so was time. Much like *le calendrier républicain* utilized in France from 1792 to 1806, early peasant calendars were organized according to the changing of the seasons and the different agricultural periods. For instance, historians have described how calendars among Germanic and Scandinavian tribes defined months by different tasks, such as the "month of wine" or the "time for going up to summer pasture."[39]

A cyclical sense of time also meant that people understood the future as something that moved forward but that then circled back, repeating the same cycles over again, generation after generation.

The linear arrow of time that we know today—the past, present, and future—did not exist. Cyclical time can be seen, for example, in how words used to signify time were taken from something cyclical, concrete, and livable in nature, such as words having to do with "tide" or "harvest." Because of this circularity, people did not view their lives as looking forward into a great uncertain future, stretching out before them in a straight line that terminates with death. The meaning of life was understood differently, as something much larger that began long before one's own birth and would continue long afterward. Although life was undoubtedly filled with many overwhelming and oppressive difficulties now long extinct, people did enjoy a freedom from the existential angst we experience today as the price of modern individualism, with its unique linear sense of time.

The future-directed outlook that so profoundly shapes people's lives today has its immediate incarnation in our escape from slowness. But there are also a number of historical factors that give us some clue about how our future directedness and the speeding up of society began in the first place. Geographer David Harvey has noted the influence of the church, for instance, writing that "Christianity broke the cyclic world view of time and substituted a more eschatological view in which there was a beginning, a culmination, and an end, such that time became 'linear and irreversible.' "[40] Along with sweeping revisions in the meaning of time, there came a shift away from the extended family—with its agrarian, public life—toward what we now call the nuclear family—with its urban, private life. Indeed, the transformation toward smaller, more isolated social units is a hallmark feature of modernity, which began to unfold rapidly in the sixteenth and seventeenth centuries.[41] Marshall Berman, in *All That Is Solid Melts into Air: The Experience of Modernity*, paints a vivid image of this age: "There is a mode of vital experience—experience of space and time, of the self and others, of life's possibilities and perils—that is shared by men and women all over the world today. I will call this body of experience 'modernity.' To be modern is to find ourselves in an environment that promises us adventure, power, joy, growth, transformation of ourselves and the world—and, at the same time, that threatens to destroy everything we have, everything we know, everything we are."[42]

Berman's double-edged description of modernity is suggestive of the excitement and romanticism that appeared on the scene after the Middle Ages and that eventually lured masses of people toward a new, urban way of life. Promises of new adventures, power, joy, et cetera were so powerful that they helped break the previously unbreakable chains that had for so long kept the extended family together. Suddenly individuals began to unearth themselves from the traditional stories, expectations, relationships, and structures of earlier times, placing their newfound hopes and dreams in an unknowable but also undeniably alluring future. Borrowing passages from a 1902 essay by the prophetic H. G. Wells on the future-directed self, Stephen Kern writes: ". . .the modern age has turned away from a dogged adherence to tradition and has 'discovered' the future as a source of values and a guide for action. While three hundred years ago people drew their rules of conduct 'absolutely and unreservedly from the past,' now they are more inclined to look ahead and consider the consequences of any action and modify the rules if the consequences merit it."[43] Statistics on urban migration document the startling results of this turn toward the future: In 1800 less than 1 percent of the world population lived in cities; by 1990 this number had risen to 33 percent. For England alone, in 1800, 10 percent lived in cities; by 1990 the percentage had risen to more than 90. Meanwhile, nearly seventy million people up and left Europe for the New World, an event altogether unthinkable a century earlier.[44]

The mass migration to the urban center—"the graveyard of the countryman"—gradually rendered obsolete the extended family and a whole host of other social relations. The extended family was refitted into the smaller social units we know today, including the nuclear family and, still more recently, the single-parent household. While the individualism of modernity was put into motion by an array of hopeful images for a prosperous new life, it was ultimately the cultural and economic contingencies of the urban arena that brought it fully into being and left little room for turning back. That is, once people moved to the cities, stories began to find their way back to the country, telling exaggerated tales of adventure and riches. Thus, once rural people relocated to the urban center, they became trapped in the economics of survival, realizing the shame they would endure if they were to return to the country empty-handed.

Meanwhile, the psychological constitution of the self, including conscious experience, continued to change. Like the French sociologist Émile Durkheim, who produced classic studies of modern alienation and suicide, an array of social theorists have stressed how urbanization and its division of labor fragment and depersonalize social life. As people's lives became fragmented, their awareness of themselves as single, solitary individuals heightened. As existentialist novelist Milan Kundera writes, there is in history a "moment when the world starts gradually losing its transparency, darkens, becomes more and more incomprehensible, rushes into the unknown, while man, betrayed by the world, escapes into his self, into his nostalgia, his dreams, his revolt, and lets himself be deafened by the voices inside him so that he no longer hears the voices outside."[45]

Urban sociologists like Peter Saunders have also described this change in the cultural evolution of the American self, noting how the individual was in earlier times integrated in his or her society, where shared community dominated aspects of his or her life. In modern urban contexts, however, "the social circles in which the individual moves become tangential to each other, and his involvement in any one of them is partial and specific." Consequently, in the highly differentiated, modern society, "the individual is constantly exposed to an infinite variety of changing situations and sensation in which his own unique personality is the only constant factor."[46] Urban life thus encourages a heightened awareness of one's "self"—an "inward turn" that sets the stage for the birth of the modern self—by stripping from the person the interpersonal relations and dependencies that existed previously in traditional life.[47]

For our purposes, what is important about this new self is that it led to a profoundly different relationship between time and society. While the self was being stripped naked on all sides, something very similar was happening with time. For the extended family, time had circled and warmed one's existence, and people lived within a cyclical temporal frame that encapsulated the present. As Aron Gurevich has described, the repetition of nature that produced a cyclical sense of time also promoted an attitude that things would not and therefore should not change. The rise of a linear sense of time came about, however, as people began to imagine and then to desire a change in what their life would become, seeing happiness as something that lay in the future. With the cycle of time broken, the imagination was then carried off into the vast uncertainties of the future, creating in turn a new and unsettling awareness of time. No longer did people live "in time," where time remained hidden within the context of human agency. Instead, they began living "alongside time," where because time is now treated as something standing between where we are and where we're headed—between the present and the future—it became an obstacle in our pursuit of happiness.

TECHNOLOGY AS TIME'S ASSASSIN

In our understanding of the hurried society, this new relationship to time has importance beyond all others. With our sights set on a distant temporal horizon, and with time now understood as that which stands between it and the present, time suddenly becomes an unexpected adversary in our lives. It begins to stand out, not as some newly abundant resource for mastering our surroundings and relaxing in the present moment but rather as something standing in the way of our newfound desires. When we anxiously await the weekend, as we do today, or when we pine away the years, waiting for school or work to end (or change), we immediately begin to experience time as something that needs to be done away with. "In being that which alienates us from the end of our striving," writes the existentialist philosopher Lorenzo Simpson, "time is at best dispensable, at worst an obstruction."[48]

With the rise of the modern age, time thus went from being hidden within the structure of everyday life to being omnipresent. Moreover, with time animating conscious experience as an obstacle between wish and wish fulfillment, the need arose to collapse the gap somehow between now and then. As suggested in the earlier example of credit cards, this is by no means the impossible task that it might appear to be. In fact, seizing upon the successes of the industrial age, technology became the principal weapon in what has since become a three-hundred-year war against time. As Neil Postman writes in *Technopoly*, time "became an adversary over which technology could triumph. And this meant that there was no time to look back or to contemplate what was being lost. There were empires to build, opportunities to exploit, exciting freedoms to enjoy, especially in America."[49] Also reflecting on the role of technology in speeding up life in America, Austrian sociologist Helga Nowotny points out that:

> There was hardly an account of a journey from the [nineteen] twenties and thirties by Europeans who had returned from the USA which was not fascinated by the hectic pace prevailing there and the cult of speed, commented on by the Europeans with a mixture of admiration and the forebodings of a cultural pessimism. The intoxication with time resulted first of all from the directly perceptible increase in speed, hastened and mediated by technology, but absorbed into the life of society as a whole, an increase which individuals could not evade. Technological change means nothing other than the accelerated sequence of social changes.[50]

A short list of some contemporary time-savers, all of which are designed to speed things up, might include ATMs, fast food, super-highways, electronic highways, remote controls, prepared foods, drive-throughs, jetliners, cell phones, home shopping networks, Pentiums, FedEx, the kitchen appliance, and minute rice.

It is indeed an ironic twist of history that just as we acquired and began to champion a new relationship to time, with a new outlook toward a brighter future, we began relying on technology to return time to a less prominent place in our lives. This complex chain of actions and reactions exposes the inherent contradictions of our modern relationship to time. Despite our mastery of technology, time is viewed more than ever as a highly scarce commodity, so much so that "time is money." Because we view time as something fixed and objective that goes unaffected by our actions, however, we unintentionally engage in technological and social practices that have the ultimate effect of accelerating time, thus making it scarcer still. Here lies one of the great misadventures in time, where our efforts to create more of it have resulted in having less of it. In the popular bestseller *Small Is Beautiful*, E. F. Schumacher draws much the same conclusion:

> The primary task of technology, it would seem, is to lighten the burden of work man has to carry in order to stay alive and develop his potential. It is easy enough to see that technology fulfills this purpose when we watch any particular piece of machinery at work—a computer, for instance, can do in seconds what it would take clerks or even mathematicians a very long time, if they can do it at all. It is more difficult to convince oneself of the truth of this simple proposition when one looks at whole societies. When I first began to travel the world, visiting rich and poor countries alike, I was tempted to formulate the first law of economics as follows: "The amount of real leisure a society enjoys tends to be in inverse proportion to the amount of labour-saving machinery it employs."[51]

Thus, while it is certainly true that technology has a powerful ability to save time, allowing us to do more, this understanding obscures its ultimate effects. The modern conquest to collapse the temporal distance between present and future succeeds in altering the pace of newness and change, but it also has an unintended transformative effect on human consciousness. Herein lies a second great misadventure in time: Technology aids us in making more happen in less time, but because human consciousness adapts almost immediately to the new sensory experience, the only lasting effect is to raise our expectations about how fast the world must go. Consequently, technology does not do away with time and its future; rather, it makes them even more salient.

Having now arrived at these two great blunders in how we produce and understand time, we are in a position, finally, to draw an initial conclusion about our temporal stance toward the future and the rise of Ritalin Nation: *By shortening the temporal gap between desire and its fulfillment, technology not only accelerates the pace at which we experience life but also raises our expectations—our need—for a hyper-paced life.* Technology has succeeded so well in making the world go faster (and become smaller) that the subjective experience of daily life has itself become compressed, creating a heightened personal demand for stimulation.

For children, this problem of temporal compression is even greater, for kids naturally experience a greater sense of temporal compression compared with their parents. That is, because a child's life experiences are as a whole much fewer than the adult's, and because one's cumulative life experiences influence one's sense of the passage of time, the child often already suffers from protracted or stretched-out sense of time in the adult-run world, regardless of the child's own exposure to constant sensory consumption. As Alvin Toffler explains in *Future Shock*, "It is hardly strange that to the boy the delay seems three or four times longer than to the father. . . . Asking the child to wait two hours for a piece of candy may be the equivalent of asking the mother to wait fourteen hours for a cup of coffee."[52]

This new sensory-demanding form of human consciousness, whether in the child or the adult, produces in turn a growing sense of urgency and impatience in human action. Rapid-fire culture leads to a compression of one's experience of time, such that brief moments left in the lurch now give rise to unmet sensory needs, then frustrations, and finally an increase in sensory-seeking behaviors. This is the social pathology we've been calling *sensory addictions.*

"A World on Time" (FedEx)

Just how obsessed we are with time can be seen in the number of expressions we have that focus on it: There's time well spent, time to kill, no time like the present, back in time, losing track of time, time in a bottle, time standing still, a fight against time, uses time wisely, time is money, time to go, time out, out of time, time off, time machine, train on time, old times, in the nick of time, enlightened times, stuck in time, *Time* magazine, sick time, time lost, times like these, in these times, the best of times, the worst of times, time's a terrible thing to waste, mealtime, night-time, daytime, maritime, anytime, terrible time, time flies, some-time, standard time, just in time, test of time, tell time, time will tell, all good things in time, a stitch in time saves nine, time frame, time bandit, time to burn, two-timing, double time, man out of time, ahead of her time, save time, from time to time, time bomb, time after time, Times Square, time warp, serving time, time's up, a time to love, a time to die, *New York Times*, time traveler, time of your life, teatime, overtime, vacation time, time clock, stolen time, find the time, make time, time won't wait, equal time, quality time, time for time's sake, good times, bad times, comes a time, time's a precious thing, all the time in the world, time's a-wastin', time tells all, time shortage, dead time, downtime, on my time, timepiece, peacetime, wartime, a time for one, a time for all, time on my hands, time waits for no one, time zone, Timex, one hell of a good time, every damn time, time to settle down, doing time, time capsule, eats up time, past your bedtime, your time will come, modern times, forgotten times, timetables, precious little time, sign of the times, the last time, tell time, only time will tell, time and time again, the end of time, and it's about time.

Speed and Its Transformation of Human Consciousness

We shape our tools and thereafter our tools shape us.

MARSHALL MCLUHAN

LET us begin this third chapter with the words of two thoughtful writers, first George Eliot, writing in her novel *Felix Holt, the Radical* (1866) and second Noelle Oxenhandler, writing in *The New Yorker* (1997):

> Posterity may be shot, like a bullet through a tube, by atmospheric pressure from Winchester to Newcastle; that is a fine result to have among our hopes; but the slow old-fashioned way of getting from one end of the country to the other is the better thing to have in the memory. The tube-journey can never lend much to picture and narrative; it is as barren as an exclamatory O! Whereas the happy outside passenger seated on the box from the dawn to the gloaming gathered enough stories of English life, enough of English labours in town and country, enough aspects of earth and sky, to make episodes for a modern Odyssey.[1]

> Among the greatest pleasures in my life has been to sit on a French train, watching each village, with its steeple and stone walls, emerge in turn from the intervening pattern of field and trees and those beautiful cows—Charolais—that are the color of silt or of cream sinking into a cup of coffee. But now, on the T.G.V.—those trains that can whip from Paris to Provence in a matter of four hours—the trees and the villages turn into a blinking pattern of stripes which gives me a headache, and I have to

look away. For the sake of speed, in the interest of not wasting time, we sacrifice the sensuous richness of the not-yet.[2]

These authors, writing more than a century apart, express an almost identical concern. Both see the acceleration of culture as undermining the simple pleasures of everyday life. Reporting from the same situation—traveling across the European landscape— each decries an accelerating world in which the past, the present, and the future have begun blurring into one incomprehensible fuzzball. No longer does the pace of life mesh with the pace at which we can accommodate it into our own conscious and memorial experience. Indeed, each of these writers believes in a profound way that she is falling out of time, trampled by the mighty force of progress.

There is at the same time, however, something strikingly different about these two passages. Although both lament the same general process, each is experiencing it at very different points in its evolution. How can this be so? How can a writer today lament the loss of something George Eliot saw disappearing while riding on last century's stagecoach: the pleasures of slowness? The answer to this question brings us directly to the matter at hand. Not only has the motion of daily life been speeding up for some time, but we have been keeping up with these changes, for better or worse, through an ongoing transformation of human consciousness. Noelle Oxenhandler can describe the same loss of meaning as George Eliot, but this is a loss that is calibrated, psychologically and societally, for her own time, not Eliot's. If we were to thrust George Eliot forward into our time and put her in Oxenhandler's rapid ride to Provence, she would suffer terribly more than does her late twentieth-century counterpart. The cultural evolution of Eliot's mind has fallen a century out-of-date, and catching up for her would be difficult and unpleasant.

While the world has been speeding up, we as conscious, temporal beings have been speeding up with it. Like the schoolchildren who unknowingly absorbed the pace and rhythm of their first-grade teachers, we cannot help internalizing and emulating the rhythm of our own surroundings. Hence, when this rhythm runs chronically fast or slow, the rhythm of consciousness also runs chronically fast or slow. As a *historical* fact, this does not mean that we cannot reverse this process; it means only that at the level of conscious experience, the process will not rewind by itself, as we know from the growing number of individuals diagnosed with "adult-ADD." Meanwhile, as the two passages above suggest, the capacity to adapt to the motion and intensity of the built world is precisely that which has allowed this intensification to go on for so long. Indeed, if we really could bring George Eliot back, her reaction would show us just how drenched our culture is from the constant downpour of stimulation and how much human consciousness has changed as a consequence.

But of course we cannot bring her back. What we can do, however, is substitute in her place our own exploration of the hurried society as it has unfolded this century, continuing with the social history of human consciousness that we began in the previous chapter. Armed with a new set of ideas about the nature and history of time, we are now in position to connect the temporal mechanics of human consciousness to the particular relationship we have developed with time and space. The fact that each day we live in a faster, smaller world has had huge implications not only for the life of the city but also for the life of the community, the life of the individual, and the life of the mind. It's not just that we can use ideas about time and space to clarify why we live and feel the way we do. We can also use them to clarify why we have *not* succeeded in turning our hard-won social and economic liberties into lives that we enjoy rather than hurry through.[3]

To understand the lure of the power of speed, one has to consider that speed actually represents two dimensions, time and space, fused into one. Greater speed means I can go more places in the same time, or I can go the same place in less time, or I can do some of both. To master speed is to simultaneously master both time and space. As we saw in the case of time, the essence of these two dimensions is at least as psychological as it is physical. Indeed, time and space can be coiled together and fused into the single dimension of speed because space also exists for us principally as a psychological category. We are aware that the physical dimensions of time can remain constant while our experience of it changes, where ten minutes can feel like an hour and vice versa. The same can be said of space. The world of a newborn child is so incredibly large that he or she has no conscious awareness of anything larger than his or her immediate physical surroundings. Families of the Middle Ages and before also experienced the world as very circumscribed; thinking the world was flat, for example, was simply a prejudice born out of inexperience. Even residents in places like the Northeast Kingdom of Vermont still experience the world as little more than a few miles square, traveling "great distances" of thirty or forty miles only on special occasions. The rest of us, however, know a world so small that phrases like "global economy" are elementary, even for schoolchildren. This is a world where the rest of the world is only seconds away by telephone or electronic highway and only hours away by high-speed train or airplane. Social psychologist Kenneth Gergen provides us with a summary of some of the changes in our world:

- A century ago, there were fewer than 100 automobiles in the United States. By the 1900s, there were over 123 million cars in use, with over 6 million new cars produced annually.
- At the turn of the century, there was no radio; at the current time, 99% of the households in the United States have at least one radio, and more than 28 million new radios are sold each year.
- Air transportation was virtually unknown until the 1920s; there are now over 42 million passengers a year in the United States alone.
- Television was virtually unknown until the 1940s; at the current time, over 99% of American households have at least one TV set—a percentage that exceeds that of households with indoor plumbing.
- Personal computers were virtually unknown in the 1970s; there are now over 80 million in use.[4]

Ultimately, as in the examples above, the cultural revolution that has transformed time and space this century has done so by transforming speed. In a literal sense, however, speed did not change the physical dimensions of time and space. The world is the same size it always was, just as an hour is an hour and a year a year. Rather, speed is transforming time and space by changing the rhythm and temporality of something inside us, human consciousness.

THE CONTOURS OF CONSCIOUSNESS

THUS far in our study of rapid-fire consciousness we have charted three of its key territories. We have first of all explored the capacity of human consciousness to assimilate new, faster modes of living. Here we saw that the mind's adaptation to the rhythm of one's surroundings, beginning at birth, creates for us the normative standard for how fast the world should go. The underlying mechanism for this transformation of consciousness has to do with the nature of temporal mechanics, where the compression of daily events—experiencing more in the same period of time—alters our experience of time's passage. With time becoming more compressed, the failure to maintain our inflated sensory expectations begins to produce symptoms of sensory addictions, including restlessness and anxiety. The end result of this temporal disturbance is that because we engage in a greater quantity and intensity of events to escape this uneasiness—*and because we continue to seek out forms of action and adventure capable of surpassing our current expectations*—we have a tendency to continue entering into even faster modes of living.

There is, however, a restriction on this formula. Because it describes a historical process, some outside force must have acted upon us in the first place to set it into motion. There remains the question, in other words, of why the pace of life began to change so rapidly with the onset of the modern era. After all, the idea is not that the acceleration of culture is an unavoidable or natural process but rather that it is a historical one put into motion by some external set of unique societal forces. What were these outside forces? In addition to the rise of individualism and a new, linear sense of time, which we saw in the last chapter, the answer to this question has to do with another change in human consciousness, namely, our core beliefs about what constitutes the "good life."

As we saw in our discussion of the premodern self and its rela-

tionship to cyclical time, belief systems have an enormous capacity
not only to shape the meaning of immediate experience but also to
define the relationship between the nature of self and the nature of
time. We saw, for example, that the self in premodern times really
had little or no sense of linear time, the future, and the possibility
of creating a separate life. This embeddedness in time and community flowed out from durable systems of belief that were handed
down, largely unconsciously, during one's formative years in the
local culture. We also saw, however, that this earlier, less
autonomous self was transformed into a new, future-directed self, as
traditional beliefs about the meaning of life and time gradually
broke down, ultimately making room for the shift toward modernity. Just as Marshall Berman describes modernity as a new "mode of
vital experience," so José María Sbert describes it as a time where "a
distinctly modern faith—faith in progress—arose to make sense of,
and give ultimate meaning to the new notions and institutions that
were now dominant." He continues: "A portentous faith in progress
is the real spiritual foundation of modern man, the tradition he
stands on. The idea has been the most influential and ubiquitous
notion in the formation of modern thought, merging the power of
the modern world with the spell of a chimerical metamorphosis of
Christian faith."[5]

In this modern context we can see the connection between the
speeding up of consciousness and the beliefs people shared about
the new meaning and structure of their lives. Technological
advances and the rapid growth of cities brought about new ideas
and norms, which in large part had to do with the new progres-
sivism. These new conceptions about the future and our place in it
eventually formed a culturally constructed, interlocking system of
beliefs that created a new context—a new existentialism and social
ethic—for how one could and should live one's life. As this developed, it gave further momentum to the rise of both the urban and
technological spheres, thus setting the stage for the rat race of the
hurried society. As this process unfolded in the United States, it was
clear, especially to outsiders, that it was here that the spirit of
modernity had it tightest grip. Indeed, it seems that nowhere else
was the sense of an open-ended future of unbridled progress less

restrained than in the imagination of the American mind.[6]

The future-oriented imaginings of modern life did not just disturb the rhythm of human consciousness, however. Once the technological revolutions of the twentieth century began to mix with the ongoing transformations taking place in the structure of work and family (including an increase in divorce and in women working both inside and outside the home), a third aspect of the human mind also began to change. A product of an emerging culture of neglect, this recent development has to do with the sudden failure of children's experiences to yield an internal system of self-governance.

As children grow older, we expect them to mature in their ability to exert more control over their own behavior, to become more psychologically independent. As self-governance develops, children outgrow their external controls, such as those embedded in normative structures of family and school. This new, internalized system of self-management serves to calm and organize the conscious mind by enabling individuals to exert self-control over their own actions. For this structure to take root internally, however, first there has to exist for the child a solid external infrastructure that can be internalized during development. As David Elkind has documented in his book *The Hurried Child*, this normative structure is really nothing more than a set of healthy family practices that, by setting reasonable limits and expectations, makes the child more psychologically secure and keeps him or her within normal standards of social behavior and cognition. By contrast, when children live faster, unstructured lives, this psychological development fails to take place, leaving children and adolescents in perpetual need of external supports. The most striking example of this developmental crisis is the use of powerful stimulant drugs, like Ritalin, which calm the individual, but in a way that only perpetuates a dependency on these externalized supports.

Taken together, these three interrelated changes in the nature of mind and consciousness provide a rough sketch of how we arrived where we are today: First, parents caught in a work ethic driven by the pursuit of material success are raising children under more trying circumstances. Despite our standard of living (or perhaps because of it), we as a whole work more than any other advanced society. This means that parents are at home less, and when at home, they (especially single parents) are increasingly distracted or exhausted by other demands. Secondly, the social and emotional refuges parents used to provide children are now being provided, if at all, by other caregivers and by passive but gripping forms of entertainment. Numerous studies have shown, for example, that children's play in the past few decades has gone from being active, social, and outdoors to increasingly passive, nonsocial, and indoors. One example is our neighborhoods, where playing in what were once safe, unhurried, and unencumbered neighborhood streets has been replaced by "safer" indoor activities, such as television, video games, and computers.[7] With the instability, inconsistency, and psychological superficiality that these changes have wrought, the external structures that now govern behavior are no longer of the sort that can be internalized by the child to produce self-governance. Thirdly, with children and adolescents occupied by the latest electronic experiences, the demand for newer, faster, and more intense activities has cultivated a shrunken attention span. We cannot keep our attention on any one thing because any one thing cannot satisfy our attention, at least not for long. Consequently, with a hurried, unstructured lifestyle undermining children's psychological development, emotional and behavioral problems begin to appear, especially under conditions of slowness. Not knowing why this is happening, we have reacted both inappropriately and ineffectively.

A NEW SPEED AHEAD

BEHIND the ascendancy of the modern, hurried self are many earlier versions of it that relate its glorious but tragic story. Looking at the rise of modern selfhood provides us with several insights. We see how it is possible that a cascade of unanticipated and unlikely events could actually overtake us. We see how this unfolded gradually, a process kept in motion by powerful institutional forces (such as economic institutions and their secularization of society) and by a persistent set of beliefs about the changing world. We also see that this gradual evolution combined in a synergistic way with our simplistic assumption about the relationship between modern life and the modern mind. This combination not only allowed a rising existential crisis to continue full speed ahead but also kept the full workings of the crisis hidden from us. As a consequence, there was little substantive change in our assumptions about the relationship among human society, human consciousness, and human motivation.

As a historical being, the self has a momentum and trajectory that tell us not only where we have been but also where we are going. We can map the evolution of modern selfhood this century by reading what early historians had to say about their own times and then connecting this to what we are currently witnessing. When this connecting of the dots is filled in, we begin to see the dramatic voyage that this historical being has undertaken. Stephen Kern, writing on *The Culture of Time and Space: 1880–1918*, drops anchor for us in the late nineteenth century: "From around 1880 to the outbreak of World War I a series of sweeping changes in technology and culture created distinctive new modes of thinking about and experiencing time and space. Technological innovations including the telephone, wireless telegraph, x-ray, cinema, bicycle, automobile, and airplane established the material foundation for this reorientation; independent cultural developments such as the stream-of-consciousness novel, psychoanalysis, Cubism, and the theory of relativity shaped consciousness directly. The result was a transformation of the dimensions of life and thought."[8]

By the end of the nineteenth century an era of cultural change had commenced in the United States that would surpass all those that preceded it. This was a time of massive technological innovation—innovation that sped up the world while simultaneously shrinking it down in size. The pace of change and the change of pace were together so disruptive that the merits of technological innovation and the hastened pace of life were hotly debated. Although things happened faster, which most found to be a virtuous thing, this quickly gave rise to new problems, including rising expectations about how much we should be doing and how fast it should all be done. The laborer might be dazzled by the exhilaration and freedom of riding a bicycle but then suffer terribly at work from new standards of productivity, efficiency, and punctuality.

These changes taking place a century ago were not only more awe-inspiring than anything seen previously, but also more profound than anything seen since. This revolutionary period saw the rise of new modes of transportation, including the automobile; new modes of artificial reality, including the cinema; and new modes of communication, including the telephone. What has happened in the years since has been almost wholly restricted to improvements upon these breakthrough inventions. In short, this era marked the beginning of a number of qualitatively new ways of experiencing the world.

The revolutionary nature of these changes helps explain why we do not see the same debate taking place today, despite the fact that high-speed trains, jet planes, and the Internet represent a considerably greater acceleration of speed and compression of time and space than did their early predecessors. One apparent exception, the computer, actually reinforces this conclusion. When personal and mainframe computers entered the market in the 1960s and 1970s, there was indeed debate over their effects on human society and human welfare. Most of this focused on how computers (and robotics) might replace people in the work force. There were also debates about how this technology might affect such things as the creative spirit, as when noted authors praised the virtues of their old Remington typewriters, swearing off the new technology. In any case, the debate was rekindled at this time because computers, like the early cinema, automobile, and telephone, represented a jarring qualitative shift in how we would live and relate to one another.

Let us look at these developments more closely.

FIFTEEN years before that fated night of April 14, 1912, when the *Titanic* was brought down on its maiden voyage by an iceberg in the mid-Atlantic, a technological race with time had commenced on the open sea. The contestants in this race were nation-states and companies that built and operated ocean liners, each wanting to lay claim to having the fastest passenger vessels. The prizewinners (and losers) were the consumers, passengers who wanted what an earlier generation might have viewed as a peculiar contradiction: to travel in the most luxurious conditions but also at the fastest possible speeds. The *Titanic*, a technological marvel of her time, would go on to demonstrate the dark side of this overzealous lust for speed, though few would learn from the experience.

Most of us know the story of the *Titanic* in terms of its reputation as an "unsinkable" ship that vanished disastrously in a night of icy waters (in fact, the true claim was "practically unsinkable"). Few realize, even to this day, that the real culprit was not a hidden iceberg or a shortage of lifeboats. Rather, the real villain was a recklessness that came from a growing obsession with speed.[9] We must remember that although today's ocean liners are an iconic image of the pleasure cruise (people wanting efficient travel now choose to "fly the friendly skies"), earlier ships represented the only mode of transatlantic passage.

Because the *Titanic* went down during a time when the virtues of technology and speedup were still being debated, the tragedy quickly prompted outrage in the United States and abroad. Describing the "arrogance of large ocean liners" and the demands of an impatient public, various historians documented the impact of rising expectations for speed on the safety of travel.[10] From the testimony of mariners who described the pressure placed on ship captains to keep unrealistic schedules to charges of recklessness expressed by public figures like George Bernard Shaw and Joseph Conrad, there was already a growing awareness of the dangers and addictiveness of speed. In Walter Lord's history of the *Titanic* disaster *The Night Lives On*, he writes:

> Knuckling under the competitive pressure of keeping schedule, most captains ran at full steam, despite strong evidence that ice was not as easily sighted as generally claimed. Especially noteworthy was the harrowing ordeal of the Guion Liner *Arizona* in November 1879. Like the *Titanic*, she was the largest liner of her day. Eastbound off the Banks of Newfoundland, she raced through a night that was cloudy, but with good visibility. Taking advantage of the calm seas, the passengers gathered in the lounge for a concert. Suddenly there was a fearful crash, sending everybody sprawling among the palms and violins. The *Arizona* had smashed head on into a giant iceberg, shattering 30 feet of her bow. But the forward

bulkhead held; there were no casualties; and two days later she limped into St. John's. In a curious twist of logic, the accident was hailed as an example of the safety of ships, rather than the dangers of ice.[11]

By the time of the *Titanic* disaster thirty-three years later, critics had painted an image of wild abandon, with ghostlike steamships marching across the dark sea at top speed with complete disregard for human life. But most people believed in the powers of technology that could build such a swift-moving forty-six-thousand-ton vessel (in its time the *Titanic* was longer than any building was tall). This faith also had the effect of promoting disregard for less romantic safety-directed technology, creating the conditions under which speed could take the lives of more than fifteen hundred people. Technology that could have guaranteed considerably greater safety was ignored because it did not enhance speed. The absence of half the needed lifeboats on the *Titanic* reveals this arrogance. Another example is the failure of the ship's crew to rely on reports using the new wireless telegraph that could help pinpoint the time and place where ice could be expected.[12] Interestingly, a third example comes from the sister ship of the *Titanic*, the *Olympic*. Although the ship was reinforced and modified for better safety following the sinking of the *Titanic*, she nevertheless also found her way to the bottom of the sea, hit by an explosive device during her recruitment into World War I. The reason she sank—and in less than one hour!—was apparently that the ship's crew failed to operate the new, "safer" technology in its intended, "unsinkable" manner.

As I think the *Titanic*'s sinking shows, speed was to have a dangerous influence on the social fabric of everyday life, not only because of the reckless nature of speed itself but also because of the intoxicating effect it has on its users.[13] The image of a sleek monster ship ripping through the sea represented more than just a single incident in the North Atlantic. At least to critics, it came to symbolize the forceful manner in which all technology would seize upon and restructure every aspect of public and private life, whether socially, geographically, or vocationally. For example, this not only diminished our capacity to appreciate the present—our ability to live in the moment—but also undermined our appreciation of nature. Relating this to the influence of science and technology, David Abram writes in *The Spell of the Sensuous*: "Oblivious to the quality-laden life-world upon which they themselves depended upon for their own meaning and existence, the Western sciences, and the technologies that accompany them, were beginning to blindly overrun the experiential world—even, in their errancy, threatening to obliterate the world-of-life entirely."[14]

Meanwhile, concerns over the hazards of speed were also appearing on land. This had mostly to do with the emergence of the automobile, but it began some time earlier with the bicycle. The bicycle evolved into its contemporary design—with wheels of equal size, pneumatic tires, and a drive mechanism that placed the pedals between the wheels—through a series of successive inventions throughout the nineteenth century. One predecessor was the hobbyhorse, a device that had no pedaling mechanism and thus had to be foot-propelled when on flat or uphill surfaces. Later came the velocipede, which had a crank and pedal on the front wheel. This was followed by still other innovations before, finally, the first bicycle appeared in England as "The Flying Dutchman" in about 1877.[15]

Certainly people had attained breathless speed on horseback long before the bicycle, but the bicycle represented something different. Aside from being more portable than the average horse, the bicycle also conferred upon its owner a greater sense of freedom and maneuverability, especially in urban areas where the streets were smoother. A writer in 1931 put it this way: "The bicycle is subservient to no time schedule; it is free. It does not follow the beaten path, rather roves along a thousand freely chosen paths. At every hour, in every direction it carries its rider. It serves nothing but individual need; it does justice to the endless variety of human desires and endeavors."[16]

The speed of the bicycle also was not to be disregarded. Its initial, imperfect form was about four times faster than walking, which was fast enough to gain attention. As one historian noted, the "speed is intoxicating, the mobility liberating, the exertion inspiring . . ."[17] There was even concern that riding at top speed against the wind might produce a kind of permanent disfigurement called "bicycle face."[18] Writing on the *l'amour de la vitesse*, the French writer Paul Adam suggested in 1907 that the bicycle had created a "cult of speed" for a new generation wanting "to conquer time and space."[19]

The most important aspect of the bicycle was, however, how it was used. If the bicycle were simply a replacement for the horse, the question of speed would have been a minor one. But the bicycle was not just in competition with the horse. It was also substituting for something considerably slower: walking. Because of its relative inexpense, the bicycle opened up a new form of rapid transit for many who, at least initially, could not afford automobiles. Indeed, the bicycle symbolized the revolutionary times that these were, with technology each day encouraging the modern spirit of personal independence, newness, and change.

As such, the mechanics and freedom of the bicycle actually paved the way for the embrace of the automobile. In *For Love of the Automobile*, Wolfgang Sachs writes, "The bicycle mobilized desire for an automobile. . . . It must be noted that not only did automotive technology—with the chain, the hub, and the air-filled tire— reap the gains of bicycle technology, but the attractiveness of the automobile in particular was nourished on the feeling the bicycle inspired."[20] Like the bicycle, the automobile got off to a slow start. Here the constraint on speed was less technological than social, however. For although the bicycle did not represent an altogether faster mode of transportation, the automobile clearly did. As drivers began to flex their new motorized muscles, the public, most of whom did not drive, quickly sought to place legal constraints on how fast cars could go. To them, such speed was an unnecessary and reckless activity. We take speed limits for granted today, but the creation of such limits late in nineteenth-century Europe marked an important moment in history, when the machine age offered up more speed than we were ready to handle. As with the race unfolding on the open sea, the corruption of speed on land began taking the lives of innocent bystanders. In England, for example, after one year with the higher speed limit of twenty miles per hour (in 1905), 1,500 motorists were charged with reckless driving, and traffic-related fatalities there rose from 769 dead in the years 1892–1896 to 1,692 dead in the years 1907–1911.[21]

Whether on land or sea, new modes of transportation were changing more than just the rhythm of life; the rhythm of consciousness was also changing, ensuring that there would be no turning back. Reminding us of the example from Chapter 1 of the rotary phone and the dual-faucet sink, Stephen Kern notes that "In an unmistakable way the new journey is faster, and the man's sense of it is as such. But that very acceleration transforms his former means of traveling into something it had never been before—slow—whereas before it was the fastest way to go."[22]

After one hundred years of the automobile's roaming the planet, many scholars of geography and urban studies consider it the single most powerful technological influence on modern society. "The automobile is much more than a mere means of transportation," adds Wolfgang Sachs. ". . .[I]t is wholly imbued with feelings and desires that raise it to the level of a cultural symbol. Behind the gradual infiltration of the automobile into the world of our dreams lie many stories; ones of disdain for the unmendable horse, of female coquetry, of the driver's megalomania, of the sense of having a miracle parked in the drive, and of the generalized desire for social betterment."[23]

The love and influence of the automobile have been especially obvious in the United States, where vast open spaces have been conquered by endless streams of concrete, rather than rail, as in Europe. With the highway and federal interstate system of the 1950s, the social distance between East and West, North and South was collapsed. This then paved the way for increased urbanization and the breakup of the extended family, including the development of suburbia, where work and home were to be connected no longer by one's local community or ethnic neighborhood, but rather by one's mobility via the automobile. As the automobile wove its way into the fabric of American society, it also maintained its role as the single greatest source of absolute raw speed. As the French critic and philosopher Jean Baudrillard suggests, "At more than a hundred miles an hour, there's a presumption of eternity."[24]

Nor was the transformation of human experience a century ago restricted to changes taking place in modes of transportation. The joy of speed had ultimately to do with motion, which meant that the moving picture would also whet the public's growing appetite for speed, action, and adventure. As one author points out in an essay on early cinema technique, ". . .the primordial basis of the enjoyment of moving pictures was not an objective interest in a specific subject matter, much less an aesthetic interest in the formal presentation of subject matter, but the sheer delight in the fact that things seemed to move, no matter what things they were."[25]

When the first Kinetoscope Parlor opened in New York City in 1894, the public lined up to look through Thomas Edison's peephole viewer, which showed a brief, continuously photographed event through a very small viewing screen. One "act" was the famous "Fred Ott's Sneeze." Such acts did not last long, however (a mere few seconds, in fact), and the public had to pay an additional twenty-five cents to continue to the next "feature." Nevertheless, the parlor made $125 on its opening night![26] A publication for the Chicago fair of 1893 summarized this device as follows: "The stereopticon shows these photographs on the screen at a rate of forty-seven per second, while the phonograph reproduces the words, and thus a life-like representation of the speaker is given, with his words, actions and gestures precisely as he delivered in the first instance."[27] This was the first American offering of the motion picture.

When people visit today's IMAX theater for the first time, they often react to the experience as if it were real. For example, viewers will try to lean backward when the projected roller coaster screams straight down its almost vertical tracks. Moviegoers often relate such experiences to others to express the bewildering power of the 3-D image. Viewed historically, however, this conclusion is misleading. When moving pictures made it to the big screen a century ago, they did so with life-size images that moved across the screen for as long as several minutes. Although most of us would experience such films today as crude and boring (and short), the evidence suggests that early viewers found them to be even more overpowering than do today's viewers of IMAX. Having never seen reality depicted in such a way, people found these images to be larger than life itself.

The initial power of the motion picture is illustrated nicely in the film *The Grey Fox*. It recounts the story of Bill Miner, who at the outset of the film has just been released from San Quentin Prison after serving thirty-three years for robbing stagecoaches. The year is 1901. In an early scene Miner attends the local movie house to see the now-classic film *The Great Train Robbery*.[28] The important moment comes when as a deadly shoot-out begins in the latter film, a man in the audience is overtaken by the excitement and shoots his revolver into the air. After the shot has been fired, the gentleman quickly realizes his mistake—it's only a movie, after all—and returns to his seat shaken. When we see the expression on the man's face (and on Miner's), it's clear that the intended effect of the scene is to show us how the action of early films could be mistaken for the real thing. Indeed, as it turns out, this account likely stems from the early French films by the Lumière brothers, who would sit a camera on the train tracks and film the train up to the lens of the camera. When the films were played back for audiences, viewers would actually leap out of the way, and that's more than we can say for the IMAX experience.

Nevertheless, these early moviegoers quickly became accustomed to the power of the moving image, just as we have come to take for granted more contemporary advances in visual technology. Consider the current popularity of installing whole movie theaters in one's living room. As the need constantly to upgrade technology suggests, each generation adapts to the current power of the image, looking for something more. As such, cinema was to make its own unique contribution to the revolution taking place a century ago. Ocean liners, bicycles, and automobiles all were speeding up the pace of life, directly in terms of sheer velocity and indirectly in terms of enabling greater independence and mobility. This alone would have been enough to alter fundamentally people's everyday experiences in the world. But with the advent of the motion picture, human consciousness was reshaped in another significant way. The initial reaction to moving pictures made it clear that this technology was capable of creating images much more real than those derived from the printed word, and thus it shattered the boundary between the real and imaginary. Among other consequences, this had the effect of giving greater depth and saliency to our imaginations about possible futures, a consequence that provided added urgency to our future-directed lives.

A final element to be considered in the speeding up of American society this century might be summarized in terms of the overall intensification of urban life. Changes in technology were instrumental in letting us go faster, but there were also larger sociological changes taking place that went with this technology. Even the following passage, written by A. B. Carson in 1928, reveals the characteristic hustle and bustle that came to signify urban life in twentieth-century America:

> Whang! Bang! Clangety-clang! Talk about the tempo of today—John Smith knows it well. Day after day it whirls continuously in his brain, his blood, his very soul. Yanked out of bed by an alarm clock, John speeds through his shave, bolts his breakfast in eight minutes, and scurries for a train or the street car. On the way to work his roving eye scans, one after the other, the sport page, the comic strips, several columns of political hokum, and the delectable details of the latest moonshine murder.
>
> From eight to twelve, humped over a desk in a skyscraper, he wrestles with his job to the accompaniment of thumping typewriters, jingling telephones, and all the incessant tattoo of twentieth century commerce. One hour off for a quick lunch, a couple of cigarettes, and a glamorous glance at the cuties mincing down the boulevard. Jangling drudgery again from one until five. Then out on the surging streets once more.
>
> Clash, clatter, rattle and roar! Honk! Honk! Honk! Every crossing jammed with traffic! Pavements fairly humming with the jostling crowds! A tingling sense of adventure and romance in the very air! Speed-desire-excitement—the illusion of freedom at the end of the day! The flashing of lights of early evening—Clara Bow in Hearts Aflame! Wuxtry! Wuxtry!—Bootlegger Kills Flapper Sweetheart! Clickety-click, clickety-click—John Smith homeward bound, clinging to a strap and swiftly skimming through the last edition.[29]

Although it may be difficult to believe today, Carson wrote this not as a spoof but as a serious depiction of the changes taking place in the psychology of everyday experience. The experiences that now define contemporary American life are simply a quantitative extension of this earlier, hurried mode of living (which probably now seems to most of us to be ordinary). Technological advances are important in understanding this, to be sure, but equally important are changes that have taken place in our attitudes toward speed and our incorporation of it into almost every aspect, every relationship of modern life.

A CENTURY OF PROGRESS

In a 1997 article in *Scientific American* two professors of social medicine at Harvard University, Arthur Kleinman and Alex Cohen, reported on the discovery of what seemed to be a bizarre cultural phenomenon. Relying on their own research and on reports from such sources as the World Health Organization, they found that dramatic improvements in the physical living conditions in developing nations were producing a crisis in mental health. As they summarize, "An evolving crisis in the developing world signals the need for a better understanding of the links between culture and mental disorders."[30] It was estimated, for example, that with safer water, better life expectancies, and higher incomes, the number of individuals struck down by schizophrenia had somehow increased more than 45 percent in just over ten years. Similar results were found for anxiety, depression, and suicide. How is this possible? The answer to this question has importance not only for today's developing nations but also for those of us living in yesterday's.

As the authors of the *Scientific American* article make clear, we cannot assume a direct connection between physical well-being and psychological or spiritual well-being. If we could, we would expect fewer suicides in wealthier families rather than more, just as we would wrongly expect a woman working long, hard hours in the rice paddies of Vietnam to be less content than a wealthy urbanite bustling about in New York City. A higher standard of living sets the stage for a better quality of life, perhaps, *but it does not guarantee one*. Despite this fact, and despite the fact that the United States is considered the most powerful and advanced nation in the world, we have yet to investigate seriously the factors contributing to mental health and personal contentment. Compare how frequently you

For the Love of Speed[31]

Founder and relentless promoter of the Italian Futurist movement Filippo Tommaso Marinetti, wrote his manifesto on speed, "The New Religion-Morality of Speed," in 1916. If not the most persuasive, it is at least the most unconditional embracement of speed ever put into writing.

In my First Manifesto (February 20, 1909) I declared: The magnificence of the world has been enriched by a new beauty, the beauty of speed. Following dynamic art, the new religion-morality of speed is born this Futurist year from our great liberating war. Christian morality served to develop man's inner life. Today it has lost its reason for existing, because it has been emptied of all divinity.

Christian morality defended the physiological structure of man from the excesses of sensuality. It moderated his instincts and balanced them. The Futurist morality will defend man from the decay caused by slowness, by memory, by analysis, by repose and habit. Human energy centupled by speed will master Time and Space.

Man began by despising the isochronal, cadenced rhythm, identical with the rhythm of his own stride, of the great rivers. Man envied the rhythm of torrents, like that of a horse's gallop. Man mastered horse, elephant, and camel to display his divine authority through an increase in speed. He made friends with the most docile animals, captured the rebellious animals, and fed himself with the eatable animals. From space man stole electricity and then the liquid fuels, to make new allies for himself in the motors. Man shaped the metals he had conquered and made flexible with fire, to ally himself with his fuels and electricity. He thereby assembled an army of slaves, dangerous and hostile but sufficiently domesticated to carry him swiftly over the curves of the earth.

Tortuous paths, roads that follow the indolence of streams

and wind along the spines and uneven bellies of mountains, these are the laws of the earth. Never straight lines; always arabesques and zigzags. Speed finally gives to human life one of the characteristics of divinity: the straight line. . . .

Speed, having as its essence the intuitive synthesis of every force in movement, is naturally pure.

Slowness, having as its essence the rational analysis of every exhaustion in repose, is naturally unclean. After the destruction of the antique good and the antique evil, we create a new good, speed, and a new evil, slowness.

Speed = synthesis of every courage in action. Aggressive and warlike.

Slowness = analysis of every stagnant prudence. Passive and pacifistic.

Speed = scorn of obstacles, desire for the new and unexplored. Modernity, hygiene.

Slowness = arrest, ecstasy, immobile adoration of obstacles, nostalgia for the already seen, idealization of exhaustion and rest, pessimism about the unexplored. Rancid romanticism of the wild, wandering poet and long-haired, bespectacled dirty philosopher.

If prayer means communication with the divinity, running at high speed is a prayer. Holiness of wheels, and rails. One must kneel on the tracks to pray to the divine velocity. One must kneel before the whirling speed of a gyroscope compass: 20,000 revolutions per minute, the highest mechanical speed reached by man. One must snatch from the stars the secret of their stupefying incomprehensible speed. Then let us join the great celestial battles, vie with the star 1830 Groombridge that flies at 241 km. A second, with Arthur that flies at 413 km. A second. Invisible mathematical artillery. Wars in which the stars, being both missiles and artillery, match their speeds to escape from a greater star or to strike a smaller one. Our male saints are the numberless corpuscles that penetrate our atmosphere at an average velocity of 42,000 meters a second. Our female saints are the light and electromagnetic waves at 3 x 1010 meters a second.

The intoxication of great speeds in cars is nothing but the joy of feeling oneself fused with the only divinity. Sportsmen are the first catechumens of this religion. Forthcoming destruction of houses and cities, to make way for great meeting places for cars and planes.

hear an economist interviewed in the news, forecasting the ups and downs of the economy, with how infrequently you hear a philosopher, psychologist, novelist, or poet measuring our psychological or social well being.[32] As this makes clear, although we do not know exactly how to turn our so-called higher standard of living into a healthier and happier society, we nevertheless assume that health and happiness will somehow naturally flow from a good economy.[33] Clearly, though, this assumption is false. As Graham Wallas already noted in 1914 in his influential book *The Great Society*, "The extension of social scale which created the Great Society was mainly due to certain mechanical inventions. Those who first developed these inventions expected that their results would be entirely good. But we now feel some misgiving when we compare *the states of consciousness* typical of the Great Society with those typical of more primitive social organizations. This misgiving leads to an effort to understand the problems of the Great Society as a whole, which runs counter to the intellectual specialisation of the nineteenth century. To that effort the study of psychology has as yet made little effective contribution."[34]

Wallas's observations apply to our development this past century just as well as they do to the experience of today's developing nations. For us as for them, the paradox of Kleinman and Cohen's article stands out as a paradox only because we have oversimplified the recipe for how to build a healthy self. If we were to see economic freedom and prosperity as means rather than as ends in themselves, then we would see the need to examine the question that social critics have been asking all along: how to use the affluent society to ensure a healthy and contented one. Each year hundreds of newly published books tell us how to get rich, how to boost our self-esteem, and how to make friends and influence others. These books are unlikely to be anything more than the book of the month, however, since they do not address the more basic question of what ultimately determines our psychological experience and the meaning of life.

As Kleinman and Cohen suggest, economic and industrial development does not mean that all else will just fall into place by default. They note, for example that, "increased rates of violence, drug and alcohol abuse, and suicide have accompanied disruptions in cultural practices, social routines, and traditional work and family roles." That is to say, the mental and spiritual health of people in both developed and developing nations is suffering because the very forces that are producing these objective gains are simultaneously undermining the traditional sources of meaning in people's lives. The Mexican writer José María Sbert connects this loss to the rise of the modern religion of progress and the future-directed self that pursues it:

> Faith in progress is entrusted with stripping the common man—who as yet has not progressed, but has already been cut off from his common land and deprived of his traditional means for autonomous subsistence—of all the cultural footholds that could give him spiritual autonomy and personal confidence as he faces the market, industry and the nation-state. Disembedded from his community and caring only for himself, free from his elders' beliefs and fears, having learned to look down on his parents and knowing he will find no respect in what they could teach him, he and his fellows can only become *workers* for industry, *consumers* for the market, *citizens* for the nation and *humans* for mankind.[35]

Once again, these observations apply equally well to both developed and developing nations. While people in countries such as India or China are currently experiencing an erosion in their fundamental sources of meaning, we in American society have long been struggling to preserve and rebuild ours. Central to this loss of meaning is the loss of "traditional means for autonomous subsistence," which defined the prominent way of life that existed for us prior to the industrial age. As one psychologist puts it, as soon as the "basic problems of survival are solved, merely having enough food and a comfortable shelter is no longer sufficient to make people content. New needs are felt, new desires arise."[36]

Today we are less likely to grow and harvest our own food, forge our own tools, build our own buildings, design our own communities, and cultivate our own moral and ethical frameworks. These achievements are usually described in positive terms as the freedom from having to work each day just to satisfy our basic needs. In and of itself, this freedom is not a bad thing. After all, it took millions of years of evolutionary struggle in a harsh world to get where we are today. But as people find themselves with greater economic security and greater options in how to live their lives, we have to consider our own contemporary problem, which is how to replace the meaning that was derived from earlier, traditional ways of being. Because we cannot go back to simpler times, when the constraints on personal freedom were so great that these larger questions were unnecessary, we must now confront head-on the question of how to cultivate a meaningful life. Indeed, this is exactly the place where the breakdown has occurred between technological and economic progress, on the one hand, and social and psychological progress, on the other. As is so clear in the case of today's developing nations, there is a need in all modern societies to cultivate new ways of living that can overcome the challenges that modern life presents, with its massive scale, complex division of labor, and its highly impersonal social relations. At least at the national and international level, there seems to be no recognition of this need today, let alone a call to action that attempts to address it.

Still, we were right to assume that transformations in the built world would yield equally dramatic changes in the psychological world. It is just that we were wrong to have assumed that so-called quantitative improvements in the physical world would mean equally positive improvements in our experience of it. Because they are made of such different stuff, these two worlds turn out not to share this kind of direct correspondence to one another. If you wonder about this, you might ask yourself why, with all the timesaving advances that have been made in the world of technology, we do not have any free time. The answer lies, I think, in the fact that as we are able to do things faster, we immediately expect ourselves, or are expected by others, to do more of them. For example, we might wait for hours for a late train, wishing for greater efficiency. And we might wish in this impatient way in dozens of daily situations. Our wishes may even come true. But as they do, we find that we have only become more impatient and still more hurried. In simple terms, we have failed to consider the possibility that short-term benefits may not actually stack up as long-term ones.

When we look back at this century of progress, then, we find that the sudden changes in the structure of daily life quickly manifested themselves as psychological and then societal problems. One of the first to address them was an iconoclast physician named George M. Beard, when, in 1881, he published his book *American Nervousness: Its Causes and Consequences*. Regarding these "causes and consequences," Beard's conclusion was clear: "American nervousness is the product of American civilization. Neurasthenia is . . . the direct result of modernity."

Beard's idea of neurasthenia was defined as a weakness of the nerves, a failing that gave rise to more psychological problems as one experienced more of what Beard referred to as "the modern."[37] The problems attributed to nervous exhaustion were vast, ranging from baldness to insomnia to mild cases of insanity. Not surprisingly, among the things Beard and his colleagues considered causal of this new nervousness was our growing obsession with time. The accuracy of clocks, the stress on punctuality, and the "watching" of watches Beard believed to be responsible for a frazzling of the nerves. Clocks and watches, he writes, "compel us to be on time, and excite the habit of looking to see the exact moment. . . . We are under constant strain, mostly unconscious, oftentimes in sleeping as well as in waking hours, to get somewhere or do something at some definite moment."[38]

Beard and his colleagues also saw the new time and tempo of American life as built into the new technology, where advances in communication and transportation were speeding up the pace of social and commercial transactions. The hazards of such changes were even correlated with death statistics. With the air of a public health official, Sir James Crichton-Browne reported in 1892 that the number of deaths in Britain from heart disease rose from 92,181 during the years 1859–1863 to 224,102 during the years 1884–1888.[39] Max Nordau, in his book *Degeneration*, summarized this "stormy stride of modern life" (in 1895), writing: "Every line we read or write, every human face we see, every conversation we carry on, every scene we perceive through the window of the flying express, sets in activity our sensory nerves and our brain centers. Even the little shocks of railway traveling, not perceived by consciousness, the perpetual noises and the various sights in the streets of a large town, our suspense pending the sequel of progressing events, the constant expectation of the newspaper, or the postman, or visitors, cost our brains wear and tear."[40]

These ideas were of course exaggerated and tainted by the prejudices of the time. Still, fears brought on by the sudden change of pace were expressive of the real impact cultural transformations were having on people's psychological constitution. In fact, Beard and others, swept up as they were by the excitement of the times, actually considered these nervous disorders an unavoidable, perhaps even positive symptom of what it meant to be civilized. While on the one hand discussing the "evil of American nervousness," Beard also claimed this new cultural pathology to be "modern, and uniquely American; and no age, no country, and no form of civilization, not Greece, nor Rome, nor Spain, nor the Netherlands, in the days of their Glory, possessed such maladies." This mixed assessment is also suggestive of how "faith in progress" could blind even the most critical minds from questioning whether progress was a more complicated thing than we first thought. For Beard as for other writers of the American nervousness, such disorders were the clearest sign that the United States had attained the highest possible level of civilization.[41]

As we come to the end of a century in which we have made brilliant economic and technological progress, it seems we have nevertheless suffered dangerous erosion on two fronts. First, the structures of daily life that give meaning to people's lives have been dismantled and then left that way. The value of slow, traditional ways of being have been undermined by a desire for a life with more action and adventure, as when we pack up our boxes and move across the country in pursuit of new careers. In many cases, this creates more isolated lives, with people finding themselves empty inside, with no real knowledge as to why. Consequently, as psychologist Philip Cushman has described, people frequently end up choosing a "life-style solution" in which the modern self "seeks the experience of being continually filled up by consuming goods, calories, experiences, politicians, romantic partners, and empathic therapists in an attempt to combat the growing alienation and fragmentation of its era."[42] Meanwhile, images of a better life continue to exaggerate the meaning of what "the good life" represents, thus eroding people's legitimate search for meaning into an existential quest for something that never existed in the first place.

HAVING offered this critique of our century of progress, it might be useful to add something of a disclaimer. It is not my intention to promote a mood of nostalgia, to grumble about how we've been duped by the slogans of progress and technology into giving up the perfect life of the good old days. The tragic aspect of American life this century is not simply that we were fooled by images of progress that never came true but rather that this progress has been antagonistic to, rather than promotive of, real changes in the quality of life. We have succeeded wondrously in many areas of science and technology, and we have widened the doors to freedom and social justice. But what we have not done is fashion this progress into a tool for creating sane and safe communities in which to live. This can be seen in what happened between the years 1957 and 1990, when the standard of living in the United States doubled. Although we would assume that this change would have at least a partial, helpful effect on people's well-being, this doubling of the standard of living actually resulted in no change in the number of people who described themselves as being well contented. Meanwhile, despite our world-renowned wealth, freedom, and quality of higher education, we now put more of our own people into prison than does any other nation in the world (per capita); we are the most violent society in the world, excluding those at war; and we have greater problems of suicide, depression, anxiety, drug and alcohol addiction, and general malaise than ever before.[43]

ON BEING AND BECOMING

ONE of the national best-sellers of 1990 was a psychological study of "optimal experience." The name of the book was *Flow*, and its author was psychologist Mihaly Csikszentmihalyi.[44] Like the *Scientific American* article discussed above, this study revealed something about ourselves that surprised many people, but was in fact something we should have known all along. What Csikszentmihalyi's book asked was, What kinds of activities are people engaged in when they experience sustained periods of contentment? In other words, what are the sources of optimal experience? This fascinating research, which has been ongoing for about two decades, dovetails with the problem identified in the *Scientific American* article; both raise questions about how to create a society that successfully promotes a rewarding quality of life.

What Csikszentmihalyi found was that passive lives of ease and comfort did not necessarily produce contentment, but that a deep engrossment in meaningful and challenging projects did. Responding to this finding, Csikszentmihalyi concluded that the American dream was in need of revision. Working long hours at a tedious job to save for a comfortable retirement can no longer be justified, according to these findings, as an appropriate model for mass society. If workers do not have an emotional attachment to their work, living for the weekend instead, they may spend twenty, thirty, or even forty years slaving away without ever experiencing any sustained periods of true contentment. In fact, they may not even know that such experiences are possible or, worse, abandon them in the search of something "better" that does not exist. Moreover, if, at the end of all these years pining away the time, we expect happiness to emerge suddenly on a Florida beachhead, we will again be sorely disappointed. Just look at how many retirees, both men and women, go back to some kind of self-chosen work after retiring, sometimes discovering for the first time what satisfaction can come from an absorption in interesting and appropriately challenging projects. As

Csikszentmihalyi points out, life in the hurried society is unlikely to produce a life of optimal experience:

> With affluence and power come escalating expectations, and as our level of wealth and comforts keeps increasing, the sense of well-being we hoped to achieve keeps receding into the distance. When Cyrus the Great had ten thousand cooks prepare new dishes for his table, the rest of Persia had barely enough to eat. These days every household in the "first world" has access to the recipes of the most diverse lands and can duplicate the feasts of past emperors. But does this make us more satisfied?
>
> The paradox of rising expectations suggests that improving the quality of life might be an insurmountable task. In fact, there is no inherent problem in our desire to escalate our goals, as long as we enjoy the struggle along the way. The problem arises when people are so fixated on what they want to achieve that they cease to derive pleasure from the present. When that happens, they forfeit their chances of contentment.[45]

Studies on flow document how, when one's awareness of oneself fades into the background of engrossed activity, the optimal, or most satisfying, experiences result. A large part of this state of consciousness derives from living in the moment, doing activities in which a person can lose him or herself. For this to happen, however, there has to be a match between one's skills and the challenge presented by the project, whether it's writing a book, reading a book, or printing a book. When someone has interest in a task and his or her level of skill matches it, a channel of flow opens up. However, if the challenge is too high, this can create anxiety and frustration; if it is too low, it can create boredom.[46]

In many ways, then, the recipe for contentment runs counter to our commonsense notions about the self. As can be seen in popular notions like "finding one's true self" (or true "inner child") or "searching for one's inner feelings," we often believe that happiness requires a turning of consciousness inward to keep a watchful eye on our private experiences. Indeed, with the straightening of circular time and the rise of the autonomous self, modern times have seen a dangerous expansion of self awareness, what Christopher Lasch cursed as the "culture of narcissism." The problem of course is that this is the very state of consciousness that goes against the flow, and that exacerbates our modern existential woes, including anxiety, mood, and personality disturbances.

Another assumption that goes against the flow is the idea that contentment comes from a life of passive entertainment. Studies show for example that time spent watching television represents far and away the greatest portion of leisure time in the United States. One statistic I saw estimated that the world watches 3.5 billion hours of television a day.[47] No wonder E. B. White once wrote that "TV is going to be the test of the modern world. . . . We shall stand or fall by TV—of that I am quite sure."[48] Television not only abbreviates one's attention span and shapes family dynamics but also leaves one in a state of mind (and body) that is good for little more than doing more of the same. Specifically in terms of flow, television and other passive forms of entertainment, including shopping, lack a crucial ingredient of optimal experience: engrossment through involvement. Television requires little concentration and requires almost no involvement on the part of the viewer. Hence, the temptations of instantaneous entertainment undermine the vigorous, hands-on experiences that people report being the most satisfying. Indeed, studies have shown that the more time one spends watching television, the lower one's self-reported level of personal contentment. Csikszentmihalyi writes, "One of the most ironic paradoxes of our time is this great availability of leisure that somehow fails to be translated into enjoyment. Compared to people living only a few generations ago, we have enormously greater opportunities to have a good time, yet, strangely enough, there is no indication that we actually enjoy life more than our ancestors did."[49]

These conclusions about the psychological impact of passive entertainment raise a larger issue. If passive entertainment stimulates an escape from reality rather than an appreciation of it, what then is the relationship between slowness, on the one hand, and passive leisure activities, on the other? Herein lies a deep confusion about the meaning of slowness. Embracing the depth and richness of slowness, of the present, does not mean we need to be passive or disengaged from the world. Rather, it means we avoid hurrying by being engaged in the present and by bringing our attention away from the future and down to what we're doing.

In his autobiography, author Stefan Zweig describes growing up in nineteenth-century Austria. Remembering his father, he writes: "Even in my earliest childhood, when my father was not yet forty, I cannot recall ever having seen him run up or down the stairs, or ever doing anything in a visibly hasty fashion. Speed was not only thought to be unrefined, but indeed was considered unnecessary. . . ."[50] What should we conclude from this? Do we believe that Zweig's father lived life at a markedly slower pace than we do today? *Yes, of course.* But do we therefore conclude that his was a passive life, lacking engagement in the world? *No, absolutely not.* Again, slowness does not, or at least should not, imply passivity. To the contrary, when we consider the stimulus intensity of our lives today, it is clear that our lives can go faster while at the same time becoming more passive. Sitting in front of the computer, hit by a cascade of constantly changing, complex stimuli, is but one example. On the other hand, our lives can become slower, avoiding both the physical and the psychological rush while we remain engaged in the world. We can work in the garden or the workshop or play with our children for long hours without ever hurrying and without ever feeling hurried. We can do this today just as we could one hundred years ago.

All this is more easily said than done, of course. For millions of people the pursuit of flow is hindered by a life in which work absorbs all the time and energy that might be spent engaged in more absorbing and rewarding activities. Indeed, our whole notion of leisure and vacation these days is premised upon the idea that we need passive relaxation, either to recover from work or to prepare for it. As Ivan Illich contends in his essay *Shadow Work*, the past two centuries have seen a dramatic shift toward working for a wage (versus subsistence living), a change that has been paralleled by a dramatic decrease in work as a meaningful and absorbing activity.

What is perhaps most paradoxical and controversial about flow is that it has no direct connection with material wealth. As life in traditional societies can teach us, once people meet their basic needs of food, shelter, and health (perhaps even if they do not), they can create fulfilling lives by doing meaningful work and by living within a stable, nurturing community.[51] Indeed, there is no convincing evidence that we need fancy cars, penthouse apartments, expensive artwork, or a constant change of fads and fashions. Nor do we need world travel or a thousand channels of television. And we certainly do not need the prospect of earning (or winning) millions of dollars to keep us from staying in bed all day. What is more, research on optimal experience suggests that people will not necessarily find satisfaction in their careers, especially if these careers cause them to become disconnected from all things except work. On the other hand, neither does this suggest that staying at home as the appointed homemaker will produce a deep sense of fulfillment. One may have close interpersonal bonds with family and friends yet still find his or her daily routine devoid of the meaning that can come from self-directed, socially meaningful engagement in the world. Contentment flows from discovering meaningful activities, whether it's working in the yard or raising children, and then structuring our lives so that we can engage in them unhurriedly and successfully.

TAKEN as a whole, then, research on optimal experience signals a conflict between two profoundly different approaches to the lifestyle question. The first of these is informed by historical evidence and research on optimal experience, which is a life of *being*. This mode of existence emphasizes social practices and thus relies on the psychology of place, permanence, repetition, and stability. The second of these represents more the contemporary lifestyle, which is a life of *becoming*. This mode of existence emphasizes technological and material improvement over social relations and relies on the psychology of newness, unbounded freedom, individual growth, and the pursuit of happiness. In terms of time, being emphasizes living with both feet firmly planted in the present, while a life of becoming is having one foot in the present and one foot scurrying off to the future.

The choice between being and becoming may be the most fundamental decision a person or family can make. So fundamental is this choice that it affects almost everything that comes afterward, from the structure of one's daily life to the long-term evolution of time, self, family, and society. Unfortunately this choice is rarely made in a conscious way. Few of us realize that there is even a choice to be made, what the choices are between, and what the choices actually represent. Families are very familiar with the long-term returns from their mutual funds, for example, but have almost no awareness of the long-term returns on their lifestyle decisions (this despite the fact that we have plenty of trustworthy information about them). A second reason has to do with our capacity to make this choice truly available in the first place. Even when we know the choice exists, the mindset, social pressures, and economic structures of the hurried society (i.e., the culture of neglect) often leave little room for choosing a slower, more holistic life of being over becoming. Under such conditions, rejecting the perpetually advertised "good life" in favor of a life of slowness has almost become a question of faith.

IN A NEW YORK MINUTE: THE GROWING INABILITY TO WAIT

HAVING reviewed how things have been speeding up, and why, we are now at our current destination in time—rapid-fire culture—where we go faster, everything changes faster, and everyone demands everything faster than ever before. With this greater understanding in hand, we can use it to develop our model of sensory addictions.

As we have just seen, the future-directed self lives a life of constant pursuit—of becoming. Throughout this century of revolutionary change, each new generation has unknowingly embarked upon this pursuit for progress under faster and more intense cultural conditions. Meanwhile, the rise of the hurried society has not been contained within the walls of the urban sphere. With the automobile and the vast array of appliances of the electronic age, a cult of speed has overtaken the entire nation, with a corresponding transformation of human consciousness.

Certainly, we are well aware of technology's ability to save time, allowing us to do more, just as we are aware that hurrying allows us to do more. But these understandings obscure the ultimate psychological consequences of a hurried, technological approach to time.

Speed and the Growing Inability to Wait

The following excerpts from newspapers offer a view into the sometimes humorous but more often tragic happenings for people once speed is everything, waiting is intolerable, and the attention span is shorter than ever.

A 43-year-old man in Issaquah, Washington, pulled a gun and shot his personal computer four times in the hard drive and once through the monitor, apparently in frustration. "We don't know if it wouldn't boot up or what," police Sgt. Ken Jones said after officers evacuated the town house complex where the man lived, telephoned him and coaxed him out of his home (August 20, 1997).

A 14-year-old boy in Orange Park, Florida, shot his 15-year-old sister, telling authorities that she was getting on his nerves by talking on the telephone too long. Officers said that when they arrived, they found the boy talking on the phone (January 14, 1998).

A woman who tried to rob a Lockport Savings Bank branch in Buffalo, New York, lost patience with a teller who took too long to hand over the cash, and snatched back her holdup note. Police said she walked to a nearby Rochester Savings Bank, where she made off with an undisclosed amount of money (November 12, 1997).

In White Plains, New York, mail carrier Mary Finn, 49, was fired after 18 years of service because her stride was too short. Finn, who is 5-foot-5, was observed walking her delivery route at 66 paces per minute, with a stride of less than one foot. Her removal notice stated: "At each step, the heel of your leading foot did not pass the toe of the trailing foot by more than one inch. As a result, you required thirteen minutes longer than your demonstrated ability to deliver mail to this section of your route" (October 8, 1997).

Identical twins Jeffery and Tom Jameson, 18, were driving their new Nissans around Alameda, California, when one of them ran a stop sign and smashed into the other, sending the car spinning into a house (October 15, 1997).

Two British motorcycle riders mistook an underground garage entrance in Amsterdam for a road tunnel, entered the parking garage at high speed and slammed into a concrete barrier inside. "The riders were more or less launched from their mounts and landed about 10 meters (30 feet) further on," said a police spokesperson. One of the men broke his arm, the other injured his shoulder (August 20, 1997).

Australian paramedics stood by helplessly while transport officials let rush-hour trains keep running over the body of a 21-year old woman who threw herself on the tracks on the Sydney Harbor Bridge after an argument with her boyfriend. "It was obvious after a few trains ran over her that she was dead," said Ambulance Service spokesperson Joe Flynn, explaining that a state rail inspector denied requests to stop trains so they could retrieve the body because he didn't want passengers to be kept waiting (January 14, 1998).

Charles Manson, 62, who is serving a life sentence in California for the murders of actress Sharon Tate and six others in 1969, told a parole board in March that he's too busy to be free. "I'm involved in too many things—I have a Web site I'm working on," he told the three-member panel, which obligingly denied his parole (July 2 and 9, 1997).

Cincinnati police accused Samantha Hicks, 24, of locking her three children in their room so they wouldn't bother her while she surfed the Internet for six to 12 hours a day. Sgt. Pete Nelson noted that Hicks left the children, ages two, three and five, in filthy and deplorable conditions, amid broken glass, human waste and other debris, while her computer area was immaculate. Psychologists said Hicks may suffer from "Internet Addiction Disorder" (July 16, 1997).

To relieve the courts, Arizona introduced the QuickCourt system: ATM-like machines for filing paperwork to get a simple divorce, change a name or file a small claim. By mid-1997, 150 will be in place. Fees range up to $30 (January 15, 1997).

German rock star Gunther Deitz died during a performance

in Hamburg when he smashed into a concrete floor after asking his fans to catch him—and they refused. Many were peeved because he showed up an hour late, then sacked his guitarist. The heavy-metal idol regularly dived off the stage into the crowd as the climax to his show, only this time when he yelled "Catch me," fans stepped out of his way instead, then roared when he hit the concrete. After hearing Deitz had died, one 18-year-old fan declared, "He got what he deserved" (December 4, 1996).

To slow rush-hour commuter traffic through the Dutch city of Culemborg, head of maintenance Hank Kievity, 33, instituted a pilot program to station six sheep at intersections in a three-block area in the Goilberdingen neighborhood. If the project succeeds, the city council said it would consider turning more sheep loose along major routes (October 9, 1996).[52]

A professor of history at the University of Colorado gave the members of her introductory American history survey course a questionnaire on reading. "I got exactly 100 responses, which put the calculating of percentages well within the reach of my quantitative skills. Twenty percent of students said they did not read for pleasure. The phrasing of their answers repeated: 'I don't have time'; 'I have NO time!' 'I have absolutely no time.' And, matching this, when asked why it was that they did not always finish assigned reading, 90% of all the students checked 'Lack of time'" (*USA Today*, April 16, 1997).

A cattle truck driver has been charged with vehicular homicide and seven other counts in the "road rage" death of an 18-year-old woman near Loveland, Colorado. The 23-year-old Hanson, the driver of the truck, is accused of running a car off Interstate 25 Sunday and forcing it into a head-on collision with an oncoming car, killing a woman and injuring three other people. The Colorado State Patrol says Hanson may have been angry about something the driver of the woman's car had done in traffic, and cut him off each time he tried to pass. Troopers say Hanson told another trucker on his Citizens' Band radio to "Stop this car because they need an attitude adjustment," then forced the vehicle into oncoming traffic and a head-on crash

(United Press International, October 2, 1997).

Motorists who run red lights in San Francisco are, by and large, highly educated, stressed-out men in a hurry who have a dozen excuses for running the light but almost never own up to making a mistake, a new behavioral survey shows. "The study suggests that people accurately see why others run red lights—they're 'in a hurry' or 'not paying attention,'" said psychologist Joe Smith, "But in terms of their own behavior, they make excuses, they deny responsibility. (*San Francisco Chronicle*, January 16, 1997).

A woman who led police on a chase on freeways from Clairemont to Mission Valley said she didn't stop for their red lights and sirens because she was in a hurry to see her lawyer. Ann Finkel, 37, was arrested on suspicion of evading arrest and outstanding warrants after she drove onto a sidewalk at Hazard Center, got out and started to run to a building. "The woman said she was trying to enter the building to see her lawyer," the police spokesman said. (*San Diego Union-Tribune*, February 14, 1996).

Until 3:13 P.M. Wednesday, the problems on Cypress Creek Road west of Andrews Avenue, in Fort Lauderdale, were minor. Drivers cut each other off as they jockeyed for position. People in a hurry lost a couple of minutes at a red light or a train. Tempers flared. Then Gary DeFarge, driving a gasoline truck, caught in a line of traffic, tried to edge his tanker across the tracks as an Amtrak train roared toward him at 60 mph. He didn't make it. The explosion of 8,500 gallons of gasoline sent fireballs exploding into the air, engulfing nine vehicles and killing six people. For the want of a few feet of road, enough for DeFarge to clear the tracks with the truck, it never would have happened (*Fort Lauderdale Sun-Sentinel*, March 21, 1993).

Whether it's the automobile, telephone, or home appliance, shortening the temporal gap between desire and its fulfillment allows us to accelerate the pace of life. More happens in less time, life moves faster, we become accustomed to faster speeds, and time becomes compressed. This means that under conditions of slowness, the same chunk of time now feels as if it has been stretched out or slowed down. Historian Stephen Kern identifies this process taking place a century ago: "As quickly as people responded to the new technology, the pace of their former lives seemed like slow motion. The tension between a speeding reality and a slower past generated sentimental elegies about the good old days before the rush. It was an age of speed but, like the cinema, not always uniformly accelerated. The pace was unpredictable, and the world, like the early audiences, was alternately overwhelmed and inspired, horrified and enchanted."[53]

The futurist Alvin Toffler has described the effect of this protracted experience of time, stressing its implication for why, because of it, our sensory needs are increasingly likely to go unmet, unless of course we manage to sustain a constant flow of incoming stimulation. Writing in *Future Shock*, he notes that "to understand why acceleration in the pace of life may prove disruptive and uncomfortable, it is important to grasp the idea of 'durational expectancies.'"[54] Durational expectancies refer to one's current sensory needs (how much sensory input our conscious mind expects), which change depending on how intense and hurried is our life. Heightened durational expectancies thus mean that under conditions of slowness one will experience time as if it were slowed down. As one minute begins to feel like ten minutes, a person is likely to become frustrated by even brief waits, encouraging even greater sensory consumption.

The unsettling consequences of being stuck in time are epitomized by the motorist who, when frozen in traffic, is actually brought to tears by the overwhelming incongruity between the motion of the dashboard clock—tick, tick, tick—and the motionless car. While those living unhurried lives of being go uninterrupted by such ecological constraints, the child or adult living a hurried life of becoming has no tolerance for, no immunity against the inevitable halts that "await" him or her each and every day. Hurrying compresses time and heightens our orientation toward the future, and thus the attempt to close the temporal gap between present and future fails to do away with time, thereby also failing to fulfill our wish to return us to a more secure temporal space.

One way to measure the development of our rapid-fire consciousness—sensory addictions—is to measure our patience, our ability to wait. The most obvious challenge to patience today seems to be traffic, perhaps because it is the most prominent place where even wealth and technology cannot overcome the forces that make us slow down. With this as our measure, the answer is clear: We are finding it more difficult to make the transition from fastness into slowness, just as we are finding it more difficult to cope with slowness over any lasting period of time. Reports show, for instance, that so many people are running stop signs and red lights today that our driving impulses have reached epidemic proportions, prompting concern in municipalities across the nation and spawning a variety of educational programs and punitive crackdowns. Sensory addictions have even created a new social pathology called road rage. The numbers alone reveal our sensory addictions: in 1991 the California Highway Patrol reported 268 deaths resulting from red light and stop sign violations. In 1992 Maryland reported 3,700 traffic accidents resulting in 20 deaths of which red light violations were the primary cause. By the first seven months of 1995 San Francisco police had recorded 462 traffic accidents because of red light violations and handed out almost 6,000 citations. New York City's red light program, which photographs and tickets violators, nabbed 63,000 motorists in its first eight months. Incidentally, adolescents and adults diagnosed with ADD are far more likely than the general public to be cited for traffic violations and to be involved in these types of traffic accidents.[55]

As being stuck in traffic tells us all too well, the ultimate problem with heightened durational expectancies is that much of the terrain on which human activity takes place remains unalterably uneven. Sometimes we have to wait! This is especially true for children, who often have to conform to the constraints of their parents' activities, time, and schedule. Not only are there physical limits to feeding the beast of temporal expectation, but as the weeping motorist shows, the resulting experience can be excruciating. Nowhere is this more true than in the case of schoolchildren having problems with attention and hyperactivity. Naturally children with low self-governance who have acquired a constant need for stimulation will have problems with the chronic slowness of the classroom. They gradually learn to avoid or escape this discomfort either by shutting down and withdrawing or by generating their own sources of stimulation; the latter can be accomplished through inappropriate behavior (hyperactivity) or by constantly turning their senses to other things (inattention), or both. By contrast, when these children are left to their own devices, allowing them to exert more control over the environment, their symptoms of sensory addictions quickly disappear. By this I do not mean to suggest that the solution to our growing sensory addictions lies in the elimination of all remaining pockets of slowness. We have already seen the results of this approach during modern times, and it has not led to the utopian life we thought it would.

WE have reached the end of this two-part history on the relationship among human consciousness, the nature of time, and the technology of speed. It seems clear that rapid-fire culture and the hurried consciousness it produces can indeed be traced to our own cultural history. The problems of sensory addictions did not come out of nowhere, suddenly appearing on the horizon, no cause and all effect. With a new future-directed consciousness, the last two centuries have seen a great race against time, born of a hopeful but misguided faith in economic and technological progress, fueled by an unquenchable thirst for speed. Now, several generations later, we live in a world in which the automobile has evolved into the plane, the phone has evolved into the fax machine and the World Wide Web, and the cinema has evolved into billions and billions of hours of television (and about one Hollywood film for each day of the year). The consequences of this indulgence of the senses have been especially tragic for the lives and minds of children, and it is to them that we turn to next.

Sensory Addictions:
How Culture Manufactures Disease

> I suggest that the hyperactive child is attempting to recapture the dynamic quality of the television screen by rapidly changing his perceptual orientation. I also wonder if it is possible that amphetamines control his behavior by producing a subjective experience comparable to the fleeting worlds of television.
>
> MATTHEW DUMONT, M.D. (1976)[1]

"JUNK science" has become a media catchphrase for faddish scientific and medical beliefs that have popular appeal but that ultimately lack scientific validation. From eugenics to cold fusion to the facilitated instruction of autistic children, junk science reminds us that the stamp of science still does not guarantee legitimacy. Science and medicine can be as flawed as the rest of human affairs, sometimes with cold, calculating animus, but more often with the best of intentions. Of course there is at the same time the possibility that the label of "junk science" will be thrown at ideas that, although valid, threaten the status quo or those who benefit from it. One thing is for certain: Both science and its critics must have their checks and balances. Neither is the embodiment of pure virtue, acting without error or ulterior motives.

One of the subjects that has attracted the label of junk science recently is multiple chemical sensitivity (MCS). This syndrome came into public view as growing numbers of people began reporting a variety of mild to dramatic reactions to their ecological surroundings. The illness has won the support of various scientists, physicians, government agencies, and noted public figures. For example, the U.S. Department of Housing and Urban Development (HUD) awards individuals diagnosed with MCS protection under federal housing and discrimination laws; in California HUD allocated almost two million dollars for special, ecological housing. MCS is also considered a disability under the Americans with Disabilities Act.[2]

The putative causes of this illness range from chemical agents, especially formaldehyde, to pesticides, solvents, paints, detergents, fumes, perfumes, cosmetics, tobacco smoke, and even electromagnetic fields. The illness is said to result from chronic exposure to such substances and can be triggered by contact with any one of them. Reports of symptoms vary considerably, including such physical problems as headaches, achy back and joints, trouble breathing, allergy symptoms, cold symptoms, and flu symptoms and such psychological problems as anxiety, memory loss, and insomnia. These symptoms are real enough to drive people—typically middle-class, well-educated women—to flee their comfortable social and physical surroundings, choosing instead the isolation of barren "glass houses." In one case a husband found himself living in the garage after his wife became so ill that even the smell of his clothes and food made her sick.[3]

Despite its apparent legitimacy, or perhaps because of it, MCS has also attracted the scorn of various scientists, physicians, and journalists. Established medical organizations have dismissed the illness as psychosomatic, claiming that studies show no relationship between exposure to chemicals and the symptoms being reported. Organizations such as the American Academy of Allergy and Immunology, American College of Physicians, the American Medical Association Council on Scientific Affairs, and the World Health Organization all agree that the data do not support the claim that these symptoms represent a real medical disorder. The symptoms, however real, are thought not to be the result of an acquired sensitivity to environmental toxins.[4] Rather, many believe they are part of a nonspecific psychological disorder, as some kind of psychosomatic illness.

The evidence that fuels critics' claims stems in part from research using a placebo test, in which those claiming to have the disorder are tested under blind conditions. This means that a person's reaction is monitored when chemicals have been applied but the person believes they have not been or, just the opposite, when chemicals have not been applied but the person believes they have. Sometimes such tests occur naturally, as in the following account: "Karen was the librarian at a newspaper in Los Angeles where I worked. When we moved to new offices, somebody told her the library's book-shelves contained formaldehyde. Soon she was suffering from a headache, aching joints, and labored breathing. But then Karen heard there was no formaldehyde in the shelves. Suddenly the symptoms disappeared. A colleague later told me that it turned out the shelves contained formaldehyde after all, but Karen remained bliss-fully ignorant of this and hence free of symptoms."[5] In another case residents of Newburgh, New York, began reporting being sick after hearing of plans to fluoridate the water supply; the problem was that the fluoridation had not yet begun.

In what is a testament to the sincerity of their claims and to the reality of their symptoms, individuals diagnosed with MCS have actually volunteered for formal versions of this kind of test, only to find that their reactions are not specific. In fact, one study, pub-lished in the *New England Journal of Medicine*, was conducted by a scientist who believed he himself suffered from MCS. What he found was that patients under blind conditions respond the same to inactive placebos as to active contaminants. As with Karen above, the results suggested that *beliefs* about what was in the air were at least as powerful in producing symptoms as what actually was. Of course this seems outrageous to those who are affected, for it appears to them impossible that being so sick could be a psycho-logical matter.

What does all this have to do with rapid-fire culture and the trans-formation of human consciousness? The notion that MCS may be built on "junk science" is first of all a warning about the rise and complexity of psychological illnesses in modern times and the possi-bility that they can be mistaken for physical illness. It is also therefore a warning about something specific to our present concerns: attention deficit disorder (ADD). That is, if we disregard the concerns we may have about the legitimacy of either of these two syndromes and focus instead on how differently MCS and ADD have been interpreted in medicine, science, and the media, we can begin to see how notions of illness and disease are constructed by "experts" for mass consumption.[6] As we shall see, the fact that the American Medical Association (AMA) considers ADD a legitimate medical disorder, while considering MCS illegitimate, turns out to have almost nothing to do with the scientific evidence. The idea here is not, however, that there is a conscious conspiracy afoot, but that unexamined institutional expectations and contingencies shape the actions of physicians, researchers, health officials, and policy makers, so that they conform to prevailing societal prejudices.

THE PROBLEM: "ADD," A CAUSE TO NO EFFECT

ATTENTION deficit disorder is unlike the syndrome of MCS in that ADD has never suffered harsh scrutiny from the medical profession.[7] But should it? After all, isn't ADD considered a well-established medical disorder, while MCS is embraced only by a fringe group of physicians and patients? As it turns out, MCS and ADD share many of the same problems of reliability and validity:

- The fundamental symptoms are vague in both cases and are very difficult to distinguish from everyday problems or problems that are altogether unrelated to the disorder in question.
- In both cases the symptoms cannot be authenticated by concrete medical tests, thus establishing each as a syndrome rather than as a medical disorder, disease, or illness.
- Both syndromes have the peculiar characteristic of affecting only certain subgroups of the population; for example, both appear to affect one sex considerably more than the other.
- The diagnosis is suspect in each case because those who make the determination clearly benefit from it since their

patients often represent a significant portion of their clientele.

These problems notwithstanding, it is important to stress that this does not mean that ADD or MCS are bogus in terms of their symptoms. In both cases these are well established. In a highly critical magazine piece on MCS, journalist Michael Fumento notes: "People with 'Multiple Chemical Sensitivity' are definitely suffering. The question is why?"[8] Similarly, Ronald Gots, a scientist and frequent critic of MCS, says that "even the most cynical observer has to admit that many of these people are suffering terribly."[9] Much the same has been said on behalf of ADD; few doubt that diagnosed children suffer from hyperactivity and inattention, at least under certain conditions; again, the question is why. To put it simply, what we want to know is whether these symptoms represent a singular medical disorder or a culture-based, developmental one.

It is also important to stress here that considerable skepticism about ADD does in fact exist, even in the United States, although this is rarely considered in the media. Consider a report "On the Epidemiology of Hyperactivity" from a professor at the University of London's Institute of Psychiatry:

> The idea of an attention deficit disorder has often been powerfully and destructively criticised. No behavioural syndrome of "minimal brain dysfunction" has been reliably identified. The DSM-III definition of "Attention Deficit Disorder with Hyperactivity" (ADDH) suggests a common, broad syndrome; but in fact this cannot be sustained as a biological entity. ADDH is not coherent in its symptomatology; it is not reliably diagnosed in practice; it has not been shown to have predictive value separately from the antisocial conduct problems which frequently coexist; and its associations are with psychosocial adversity as much as with biological disadvantage. [Moreover,] the response to amphetamines is not different in kind in children with hyperactivity and those without.[10]

Clearly, the key difference between ADD and MCS is not going to be that one is supported by clear-cut scientific evidence while the other is not.

SYMPTOMS OF WHAT?

CRITICS of MCS stress that its symptoms are ubiquitous and could be used to support any number of conclusions. "We all have these symptoms sometimes—headaches, tiredness," notes one journalist. "If a doctor tells you, oh, it's those chemicals, it's this thing that's causing it, it's easy to start seeing patterns and make yourself sick."[11] Another journalist notes that, "the difficulty, of course, is that the symptoms are so vague and there are no laboratory tests to diagnose the condition."[12] Meanwhile, others have drawn the same conclusions about ADD. A brochure by the American Academy of Pediatrics states: "ADHD can be very hard to diagnose since it shares many of the same symptoms as other disorders."[13] Similarly, psychiatrists Edward Hallowell and John Ratey write in their best-selling book on ADD, *Driven to Distraction*, "[T]he hallmark symptoms of ADD—distractibility, impulsivity, and high activity—are so commonly associated with children in general that the diagnosis is often not considered . . . How can we tell a spoiled child from an ADD child? How can we tell a child with emotional problems from a child with ADD?"[14]

The criticism that ADD is really nothing more than a set of heterogeneous symptoms that may or may not constitute a real medical disorder comes from multiple sources. Perhaps most striking is the history of the diagnosis, which shows remarkable inconsistency. The early diagnoses, which focused solely on hyperactivity (such as the diagnoses "minimal brain damage" and "hyperkinesis") were followed by a shift toward problems of attention ("attention deficit disorder") and then by an either/or diagnosis of hyperactivity or inattention (this is the current diagnostic category, "attention deficit hyperactivity disorder"). On this note, the professor of psychiatry Gerald Coles points out: "The whole notion has gone through so many metamorphoses as to suggest a catastrophe in terms of conceptual integrity."[15]

It is important to realize that throughout all these changes in the mind of psychiatrists, the diagnosis has always been grounded solely on "soft" symptoms. It has been based not on independent medical tests but rather on a collection of symptoms, none of which is unique to the disorder. Both hyperactivity and inattention can result from a variety of psychological problems, including depression and behavioral problems; they also represent part of the normal spectrum of behavior. Indeed, because the symptoms of ADD occur in most children to some extent, it is only when there are enough of them in combination, when the child finally upsets his or her caregivers, that a diagnosis is deemed warranted. In short, the diagnosis is based on a vague system of counting the frequency of what would otherwise be considered normal behaviors. According to the current diagnosis, a child must show six of nine conditions for hyperactivity (such as the child fidgets) or six of nine conditions for inattention (such as the child is easily distracted). How it is that two separate sets of symptoms can stand for the same disorder is not explained.

Why is there a problem with a diagnosis based on soft symptoms? This question brings us to a second concern with how ADD is defined, which is that the diagnosis simply does not work. Physicians, even professionals specifically trained for this type of diagnosis, have been repeatedly shown to be unreliable. How do we know this? We know this, first of all, from formal studies that compare diagnoses made by several trained individuals relying on the same profiles of behavior.[16] One study used videotapes to compare the rating of hyperactivity by professionals from four different countries and concluded that ". . . perceptions of hyperactivity vary significantly across countries even if uniform rating criteria are applied."[17] In another study, conducted solely in Britain, 12 percent of the "normal" children were misdiagnosed as hyperactive. This may sound like an acceptable degree of error, but it is not. If the actual prevalence of hyperactivity in children today is, say, 5 percent (regardless of the cause), this means that 95 percent of children fall within normal levels of hyperactivity; thus, if 12 percent of this 95 percent is misdiagnosed, a majority of all kids diagnosed with ADD would actually be "normal."[18]

Perhaps the most damaging evidence of how vague the idea of ADD really is comes from studies that look at whether physicians can reliably diagnose children in their offices, the most common locations for diagnosis today. Because children who behave within the boundaries of acceptable behavior sometimes look hyperactive and because hyperactive children often look "normal," especially in the doctor's office, this poses a grave problem. One study, reported in the journal *Pediatrics*, found that 80 percent of the children thought to be hyperactive, according to home and school reports, showed "exemplary behavior and no sign of hyperactivity in the office." This finding is consistent with numerous studies showing, and dozens of newspaper articles reporting, considerable disagreement among parents, teachers, and clinicians about who qualifies for a diagnosis.[19] This can only raise questions about the existence of ADD as a real medical phenomenon since it is these symptoms alone that are the basis of the diagnosis. As noted in the passage quoted above, ADD "is not coherent in its symptomatology; it is not reliably diagnosed in practice."

A third source of evidence that ADD is a vague mélange of symptoms comes from epidemiological estimates of its prevalence. While critics point to prevalence rates in European countries that run as low as one-tenth of 1 percent, others on this side of the Atlantic suggest a rate in the United States as high as 20 percent; the estimate here in the United States has also dramatically increased during the latter half of this century. Whatever the current prevalence of these problems, the point here is that this variability reflects how impossible it is to draw a sharp boundary between those who are to be considered "normal" and those to be "ill"; it seems much more accurate to say that rather than representing two well-defined black-and-white categories of "normal" and "abnormal" these symptoms reflect a continuum made up of many shades of gray.[20]

This conclusion— that the diagnosis of ADD is defined by problems that also occur for other reasons—is of course the very same conclusion that has been drawn about MCS. Again, this does not mean the symptoms do not exist; they may even be on the rise. What it does mean is that the scientific evidence for a biologically proved medical disorder is not at all compelling. The difference that does exist between ADD and MCS lies instead in how this ambiguity is interpreted. In the case of MCS, the fact that the symptoms could occur for a variety of other reasons has been key in arguing that it is a psuedomedical disorder. As we have seen, the symptoms are thought to occur because of other illnesses or because of a psychosomatic syndrome. By contrast, in the case of ADD, these vague symptoms have been used, and successfully so, to argue just the opposite: to prove the existence of the disorder. How is this done? Proponents use the ambiguity of ADD to explain its sudden rise, saying it existed all along, but without being adequately identified and treated. This is exactly what we find in Hallowell and Ratey's *Driven to Distraction*: "Once you catch on to what this syndrome is all about, you'll see it everywhere. People you used to think of as disorganized or manic or hyper or creative but unpredictable, people who you know could do more if they could just 'get it together,' people who have bounced around in school or in their professional lives, people who have made it to the top but who still feel driven or disorganized, these may be people who in fact have attention deficit disorder. You may even recognize some of the symptoms in your own behavior."[21] Here we're faced with a clear and dangerous contradiction. We cannot discredit one disorder for being vague and speculative and then turn around and use another disorder's vagueness to prove its existence. What is more, the idea that when you know what to look for, diagnosing ADD can be as easy as 1, 2, 3 shows a disturbing arrogance on the part of some psychiatrists, one that may remind us of a moment in psychiatry's history that many in the profession would like to forget.

In the early 1970s D. L. Rosenhan decided to test the possibility that psychiatrists do what Hallowell and Ratey appear to be doing in the passage above: interpret human behavior through a distorting lens that confirms their own particular prejudices about who has a medical problem and who does not. What Rosenhan did was send a variety of perfectly normal people—some psychologists, a psychiatrist, a painter, a homemaker, et cetera—to a variety of psychiatric hospitals in the San Francisco area and elsewhere. They were instructed by Rosenhan to act as normal as possible, to be totally courteous and cooperative, and to answer all questions honestly. The only exception was that upon checking in, they gave false names and professions and reported recently hearing a voice saying the words "hollow," "empty," and "thud." Once admitted, they made no further reference to hearing such voices.

What Rosenhan wanted to know was how many of his mock

patients would succeed in being admitted and, if so, how long it would take before they would be discovered as perfectly sane. In the report of his study, published in *Science* in 1973 ("On being Sane in Insane Places"), Rosenhan reported findings that surpassed even his grim expectations. All his confederates were admitted, and they were kept for an average of nineteen days.[22] Ironically, although seven of the eight were diagnosed as schizophrenic and, even upon release, were still labeled as "schizophrenic in remission," many of their "fellow patients" were convinced they were faking. On occasion, patients complained that the mock patient was probably a journalist, investigating the hospital. As Rosenhan concluded, trained and experienced professionals repeatedly failed to discriminate between sane and insane behavior, despite the normal behavior on the part of his confederates. Instead, the psychiatrists showed what has been defined in social psychology as perceptual assimilation, which is the tendency to "read in" what you want to see, rather than see what is really there.

Now consider this in terms of the problems associated with ADD. When Hallowell and Ratey tell us that "once you catch on to what this syndrome is all about, you'll see it everywhere," it seems they are correct. After all, once psychiatrists, pediatricians, teachers, and parents are conditioned to view disruptive rates of otherwise normal behaviors or psychological withdrawal as an inborn illness, they are certainly more likely to see ADD popping up everywhere. They are also likely to forget that these problems alone constitute the label of ADD, allowing them to begin using ADD as an explanation of them. This is of course a patently circular explanation because in the absence of biomedical tests, we have no evidence for the existence of ADD beyond the symptoms we use to define it. How psychiatrists, pediatricians, or anyone for that matter can distinguish between someone with inborn restlessness and what Hallowell and Ratey have referred to as "culture-induced ADD" thus becomes a pressing social question.

This double standard in how we interpret the ambiguity of ADD versus MCS can be seen in a report on MCS that aired on the ABC newsmagazine *20/20*. Highly critical of MCS, *20/20* sent two healthy confederates to a physician known to support the diagnosis of MCS. After completing a number of questionnaires honestly and an interview with the physician, both individuals were given the diagnosis of MCS. Of course this was just what the journalists wanted. Now the disorder and the physicians who support it could be shown on national television as a silly hoax. Knowing that ADD has been spared this kind of televised embarrassment, we may wonder what would happen under the same circumstances. What would happen, in other words, if we sent a few of our everyday "boys will be boys" to a pediatrician or child psychiatrist? As it turns out, we already know the answer to this question, and it is the same as the one reported by 20/20 for MCS. As the studies above suggest, we might expect a misdiagnosis even if the children were sent to physicians who did not specialize in these kinds of problems. If, however, as in the 20/20 report, we sent the children to a physician who specializes in treating ADD—and who regularly prescribes Ritalin—we could almost certainly expect a diagnosis of ADD. Again, as this example shows, the difference between MCS and ADD lies not in the scientific evidence but rather in how they are constructed by the media, as well as by science and medicine.

Of course vague symptoms do not by themselves prove that either MCS or ADD is a pseudodisorder. Numerous medical illnesses such as AIDS can have hard-to-interpret symptoms. However, what makes this a serious problem in the case of ADD (and MCS) is the lack of hard medical evidence to confirm the meaning of these symptoms. It may seem obvious to you, and rightfully so, that an accepted medical disorder should be supported by medical evidence, but this is not the case for either of these two syndromes, which is why they are *syndromes*.

THIS THING CALLED ADD

To say someone has a medical illness, disease, or disorder has become a much more liberal enterprise in recent times. As Stanton Peele notes in *Diseasing of America*, we as a nation have become obsessed with labeling every persistent behavioral and psychological problem as a disease, from ADD to alcoholism to depression to obesity.[23] Meanwhile, even a casual examination suggests that this medicalization of psychological phenomena has gone too far, especially when we consider how much these problems have varied throughout history and across cultures and subcultures.[24] Unless this variability is a result of infectious disease, we would not expect the prevalence of biologically based problems to change in this way. Of course one way to prove the medical basis of what looks to be a psychological problem is to find biomedical evidence for it. Because of the discovery of "hard" evidence of disease, the madness produced by untreated syphilis, the paranoia and forgetfulness produced by Alzheimer's, and the erratic behavior of someone with a brain tumor are no longer mistaken as psychological problems. But as we've seen, there is in fact no evidence of organic disease for either MCS or ADD.

In considering MCS, Michael Fumento writes, "The traditional definition of organic disease would lead us to expect a fairly narrow range of symptoms, of causes, and of treatments (if any). Furthermore, there should be biological tests to confirm the disease."[25] He goes on to show that "by all traditional standards of illness—symptoms, causes, treatments, and tests—MCS comes up wanting."[26] Similarly, scientist Ronald Gots criticizes MCS because after "all kinds of blood testing, immune system testing, and brain testing . . . they don't have any physical evidence of disease associated with these exposures."[27] Even the American Medical Association's Council on Scientific Affairs, which looked specifically at the MCS claims, concluded that there was no hard evidence for the disease and that medical tests were at best experimental.[28]

Without biomedical evidence for MCS, its diagnosis as a biomedical disorder can be viewed only with suspicion. In the case of ADD, however, no such logic holds. All the above criticisms apply to ADD, yet it is still embraced and defended by the American medical establishment. Indeed, ADD has never had a known biomedical cause and has never had a reliable diagnostic exam (with the exception of those very few diagnosed because of childhood illness or injury), but this has not slowed the medicalization of these childhood problems by the American Psychiatric Association (APA) and the AMA. As Katherine Tyson, a professor of social work, wrote in 1991:

The vast majority of research on childhood hyperactivity has been based on one pervasive, reductionistic, and unwarranted assumption . . . [which] holds that the child's behavioral and cognitive symptoms can be best understood and treated by prioritizing the central nervous system as the relevant etiologic variable. . . . Even though thousands of studies have been conducted in the effort to find the organic defect, no one has ever identified a neurological lesion specific to children labeled hyperactive. . . . [Also,] despite 20 years of searching, no defect in neurotransmitter activity specific to children labeled hyperactive has been identified [and] many techniques for measuring parameters of cerebral neurophysiology . . . have not identified any neurological dysfunction specific to children diagnosed as hyperactive.[29]

The history of defining these behavioral problems as biological ones actually had an honest beginning. This is because the first observations of hyperactivity were identified closely with children who had clearly suffered some kind of rare illness or trauma, such as from congenital defects of the brain, birth trauma, postnatal head injury, meningitis, encephalopathy, or epilepsy.[30] Naturally, the observation of hyperactivity in these children was attributed to the physical injuries they had suffered. As was the case with a study published in 1937 in the *Archives of Neurology and Psychiatry*, early studies of children with hyperactivity often found an associated biological origin for hyperactivity; what is equally interesting, however, is that when no minimal brain dysfunction could be located, the causes were often believed to be (and sometimes clearly shown to be) "environmental disturbances."[31]

This last finding is interesting because very few children diagnosed with ADD today suffer from any such "minimal brain disorder." This change is due not to the fact that these problems have ceased to occur, but rather that the proportion of children diagnosed with ADD who are otherwise healthy has skyrocketed. In 1980 the APA, which is responsible for the diagnostic category of ADD (now ADHD), noted that *no more than 5 percent of the children who might be diagnosed with ADD actually have such an identifiable neurological basis*.[32] This raises two troubling questions. First, why has this problem gone from a rare disorder associated

with identifiable childhood illnesses and brain injuries to a ubiquitous one associated with some unidentifiable brain imbalance with
no known cause? Second, given that early views of hyperactivity
would suggest this huge increase in ADD is due to environmental
rather than biomedical causes, why do we view ADD as a medical
disorder? After all, there remains no medical evidence to support
such a claim.

The failure to find a neurological or biochemical dysfunction in
most ADD-diagnosed children has not prevented the constructing
of a medical disorder to explain hyperactivity and, more recently,
inattention. The current account goes something like this: The past
fifty years are marked by immense scientific progress. Many individuals suffer from a neurobiological disability that only recently
has been scientifically characterized, diagnosed, and successfully
treated. While there remains no precise biological explanation of
the causes or mechanisms that underlie it, the efficacy of Ritalin—
most people show an immediate response to the drug—demonstrates the existence of the disorder and its inner, organic cause.
Like diabetes, ADD will remain for most a lifetime disability, requiring permanent medication and specialized social services. Thus,
while overdiagnosis, overprescribing, and recreational Ritalin abuse
may occur and may even be on the rise, these abuses in no way dis-
prove the fact that ADD is both a recognized neurobiological disorder and a crippling disability.

The truth of the matter is not anywhere near this simple. As
numerous critics over more than two decades have noted, the persistent search for a biological cause has done little more than prove
the long-standing bias that exists toward medicalizing children's
problems. Child advocate Alfie Kohn, examining the myth of ADD,
concluded that "the medical journals are littered with the remains
of discarded theories that purported to explain restlessness in children as a symptom of disease. . . . What is remarkable here is not the
series of failures to find a biological cause but the tenacity with
which this line of investigation continues to be pursued."[33] In taking
this tack, the medical profession has repeatedly violated a basic
tenet of its scientific principles, insisting that ADD is biological
despite the absence of evidence to support the claim. Science

demands that while searching for an explanation, we remain neutral enough to consider all the possibilities. In this case the alternative possibility, which the evidence *does* support, is that the vast majority of children (and adults) diagnosed with ADD suffer from a developmental problem.[34] Yet what we hear instead from the medical establishment (and now the media) is the paradoxical statement that ADD is without question a biomedical problem, although "the causes of [it] are not clearly understood."[35]

What this diagnosis by fiat really signifies is that the authority of American psychiatry operates largely as a social and political force, relegating to science only an affirming role. Hence, when biologically oriented psychiatrists declare that "most practitioners in the field now agree that the characteristic problems of people with ADD stem from neurobiological malfunctioning,"[36] what they are really saying is, "have faith in us; we know what's best." The only reason we are being asked to trust them, though, is that they lack the science to support their own professional opinions. If they had the scientific evidence, we can be sure they would use it in place of a mere opinion poll. Instead of the above sentence, we would read, "Most studies indicate that the characteristic problems of people with ADD stem from neurobiological malfunctioning." Without the confirming evidence from such studies, however, they rely instead on the public's trust, abusing the privilege by preying on people's need for quick answers to what are ultimately very complex problems.

PERHAPS the most illustrative case of this scientific malpractice, documented in detail in the adjacent box, is a study reported in the *New England Journal of Medicine* in 1990. This report, conducted by Alan Zametkin and colleagues at the National Institute of Mental Health, declared a statistically significant difference in the brain's metabolizing of glucose in adults with ADD symptoms.[37] As some scientists have discovered, however, this widely cited and celebrated study did not demonstrate any such relationship between brain function and hyperactivity.[38] In fact, when this research team attempted to replicate the alleged findings, it was forced to conclude, in a 1993 report, that no such relationship actually existed

How to Manufacture Disease

Start with Research That Is Weak in Methods and Strong in Bias

"In a landmark study that could help put to rest decades of confusion and controversy, researchers at the NIMH have traced ADHD . . . to a specific metabolic abnormality in the brain." This conclusion, from the November 26, 1990, issue of *Time* magazine, refers to a study conducted by a team of researchers led by Alan Zametkin at the National Institute in Mental Health.[39] The study, published in the *New England Journal of Medicine*, used positron emission tomography—PET scans—to examine cerebral glucose metabolism in hyperactive and non-hyperactive adults while performing an attention task.[40] Results showed that the rate of metabolism was 8.1 percent lower in the hyperactive adults, which represented a statistically significant difference between the two groups. This result led Zametkin and colleagues to conclude that after many years of searching, research had finally located a biological cause of ADD. As Zametkin remarked in the *New York Times*, "there are people who say you should not use medications, that it's a matter of upbringing. We're hoping that this will put an end to that kind of thinking."[41]

But are these results in fact valid? Should we really stop looking for the causes of ADD, as Zametkin instructs? A number of factors suggest we should not. First, efforts to replicate the findings reported by Zametkin et al. have failed; numerous studies have followed up this report, with little to show in return.[42] Second, the participants were adults rather than children, thus limiting the applicability of this study for children. Third, there remains no evidence that a mere 8.1 percent difference in metabolism would produce clinically significant difference in behavior, including hyperactivity; as students of statistical testing know, statistical significance should not be interpreted to mean clinical significance. In fact, the differences between the two groups in metabolism did not correlate with any difference between their performance on the attention task. Fourth, it appears that the findings themselves were likely the result of a confounding variable that had nothing to do with ADD. While 72 percent of participants in the hyperactive group were men, in the control group this number was only 56 percent. This means that if men have a lower glucose metabolism in this particular area of the brain than do women, the difference between the two groups could be the result of there simply being more men in the hyperactive group. Indeed, another group of researchers compared the metabolism between the men and women in the control group of the Zametkin study and found just such a statistical difference in metabolism.[43] Finally, even if there was a valid difference in metabolism between these two groups, this study tells us nothing about the causes of these differences. Either the hyperactivity may have nothing to do with the metabolism or both these phenomena could be the product of some other set of childhood factors.[44] Consider another study that used PET scans to determine brain glucose metabolism. This study, conducted by a team of researchers studying obsessive-compulsive disorder (OCD), found that both drug (Prozac) and behavior therapy had the same effect on both OCD behavior and the rate of glucose metabolism in individuals suffering from OCD.[45] There is clear evidence, in other words, that the rates of glucose metabolism found in the Zametkin study could have been the result of environmental forces rather than biological ones.

Publish the Flawed Results in a Prestigious Medical Journal That Shares This Bias

Despite the many limitations of the study by Zametkin and colleagues, it was nevertheless published in the prestigious *New England Journal of Medicine*. One can only speculate as to how "junk science" makes its way into a highly visible journal, though it seems clear in this case that much of this has to do with the researchers' treatment of ADD as a biomedical problem (rather than a developmental or societal one), a bias that is undoubtedly also shared by the journal.[46] The fact that this same team of researchers has published even more misleading results along these lines in this and similarly prestigious journals suggests that this bias toward reductionism and medicalization is in fact common to most psychiatric research and publications.[47] Moreover, given the weaknesses of the study and given the journal's knowledge that such data will be interpreted by the media as clear evidence that ADD is biological, publishing them suggests a reckless disregard of the truth on the part of both the researchers and the journal.

Feed These Seemingly Important Findings to an Uncritical Media That Are Blinded by Science

The publication of these results in the *NEJM* did indeed prompt considerable media attention.[48] Just as *Time* called it a "landmark study" in an article entitled "Why Junior Won't Sit Still: Researchers Link Hyperactivity to an Abnormality in the Brain," the *New York Times, Washington Post,* and *Newsweek* all were quick to report on the apparent breakthrough.[49] Taken as a whole, the media coverage of this so-called discovery was accepted uncritically as proof for the long-standing assumption that ADD is an innate disorder or the brain. As Hallowell and Ratey conclude in *Driven to Distraction*, the Zametkin study is "one of the landmark studies in the entire ADD area, a study which really marked a turning point in establishing a biological basis for ADD, . . . [and which] created a bridge where before there had been only a leap of faith."[50] If this study is the best proof for saying ADD is a biological disorder, it seems that believing ADD is a biological problem is still a leap of faith.

between its measures of brain metabolism and ADD.[51] One year later these researchers reported on yet another attempt to link ADD with the brain's metabolism of glucose; in this instance the idea was to show that if ADD was a result of the brain's failure to metabolize glucose, Ritalin should work by increasing that metabolism.[52] Once again, the results were a failure: Although administration of the drug had the usual effects on subjects' behavior, it did not correspond to changes in brain metabolism. Meanwhile, the most reputable newspapers and magazines, the medical profession, and the ADD industry continue to hail this research as the most definitive evidence of ADD as a biological disorder.

Had these studies actually shown a valid relationship between brain metabolism and ADD, the researchers would immediately have been facing an even greater challenge. Not only had they studied adults and adolescents, rather than children, and not only did variations in brain metabolism fail to vary along with the behavioral performances of the subjects, but the authors also failed to acknowledge that differences in brain metabolism would most likely represent a *result* of what was causing the hyperactivity or inattention, rather than their cause. "The authors do not recognize that demonstrating the presence of an organic anomaly is not the same as demonstrating the instigating cause of an illness," writes Katherine Tyson.[53] Because future studies will no doubt continue to rely on the same spurious logic, let us consider this question of "cause" and "effect" more closely.

Not only in the case of ADD, but throughout much of psychiatry and in the media, there is the assumption today that any correlation between psychological problems and neurophysiology proves the problems have a biological basis. Psychiatrists and neuroscientists often fall into this trap by relying on an old-fashioned dualism of mind and body, where mind has no matter and body has no mind. The noted physiologist Candace Pert summed up the limits of this dualism while testifying on Capitol Hill: "I believe that the data clearly show that the mind is not confined to the brain, but impacts on every organ in the body. . . . One day we will look back regretfully on this strange mindless era of blatant over-medication and cavalier surgery for pain with psychological roots as we now regard the ignorant era of medicine in the 19th century when germ theory was unknown and physicians scoffed and persecuted those who thought washing the hands was important."[54]

The problem with dualistic thinking in the mental health field is that, as we shall see in this second half of this chapter, the factors that yield durable psychological characteristics also yield pronounced changes in the brain.[55] Not only is it true that differences at the level of physiology may implicate either a biological or a developmental problem, but it is also true that whatever the cause, significant differences in children's behavior will always be correlated with significant differences at the level of biochemistry and neurophysiology. Despite these facts, the biological reductionism Pert decries persists in psychiatry in large part because it is an effective way of medicalizing psychological and developmental problems. Once we see the problem as biological or physiological in origin, we are likely to conclude that its treatment should also be of an individual and medical nature. To put it simply, it fits psychiatry's way of understanding the world, and it certainly makes good business sense in a world of managed care.

A study reported in 1971 offers a good example of why we must be more cautious in our interpretation of research findings on mind and body. This study examined the levels of the brain chemical serotonin in more than two dozen hyperactive children.[56] Why these children were hyperactive was unclear in that none of the children had any known history of severe illness or injury. To determine whether their levels of serotonin were abnormally low, the hyperactive children's levels were compared with the levels of serotonin in a group of children who were similar except they showed no signs of hyperactivity. As anticipated, even the children with the lowest serotonin levels in the "normal" group had higher serotonin levels than all the children in the hyperactive group. In other words, by biochemical measures alone, we could tell the hyperactive kids apart from the nonhyperactive ones.

In contemporary times this result would have led immediately to the conclusion drawn by A. J. Zametkin and colleagues: that ADD is a result of some inborn biological disorder. However, this study did something none has done since. It took the two most hyperactive children and tested if their levels of brain biochemicals would change as they spent time at the research hospital and away from their usual lives. What happened was striking. As time went on, the children's low levels of serotonin began to return to normal, higher levels. Then, one month after the children left the research hospital, researchers found that the biochemical levels in both of them had returned to their previous low levels. Perhaps most important was the fact that unlike the results in the study by Zametkin et al., these changes in the brain were correlated with the expected changes in hyperactivity: As serotonin increased, hyperactivity decreased; As serotonin decreased, hyperactivity increased. Thus, rather than affirm the idea that different brain states mean that ADD is inborn, this study offered hard evidence *that the conditions of our lives can simultaneously alter both our brain chemistry and our behavior*; measures of the brain states alone only beg the question of whether such measures represent a cause or an effect of ADD-like symptoms.

The uncritical acceptance of studies that purport to show a biological basis for ADD reveals the bias toward individualistic solutions in the medical profession. While the American Medical Association has gone on to dismiss MCS, citing a lack of biomedical evidence, it has at the same time both embraced "junk science" in favor of ADD and shown a dangerous disregard of the evidence against it. This does not mean, however, that individuals—whether in medicine, science, or the media—are consciously conspiring to manipulate scientific knowledge. Although this certainly happens, it is much more probable that the process flows from tacit individual and institutional assumptions and biases.[57] Much as a social stereotype is confirmed when people pay attention to evidence in its favor while unconsciously ignoring evidence against it, so the manufacturing of disease develops historically according to certain unexamined cultural prejudices. Once these assumptions operate as part of the common sense, as we saw in Rosenhan's study of psychiatric hospitals, medical practitioners begin to perceive the world in a manner that confirms them. *Thus, for ADD, early evidence showing that hyperactivity can result from childhood illnesses or injuries paved the way to the assumption that all cases were biological.* That there has never been any hard evidence to support this expanded claim has not led to its questioning; rather, it has encouraged only a more intensive search for this evidence, which at this point still does not exist.

WHO GETS SICK?

THE third similarity to be found between MCS and ADD—that they affect only certain subgroups—also supports our general conclusion about how culture manufactures disease. In the case of MCS, the criticism has been that those most likely to be diagnosed—middle-class, well-educated women—are not the ones we would most expect to be suffering from chemical exposure. Studies have long shown that blue-collar workers (and their families) are much more likely to be exposed to toxic levels of chemicals, and for obvious reasons: These are the people who most often work in the industries that manufacture and use such substances. We have also long known that the individuals most likely to suffer from psychosomatic illness are, for whatever reason, women.[58] This profile of who becomes sick with MCS suggests that it is a psychological and cultural syndrome, not a biological or medical illness.

The same can be said of ADD. Here, however, the profile looks different: Boys are three to five times as likely to be diagnosed with ADD as girls—although the gap appears to be closing. While it is certainly true that we might expect boys to be naturally more hyperactive and inattentive than girls, this "boys will be boys" sensibility has at least as much to do with how boys are raised as it does with their boy genes. However, rather than ask why boys are more likely to be diagnosed with ADD, scientists and physicians simply assume that boys are prone to such problems. But as Natalie Angier writes in the *New York Times*, ". . . biological insights can only go so far in explaining why American boyhood is coming to be seen as a state of proto-disease. After all, the brains of boys in other countries also were exposed to testosterone in utero, yet non-American doctors are highly unlikely to diagnose a conduct disorder or ADHD."[59]

A developmental and cultural approach to ADD does a better job of explaining these gender differences, why the gap is closing between the sexes, and why increasing numbers of adults are now being identified with ADD. If the psychological and cultural conditions that produce these symptoms are becoming more virulent, as they certainly are, it should be no surprise that girls will begin showing up on the radar screen more often; from the point of view of sensory addictions, because girls tend to be more mature than boys overall, they may be more resistant to the effects of rapid-fire culture, but they will not be spared. Much the same is true of adults diagnosed with ADD. A generation ago most children on Ritalin actually gave up the drug and the diagnoses as they climbed through adolescence and into adulthood. As one study concluded in 1957, "in later years this syndrome tends to wane spontaneously and disappear. We have not seen it persist in those patients whom we have followed to adult life."[60] Another study, which conducted a fourteen-year follow-up of hyperactive children beginning in 1965, concluded that this syndrome is ". . . restricted largely to childhood and adolescence, and then mostly to school-related areas."[61] How such a mysterious disappearance of a medical disorder was possible was never explained. Now, a generation later, it no longer has to be. Most children today continue with the diagnosis and the drugs, taking them into adolescence and adulthood. Still, other questions remain: How can the prognosis of a such a disorder all of a sudden become worse? How can a disorder that once affected only childhood now cripple these children for a lifetime? Why is the disorder now suddenly on the rise in adults? Historically ADD was solely a problem associated with childhood, so why do we now have a new adult disorder that doesn't exist outside the United States?

These questions are perplexing, but this is only because we view them from a medicalized perspective. If we look at them from a developmental viewpoint instead, the confusion vanishes. First, we realize that as a culture-based phenomenon, the diagnosis of ADD can shift radically merely as a result of changes in the acceptability of the "disorder." Second, we no longer expect that hyperactivity and inattention will disappear during adolescence, and neither will the use of Ritalin, since the developmental conditions that produced these responses in the first place are worsening. The world is more saturated than ever with constant motion, and the structures of everyday life continue to become more fragmented and sped up.

Hence, if more children are being diagnosed with ADD, it makes perfect sense that more will carry their problems into adulthood, just as it makes sense that some will not show signs until adulthood. Each of these developments is consistent with the idea that the impact of sensory addictions, both direct and indirect, is widening, catching more in its invisible net. For the most vulnerable, this means more severe and more enduring problems; for the less vulnerable, it means having them for the first time in adulthood.

IN THE EYE OF THE BEHOLDER

THIS brings us to a final similarity to be explored between MCS and ADD. As critics have questioned the basis of MCS as a legitimate medical disorder, they have also questioned the motives of the physicians who diagnose it, charging that they have a professional and financial interest in it. Michael Fumento writes, "Clinical ecologists have an investment in keeping people sick. They want to keep patients. And so, they say, 'Look, you know, I'll keep you going from week to week, but you're probably going to have to see me for the rest of your life.' And they'll tell you Multiple Chemical Sensitivity at this point in medical science is incurable. . . ." Now it is true that this charge could be thrown at any number of medical professionals, including those who treat Alzheimer's, Parkinson's, or cancer, since each of these groups makes a living treating chronically ill patients. But because MCS lacks the scientific evidence for its claims, whereas the others do not, the question of motivation takes on greater significance.

Notice, however, that this concern has not been applied to ADD, even though the physicians who embrace the diagnosis of ADD are open to the same critique. If we rewrite Fumento's remarks in terms of ADD, it would read: "Some psychiatrists and pediatricians have an investment in keeping people sick. They want to keep patients. And so they say, 'Look, you know, I'll keep you going from week to week, but you're probably going to have to see me for the rest of your life.' And they'll tell you attention deficit disorder at this point in medical science is incurable." Although I would stress that there are many physicians who believe Ritalin's use is out of control, this hypothetical statement is, for much of psychiatry, perfectly accurate. To give just one example, there is a psychiatrist in my community who writes as many as two hundred prescriptions for Ritalin per month. Steeped in the biological worldview of the APA, she not only has an investment in keeping these children sick, but also tells them that medical science believes the disorder to be incurable.

A TISSUE OF FICTION

WHY, if all the above is true, do we not find anyone in the public realm and in the media challenging the medical basis of ADD? Although the voices of dissent are beginning to be heard, it is true that public concerns continue to be focused only on whether too many children are being diagnosed. The problem we face here is that while critics may charge that MCS is based on fringe medicine backed up by junk science, this is a much more difficult claim to make against ADD, however true it may be. This is not because of differences in the scientific legitimacy of these two syndromes but because of nonscientific factors, including the immense power, resources, and momentum of the pro-ADD medical establishment, the huge commercial push by pharmaceutical companies, the growing prevalence of the problems of hyperactivity and inattention, and the apparent lack of a credible alternative explanation.

However fictitious the ADD diagnosis is, those who use it certainly are not a fringe segment of American society. Supporting the AMA are the thousands of practicing psychiatrists and pediatricians who rely on the diagnosis, the pharmaceutical companies that make many millions of dollars each year from ADD-related drugs, and the hundreds of thousands of families and teachers who, under the assault of rapid-fire culture, seek shelter behind the diagnosis and its so-called treatment. As noted in Chapter 1, in 1988 there were a mere twenty-nine chapters of CH.A.A.D. (Children and Adults with Attention Deficit Disorder), the ADD advocacy group. With the continued financial boost of Ritalin's manufacturer, Novartis, however, there are now more than five hundred chapters of CH.A.A.D., with more than thirty-two thousand members (Ritalin's maker increased its funding for CH.A.D.D. from fifty thousand dollars in

1992 to almost four hundred thousand dollars in 1994.) Given that the public believes ADD to be a credible medical disorder, it is hardly a surprise that defenders of the faith can keep it going.

The powerful influence of the Ritalin solution on the acceptability of the ADD diagnosis is also suggestive of something we examined in the previous chapter: people's faith in technological progress as the solution to our social problems. Today there is a pervasive sense, in the public and in the media, that miracle breakthroughs are being made in medical and pharmacological science and neuroscience. As we shall see in Chapter 5 for Ritalin, this is not all that it seems to be. With all the persisting psychological and social problems that American children and adults are facing, combined with the fact that no psychotropic drug will ever cure them, it seems unlikely that medical progress will be our salvation. Ritalin is a very good example since it is often viewed as a special medication for ADD-diagnosed children, yet in fact it is merely a run-of-the-mill stimulant, developed for reasons having nothing to do with its current use.

There are other differences between MCS and ADD that are also crucial to understanding their different fates. Perhaps most important is the credibility ADD has received from its putative medical treatment. In the absence of medical evidence proving ADD to be biological, advocates have relied heavily on the "treatment" effects of Ritalin to give it legitimacy. As psychiatrist Ted Hallowell wrote in 1997, the most impressive evidence for the "biological basis" of ADD "is the clinical evidence from records of millions of patients who have met the diagnostic criteria and who have benefited spectacularly from standard treatment."[62] This is a tissue of fiction, however, because many of the most prominent researchers in this area readily acknowledge that the effects of psychostimulants ("standard treatment") are at least as pronounced in nonhyperactive children.[63] Nevertheless, there can be little doubt that the Ritalin solution—coupled with the tens of millions of dollars spent for advertising by the manufacturer of Ritalin since the early 1960s—has been the single most important ingredient in ADD's respectability. This is a big difference between ADD and MCS since MCS has had no "magic bullet" solution.

The rise of ADD benefited from another important attribute that promoted its acceptability in American medicine, one that shines a bright light on how concepts of disease and illness are constructed by institutions of health, media, and government. Unlike MCS, ADD is defined as a medical problem that originates within the individual. Whereas the existence of MCS would demand a radical change in industrial and environmental policy, ADD fits perfectly within the rubric of a medical problem with a well-defined, individual-based solution: Ritalin. In this sense the American medical establishment has been wholly consistent. Rejecting a psychological explanation in the case of ADD ("ADD is a developmental problem") while accepting one for MCS ("MCS is a psychosomatic illness") appears to be contradictory, but it actually conforms to the same overarching institutional goal, which is to deny that the symptoms represent a societal problem. Persons with ADD and MCS need psychiatric help, say doctors; they are indeed sick, but not from something in the world outside them that needs changing.

AN EXPLANATION STRANGER THAN FICTION: SENSORY ADDICTIONS

MY objective in undermining the public's belief in ADD is *not* to convert it to some other dogmatic position. Instead, the ultimate goal must be to encourage a critical pursuit of the facts and a relentless search for what can be done to give children, and their children, more wholesome lives. Getting used to giving your children powerful, mind-altering drugs or taking these drugs yourself should not be a desired "solution." It is truly too big a pill to swallow. Nevertheless, at this time, much of the public still embraces the rigid view that all cases of ADD represent an incurable disease with which millions of American children are affected and thus required to take chronic doses of powerful and potentially harmful drugs. If 7 percent of the population around the world were really to have ADD, as drug companies and some medical "experts" have suggested, this would mean four hundred million people, more than the combined populations of the United States, Mexico, and Canada, could be taking Ritalin.[64]

The Ritalin solution has become so common today that we no longer feel outraged at how crippling and destructive it is in the long run. Evidence of this normalization, of how we have become oblivious to the threat of Ritalin, is not hard to find: In contrast with us today, many in the 1970s expressed outrage, as the number of children being put on psychostimulants grew beyond one hundred thousand. Among them were Peter Schrag and Diane Divoky, who in 1975 wrote *The Myth of the Hyperactive Child*: "An entire generation is slowly being conditioned to distrust its own instincts, to regard its deviation from the narrowing standards of approved norms as sickness and to rely on the institutions of the state and on technology to define and engineer its 'health.' In enhancing the power of the state, and in destroying even the ability to imagine the alternatives and understand the liberties which might once have been exercised in defending them, the impact of that conditioning is almost incalculable."[65]

Similarly, while in 1997 *Psychology Today* ran a cover story entitled "ADD, Why I'm Glad I Have It," twenty some years earlier it ran critical pieces like "We're Too Cavalier about Hyperactivity," "A Slavish Reliance on Drugs—Are We Pushers for Our Own Children?," and "Big Brother and Psychotechnology." In the 1970s we could also learn from reading popular magazines that in the late 1960s Sweden banned the use of Ritalin after rising street abuse and that in 1971 the FDA and the National Academy of Sciences in the United States warned strenuously of the risk of abuse; in 1978 *Newsweek* reported problems with Ritalin abuse in an article, "Boom in Illegal Pills." Little of this important information is reported in the mainstream media today, however, lingering instead in professional journals of sociology and social work.

WE have seen that a critical pursuit of the facts undermines the blanket assumption that ADD is a singular biological problem: the very criticisms that professional organizations have used to discredit MCS apply equally well to ADD. Hence, the alternative viewpoint presented here: that ADD is really a cluster of developmental problems, many of which stem from the hurried society and its cultivation of sensory addictions. Again, this alternative viewpoint is not offered as a fait accompli but rather as a way of putting some distance between us and the blinding assumptions powered by the ADD industry. As we know from research on the development of people's scientific beliefs, scientists and the public will not abandon one theory, however inadequate it is, unless a more reasonable one is readily available. In this sense the present account is like an island off the coast of the prevailing conventional wisdom, from which perhaps we can begin to see things more clearly. The question for us becomes whether a developmental perspective provides us with a better account of what we see when we look at the problems associated with the ADD diagnosis.

HOW CULTURAL PROBLEMS BECOME PSYCHOLOGICAL ONES

ONE of the most heralded stories of 1997 offers a powerful insight into the development of sensory addictions. As reported first on the cover of *Time* ("Fertile Minds") and then in a special issue of *Newsweek* ("Your Child, from Birth to Three") and a special ABC report ("I Am Your Child"), a new social movement has materialized that focuses on the significance of development in the child's formative years.[66] The principal impetus for this renewed concern over the lives of young children (from birth to age six) is the growing evidence that much of the development of a child's brain takes place in real time *after* birth. We have long known that newborns and very young children need special attention for normal development to occur, but not until recently did research in neuroscience make it clear just how much development really takes place. "Scientists are just now realizing how experiences after birth, rather than something innate, determines the actual wiring of the human brain," an article in *Newsweek* says, "A baby is born with a head on her shoulders and a mind primed for learning. But it takes years of experience—looking, listening, playing, interacting with parents— to wire the billions of complex neural circuits that govern language, math, music, logic and emotions."[67]

There are really two important findings here. The first is that the mind represents the combined activities of about ten to one hundred billion interconnected neurons in the brain's cerebral cortex. Because these nerve cells of the brain make sometimes hundreds or thousands of connections with other neurons, together they create a massive jungle of neural wiring—about one million billion connections in total. This means that in a space in the brain the size of a large match head there are about one billion neural connections, and this represents only the specific connections we might find inside one healthy child. Since at the level of neural connections each brain develops differently, the total number of *possible* connections in a healthy human brain is a number so astronomically large that it is difficult to fathom. Nobel laureate Gerald Edelman describes this as the number ten with millions of zeroes trailing behind it.[68] In short, consciousness and the human mind are emergent products of a brain that has almost unimaginable complexity—complexity that also translates into enormous flexibility.

This flexibility represents the second important aspect of these findings. We used to think a child's brain was largely intact at birth. We really had no idea that for each minute in the newborn child there is something like 4.7 million branches growing out from neurons, making connections to the many neighboring branches of other neurons.[69] The brain's connections proliferate widely after birth, and experience then directs and prunes these connections accordingly.[70] Knowing this is taking place inside the child is almost shocking, especially when we realize why this development must happen after birth, since the brain needs real-life experiences to steer its growth. Of course our genome plays a fundamental role, but it cannot possibly have the knowledge to instruct ten billion nerve cells on where to make their seemingly endless combinations of neural connections.[71] This developmental process is thus so striking because of how directly linked it is to the moment-to-moment experiences the child is having right under our noses. As an article in *Time* puts it, "parents are the brain's first and most important teachers."[72]

In large part because of the vividness of these pictures of the developing brain, parents and others have become more convinced than ever that early-childhood experiences cultivate (or erase) the child's possibilities for the future. Individuals and society both pay a huge price for what does or does not happen during these critical years. Hence, investing time and energy in the education of the child's senses, rather than having them flattened out by a hectic, electronically amplified lifestyle, should reap exponentially larger dividends than later investments, since much of the brain's organization of mind and body would have already taken shape. This brings us to the question at hand: What are the implications of this early critical period for what we are seeing in the lives of children growing up in the hurried society? If what we are calling ADD is primarily a developmental problem, retained at the level of neurophysiology, these neuroscientific findings could provide the basic scientific evidence for how rapid-fire culture transforms human consciousness, leaving sensory addictions in its wake.[73]

To understand the possibility that children's brains are different today, we can begin by asking in what way problems with attention, impulsivity, and hyperactivity look like developmental problems. Are they evident at birth, as a genetic viewpoint would predict, or do they appear gradually over time during early and middle childhood? Furthermore, if these problems are principally genetic, changes in societal circumstances should not alter their magnitude, their frequency, or the course of their evolution. If we look at the current diagnostic criteria for ADD, however, we find this conclusion: "It is especially difficult to establish this diagnosis in children younger than four or five years."[74] Because psychologists have established that early genetic influences on temperament can in fact be observed in the newborn child, we should expect that signs of poor attention or hyperactivity would be present early on—that is, if the disorder were in fact genetic. But as this aspect of the ADD diagnosis makes clear, these problems cannot be located in very young children. Indeed, the one behavioral measure during infancy that might predict ADD—temperament—turns out not to be predictive of latter hyperactivity or inattention.[75] Although it is unlikely that genetic background plays no role whatsoever, it appears that these problems are contingent upon certain developmental experiences—events that ultimately determine if a child (or adult) will end up with an ADD diagnosis.

As has been pointed out, for every study that considers possible developmental factors involved in ADD, there are dozens searching for physiological or genetic causes. What is still badly needed are longitudinal studies that chart the course of a child's development in real time, from before the symptoms of ADD begin until after they appear. The virtue of this methodology lies in the ability to take account of factors early in the child's life that may develop into hyperactivity and inattention, thus escaping the limitation of retrospective studies, which cannot distinguish very effectively between cause and effect. In what may be the only study to examine childhood hyperactivity and inattention prospectively, the results were quite convincing. This study, which began in the 1970s and was published in 1995, examined the same 191 children at six months, during early childhood, and during middle childhood. At each time measures were taken for a variety of behavioral, psychological, and family variables.[76]

Researchers found first of all that variables operating at the level of the family were predictive of which children would and would not have these problems. Their overall conclusion: "In early childhood, quality of caregiving more powerfully predicted distractibility, an early precursor of hyperactivity, than did early biological or temperament factors. Caregiving and contextual factors together with early distractibility significantly predicted hyperactivity in middle childhood."[77] Marital status at the time of the child's birth, the emotional supports provided to the caregiver(s) during the child's development, and the caregiving style were the most powerfully predictive factors.

Needless to say, all these factors are themselves either directly or indirectly impacted upon by rapid-fire culture and the culture of neglect. Single parenting and poor external supports for such parents are obvious examples of the stressed conditions encouraged by the priorities of today's hurried society. As David Elkind writes, "These crumbling boundaries and mounting pressures, combined with an appalling lack of institutional support for families, certainly does not make life in a permeable family easy for many postmodern parents."[78] These general contextual factors also create the conditions for a restless and sensory-laden lifestyle for children. In fact, the most significant factor of this study—caregiving style—addresses this very possibility since it refers to overstimulation received by the child during infancy and during early childhood. Overstimulation refers here to parents' unintentional practice of imposing their sense of timing on their child, thereby interrupting his or her normal pacing and interests. Chronic exposure to this caregiving style appears to increase the child's overall levels of distractibility, which correlate with later hyperactivity. The effects of the parents' hurried and hectic life become a disruptive force in the child's self-paced discovery of the world.

Of course the family circumstances that make for this kind of overstimulation are likely also to correlate with other distracting sources of stimulation in the child's environment, including the pacing of activities throughout the day and a reliance on plugged-in activities (such as television). As one study showed, not only do children watch a greater quantity and more intense genre of programming than do infants and adults, but ADD-diagnosed children in particular often watch more television relative to their peers. This study, published in *Child and Adolescent Social Work*, reported that both ADD children and their parents are often avid TV watchers. When television viewing was compared across five groups of children, all of whom were diagnosed with a specific childhood disorder (such as ADD, conduct disorder, or adjustment disorder), authors James Shanahan and Michael Morgan noted that "children whose primary diagnosis is [ADD] spend more time watching than any other group, almost a full hour [a day] over the sample mean . . . [and that] children of heavy-viewing parents are more likely to be judged as having ADD."[79]

On top of this, parents whose children have started on the way to sensory addictions may encourage this development more and more by relying on stimulation that, at least in the short run, soothes the child. According to psychiatrist Michael Gordon, "some parents have compensated for their child's impulsiveness and distractability by adjusting their family's lifestyle to minimize situations bound to cause problem."[80] One parent says, "We don't make him sit with us [at meals] because he fidgets terribly in his chair, gets out of his seat every ten seconds to run for juice or check out a noise in the living room, or change channels on the TV a million times. And he interrupts conversations so much that it's just better if he eats when he's done playing."[81]

A related developmental problem addressed by the longitudinal study above is the child's need to learn self-regulatory skills, defined earlier as children's need for self-governance. As one of the authors, Alan Sroufe, documents in his book *Emotional Development: The Organization of Emotional Life in the Early Years*, parents, whether they realize it or not, play a crucial role in the child's internalization of healthy regulatory practices, which in turn affect behavioral self-control, emotional development, and self-esteem.[82] In simple terms, dysfunctional ways of regulating and organizing the child's behavior, such as the overstimulation reported in the longitudinal study above, tend to undermine such development.

This longitudinal study demonstrates plainly that hyperactivity and inattention correlate with identifiable characteristics found in the contemporary American family. This type of study can go a long way toward redirecting the question of where the symptoms of "ADD" come from, and that is of course why we need more of them. Consider, for example, how parents sometimes report that their child "was always" hard to manage, seeing this as evidence of a biological cause. Yet we know that many children are considered out of control during the terrible twos. Moreover, about 40 percent of all four-year-olds are described by their mothers as hyperactive, and about 25 to 35 percent of all six- to eight-year-olds are described by their parents as either impulsive or hyperactive.[83] Additionally, longitudinal data suggest that this early evidence of a problem is the same evidence we would expect to find for a developmental problem, especially for one that can be predicted using measures of the family context at birth and at sixth months. We must remember, after all, that a developmental problem is likely to begin early and then slowly worsen until it reaches a crisis level. Early signs of behavioral problems often predict later problems because the contextual factors that produced them in the first place also persist. As was concluded in the longitudinal study, "While early hyperactivity best predicted later hyperactivity in elementary years, caregiving and contextual factors contributed to the maintenance of hyperactivity across this childhood period and, independent of earlier hyperactivity, predicted later AD/HD. The findings suggest that once established, the disordered behavior cycle may be self-stabilizing."[84]

"A MOVEABLE FEAST"

ANOTHER reason why we should view ADD as a developmental problem is that its prevalence has varied both historically and cross-culturally. Only since the 1970s have we witnessed a remarkable, exponential rise in children being medicated with Ritalin, even though stimulants have been an accepted treatment for hyperactivity since the 1950s. Even more remarkable are the rising numbers of adults lining up for Ritalin and the requisite ADD diagnosis. Both these historical changes have been dismissed by ADD advocates, who insist that advances in medical understanding are responsible for these changes.

The problem here is that experts from European countries argue for a considerably lower incidence of ADD than is currently reported in the United States (in Britain, for example, use of drugs like Ritalin is far less common than in the United States, although its use has increased twenty-fourfold since 1990[85]). Indeed, children are estimated to be anywhere from ten to fifty times more likely to be diagnosed with ADD in the United States than in Britain or France. Even among Western European health professionals who believe in ADD, most still note a much lower prevalence in their own countries than here. Some of these cross-cultural differences have to do with the fact that in contrast with the U.S. bias, Europeans view these problems as developmental and psychological, rather than biological and medical, but much of them also have to do with the fact that such disturbances as hyperactivity, impulsivity, and inattention are considerably less common in Western Europe than in the United States.[86]

Differences between American children and their European counterparts do not worry only critics; they also worry ADD advocates, who see cross-cultural difference as potentially damaging evidence against categorizing ADD as an inborn illness. Once when speaking on the radio about these matters, I was taken by surprise when my psychiatrist colleague confidently told listeners that such disparities could be explained by genetic differences in those who first emigrated from Europe to the United States. My immediate reaction to this was dumbfounded silence since I could not imagine a more ridiculous explanation. Not only does this not explain why ADD is as common for racial minorities as for those of European descent in the United States,[87] but it also does nothing to explain why radical changes have taken place in the prevalence of ADD over the past forty years. Moreover, although psychiatrists repeatedly cite the earliest-known study on hyperactivity—a paper by George F. Still, published in 1902—these observations were actually of British rather than American children. If ADD is genetically unique to the United States, why should the earliest observations have come out of Britain?

At the time I dismissed this imaginative explanation as a desperate move by a psychiatrist heavily invested in the ADD industry. I later found out, however, that this is a widely held myth in the popular ADD literature. Psychiatrists Hallowell and Ratey reach for this explanation in *Driven to Distraction*, for example, writing that "one possible explanation [for differences in the United States and Britain] is that our gene pool is heavily loaded for ADD. The people who founded this country, and continued to populate it over time, were just the types of people who might have had ADD. They did not like to sit still."[88] Self-serving stories such as this not only demonstrate the concern pro-ADD physicians have with the implications of cross-cultural differences in hyperactivity—indeed, studies that examine such differences are rare—but also suggest the utter impenetrability of their faith to evidence to the contrary.

As we saw in Chapter 1, the steadfast refusal by psychiatry to consider the significant changes taking place in children's lives stands in sharp contrast with what child advocates and developmental studies are saying. One of the most comprehensive of these, a 1989 study that examined children and adolescents over a thirteen-year period, reported a significant increase in problems concerning not only attention but also sociability, anxiety, delinquency, and aggression.[89] Another study, reported in 1993, found that as much as 25 percent of all school-age children experience real physical symp-

toms that are largely psychosomatic in nature.[90] Such studies led
Daniel Goleman to write in *Emotional Intelligence* that "unless
things change, the long-term prospects for today's children marry-
ing and having fruitful, stable lives together are growing more dismal with each generation."[91]

With all that is taking place in modern American life—with our
divorce rate 50 percent higher than in any other country, with 25
percent of our children under six living in poverty, and with 45 percent of children under the age of one in day care (and two-thirds
under the age of seven)—there is every reason to be concerned
about what is going on in children's lives. Moreover, when we consider the effects of the hurried society on children's brain development, as we now understand it, it's easy to see why people have
started questioning whether American society might be becoming a
toxic place in which to raise a family.

ADAPTATION AND ADDICTION

AT the heart of the crisis in child development lies the problem of
sensory addictions. Indeed, we might well wonder about the relationship between sensory addictions and what we have just learned
about the sensitive minds of infants and young children. As I began
writing this chapter, for example, President Bill Clinton proposed a
twenty-two-billion-dollar program to help eliminate the inadequa-
cies endemic to the child care industry throughout the nation; and
as Mr. Clinton emphasized the need for employers to create a more
flexible workplace for working parents, the First Lady was speaking
to groups about the connection between family life and research on
children's brain development.

Regarding the research, we know, first of all, that the brain has an
incredible capacity for adaptation to the stimulus world. The primary purpose of this process, evolutionarily, has probably been to keep
our attention directed toward important stimuli and away from irrelevant ones. As researchers of perception have long known, the world
is full of such a myriad of stimuli that we can attend to only a small
portion of what's actually out there; if we were conscious of all the
stimuli in our perceptual field, we would lose the ability to discrim-

inate between what's important and what's not. Have you ever noticed, for example, how, not long after you pin up a note on your fridge, you become accustomed to its being there and can no longer "see" it? In a few days the note becomes familiar and fades into the background, blending in with all the thousands of other stimuli that could attract your attention but don't. We continue to attend to red and green streetlights, yes, but most of what we "see" each day is no longer seen. Cognitive psychologist Shelley Taylor reflects on this process in infants: "Within weeks after birth, an infant actively explores the environment, responding to a new stimulus, such as a brightly colored rattle, with rapt attention and babbling. Soon, however, when the rattle has been fully explored, the infant shows little response when the rattle is again dangled before her, but may react with the same excitement to a new checkerboard that she has not previously seen. . . . Exploration and the ability to bring about change in the environment are their own rewards. . . . Moderately new environments that include objects the child has not seen before are far more interesting and stimulating than either radically different environments or environments full of familiar objects."[92]

Built into the idea of sensory adaptation are several important phenomena. First, research clearly suggests that a child will gradually adapt to simple sensory pleasures, creating a growing demand for stimuli that have a greater impact on the senses. Historically this elusive chase has not been problematic since there was a natural constraint on how "loud" stimuli could be. However, with the technological changes in transportation and the rise of the electronic age, this limit has been shattered. As the creators of film, video games, and MTV either knew or quickly discovered, there is always an audience, usually a young audience, out there waiting for a stimulus world to open that offers ever-greater complexity and velocity. The revolution in speed we have experienced this past century thus leads to a particularly modern question: How frenetic must our experience be before it becomes unpleasant or maladaptive? After all, the same studies on children's brain development suggesting that chronic stimulation may lead to sensory addictions also tell us that a normal range of stimulation during early development is necessary for normal development. Today, however, with technology advancing by leaps and bounds, and everyone assuming it has no effect on the nature of consciousness, this process of adaptation is spinning out of control. Indeed, we are now generating such a demand for stimulation that many of our pastimes are becoming passé, leaving in their place only the symptoms of sensory addictions and the virtual realities we create in order to escape them.

To see that sensory addictions are actually just the perversion of an everyday process, consider them in comparison to drug addictions. On the latter, we know from hundreds of laboratory studies with animals (and humans) that it is perfectly normal for psychoactive drugs to create experiences that encourage and maintain their self-administration, especially under conditions in which other desirable activities are unavailable (such as the opportunity for social interactions). In fact, perfectly healthy animals will voluntarily work to self-administer the same psychoactive drugs that humans use and abuse (a discovery that we'll take up in the next chapter with regard to Ritalin). These studies provide scientific evidence that drug-seeking behavior is a normal rather than, as was previously believed, a pathological process (for example, a defective personality trait). As Andrew Weil documents in *The Natural Mind*, although drug addiction is sometimes a consequence of drug use, it is not abnormal to seek changes in one's state of consciousness, whether with mind-altering drugs, meditation, or other forms of stimulus change.

On the basis of this conclusion, we can anticipate that the fundamental desire to change one's state of consciousness via the pursuit of novel and complex stimuli is a perfectly natural response. Moreover, just as a desire for drugs creates the possibility of drug addictions, so the desire for new sensory experiences creates the possibility of sensory addictions, especially under conditions of rapid-fire culture. When we look around the world today, we see widespread use of psychoactive drugs in many parts of the world, although we see serious problems of addiction in only a few. The same holds true for the consumption of the world's sights, sounds, tastes, and touches: We see it in all parts of the world, although we see serious problems of sensory addictions in only a few. That we find drug addictions and sensory addictions coexisting in the United States should thus come as no surprise. Nor should it surprise us that these two worlds collide in the case of Ritalin, where psychostimulants function as substitutes for desired external stimulation.

The natural allure of new sensory experiences, and the normal tolerance that develops to them, can be seen in the tendency of newborns to seek out sensory experiences and display sensory adaptation to familiar ones. We have also witnessed this in the laboratory with animals. Just as laboratory animals freely respond to obtain the administration of mind-altering drugs, so they respond to obtain the presentation of more complex stimuli and to obtain changes in their levels of stimulation. For example, psychological studies with both rats and chimpanzees have demonstrated a preference for progressively more complex stimuli.[93] When animals are introduced to an experimental setting and then reintroduced to it after some minor changes, they spend significantly more time investigating the new, unfamiliar areas.[94] Similarly, when animals are allowed to choose between two activity areas varying in visual complexity, animals choose the more complex one.[95] What is more, animals will try to produce changes in their stimulus surroundings. For example, studies with monkeys and pigeons have shown that they will work for the opportunity to look outside their experimental chamber,[96] suggesting that, as Shelley Taylor wrote about the infant child, "exploration and the ability to bring about change in the environment bring their own rewards."

Still, like infants, animals do not prefer stimuli that are too complex or unfamiliar.[97] Here it is important to realize that what counts as "too" complex is relative to a person's (or animal's) past experiences. As D. E. Berlyne notes in his work on curiosity, whether a stimulus is novel or complex cannot be determined without knowledge of the animal's or person's history.[98] The tendency to prefer more rather than less complex stimuli is constantly changing because what registers as novel or complex also changes with exposure. This explains the parent who complains to the adolescent child, "How can you listen to that crap?" since what the son or daughter hears as music the parent hears only as noise.

This notion that the complexity of a stimulus is relative to personal experience also draws another connection between drug and sensory addictions, since sensory adaptation is akin to drug *toler-ance*, in which more of the same substance is needed to produce the same effect. Consider the results of studies that examine peo-ple's habituation to background noises. They show that our senses readily adapt to the prevailing intensity of the stimuli surrounding us, from smells to sounds. One such study asked subjects to adjust the loudness of a jet noise so that it was perceived as comparable to a propeller noise. Although during the first set of trials the subjects required a decrease in jet noise of about fourteen decibels, on the second set of trials this number had already decreased to about ten decibels, and by the third set of trials, only a drop of 8 decibels was required. Adaptation to this noise was found to be both rapid and pronounced. It seems individuals quickly become "tolerant," even to noxious stimuli in the environment.

We have already seen a vivid example of this adaptation in the two passages that began Chapter 3, in which one writer in 1997 reported a different idea of what it meant for the world to be going too fast from that of another author writing more than a century ear-lier. The noted sensory adaptation theorist Harry Helson draws a similar conclusion with regard to people's experience of modern art. Concluding with a passage from Rudolf Arnheim's noted text *Art and Visual Perception* (1954), he writes:

> Most individuals are not aware of the highly complicated and specific style of many works of art produced in their own period or in preceding periods with which they are familiar. Unfamiliar works of art from any period strike us with their unusual features. We accept Cézannes and Renoirs today, but only a few decades ago they looked offensively unreal to the people of that genera-tion. Arnheim ventured the following prediction in line with this analysis: ". . . Anybody who is concerned with modern art will find it increasingly difficult to remain aware of the deviations from realistic rendition that strike the newcomer so forcefully. Even though our daily life is being permeated with all the devices of modern art by designers who use them for wallpapers, store windows, book covers, posters, and wrappers, the man in the street has hardly gone beyond the reality level of 1850 in painting and sculpture. I must emphasize that I am not referring here to

matters of taste, but to the much more elementary experience of perception. When confronted with a still life by Van Gogh, a modern critic actually sees a different object than his colleague saw in 1890."[99]

As these real-life examples suggest, today's meaningful symbols are likely to become tomorrow's shallow stimuli, just as what is "too" overpowering today is likely to become the preferred medium of tomorrow. Naturally, this happens more intensely with those belonging to the younger generation, since they are the ones who grow up in sync with the latest culture of speed. As for the infant, we can be assured that she is already losing interest in her close quarters and will soon be off crawling, walking, running, and then riding and driving in search of new and more intense sensory pleasures. Furthermore, because she is no longer constrained by the natural limits on how intense her stimulus worlds can become, she and her parents are faced with the problem of imposing the constraints themselves. However, because we have failed to do this historically, we now find ourselves living under conditions of extreme sensory inflation, conditions that are designed to satisfy our heightened sensory expectations, but don't. They don't because they simply cannot, at least not in the long run.

THE ANATOMY AND PHYSIOLOGY OF SENSORY ADDICTIONS

HAVING connected sensory adaptation to both rapid-fire culture and the development of hyperactivity and inattention, we can now conclude by drawing a final connection between sensory adaptation and our knowledge of children's developing minds. Further research exploring how the mammalian brain works through adaptation to filter out unimportant stimuli, so that we can attend to important ones, gives us a firsthand view of how sensory experiences may change the physical workings of the brain so that the brain becomes less and less attentive to familiar stimuli. If we return to our basic model of adaptation, we know already that both novel and important stimuli trigger the mind to notice them, whereas familiar and uninteresting stimuli go ignored. But how exactly does experience change the brain so that it reflects this learning? What research on visual attention in monkeys now tells us is that the nerve cells of the brain work in relation to one another in a kind of Darwinian competition.[100] As in real life, there are three basic kinds of stimuli used in this research. Depending on the current situation and past learning experience, stimuli function as either familiar and unimportant, familiar and important, or novel. Competition works by making sure that when there are several of these stimuli in the visual field, as is typical, only the novel and important ones will succeed in having a physiological effect at the higher levels of the brain, thus taking the stimulus from mere sensation into the realm of conscious perception.

To clarify this, start with the basic fact that if a stimulus falls on our retina, it is going to cause some initial neural response in the visual pathways of the nervous system. But since all stimuli cannot attract our attention, somewhere and somehow the nervous system must decide whether to encourage this neural response or to snuff it out. This has to be an unconscious process, by definition, because we cannot experience stimuli to determine which to experience. What happens works very much along these lines: All visual stimuli that fall on the retina do in fact have their day in court, but the jury tends to be very biased by past experience. If that stimulus has shown up before but has not made much of a case for its importance, other nerve cells in the visual cortex will vote it down by suppressing its activity. If, on the other hand, a new or important stimulus shows up, not only will the stimulated nerve cells remain active, but they will also activate additional neurons, thereby energizing the neural impact of the stimulus.[101] When the neural impact is enhanced in this way, the stimulus will be attended to and perceived.

In one study of this process, researchers at the National Institute of Mental Health monitored the activity of specific neurons in the brains of monkeys learning a visually based task. When the monkeys were presented with multiple stimuli, only one of which was significant for responding appropriately, researchers found that all the stimuli gained an equal amount of neural attention, thus leading to

Psychology's Theory of Relativity

Over the past several decades psychologists have fashioned their own theory of relativity, called adaptation-level theory. According to this school of thought, not only do we become adapted to the levels of sensory stimulation that surround us, such as the faster and more complex stimuli that come from our televisions, but we also become adapted to our conditions of living, to our lifestyles. As strange as it may seem, the satisfaction and dissatisfaction we find in our own lives turn out to be a relative rather than an absolute matter. The expectations we grow up with, the expectations provided to us by advertisers, and our own expectations set a standard that we must meet if we are to feel successful and content. As psychologist David Myers has written, adaptation means that "what formerly felt good registers as neutral, and what formerly felt neutral now feels like deprivation. This helps explain why, despite the rapid increase in real income during the past several decades, the average American is not happier."[102] As mothers sometimes say, "Don't get your hopes up; you'll just be disappointed." For this reason, a fashion model is not likely to be any happier than a heavy set women, since the model will have very high and probably unsustainable expectations about what her "attractiveness" will bring. This holds true for the victim of an auto accident who loses the use of her legs; fortunately, after some period of loss, she will adapt to new expectations and form a new kind of happiness. Adaptation-level theory warns us, however, that once we achieve our expectations, we are apt to raise them, creating what can become a winless pursuit of happiness. Consider studies of people who have won lotteries, which have consistently demonstrated that winning huge sums of money creates such high expectations that the small pleasures of life are quickly lost (not to mention friends and relatives). Consequently, these studies show no net improvement in people's levels of life satisfaction. One such study was aptly titled "Lottery Winners and Accidental Victims: Is Happiness Relative?"[103] Taken as a whole, psychology's theory of relativity goes a long way toward explaining the hurried society: Constantly rising lifestyle expectations motivate us to cram more "living" into our lives. This then produces rising sensory adaptations and expectations, not to mention an accelerated and compressed experience of time. Hence the problem with searching for absolute bliss in a relative and rapidly changing sensory world.

behavior that was inappropriate for the task. However, after the animals began to experience the consequences for inappropriate behavioral responses, researchers found that the neurons responding to the irrelevant stimuli were quickly suppressed by neighboring neurons. Thus, on the basis of experience, the brain began to filter out what stimuli would surface at the level of consciousness.[104]

As this research suggests, whether stimulus events in the environment do or do not sustain our attention appears to be the net result of a competition taking place across the billions of neural connections in the learning centers of the brain. This competition is a powerful built-in mechanism for promoting adaptation, a mechanism that ensures that one's personal experiences in the world help decide what will be consciously experienced. These adaptive changes are not just fleeting ones that occur only on the brain's periphery; ultimately they affect the core workings of the brain. As one report concluded, "Recent studies show that neuronal mechanisms for learning and memory both dynamically modulate and permanently alter the representations of visual stimuli in the adult monkey cortex."[105]

This research on neural adaptation thus provides initial physiological evidence that experience changes the brain so that it will be more responsive to some stimuli and less responsive to others. It is only a small step from here to the conclusion that chronic exposure to rapid-fire culture during development can produce a chronic state of human consciousness that is highly adapted to the rapid-fire sensory world, thus creating a protracted sense of time and a restless pursuit of constant stimulation. We already know the mind quickly adapts to the intensity of incoming stimuli, and we have now seen that there is a specific process that keeps stimuli from reaching the conscious realm of attention. Taken together, these findings suggest that growing up in the throes of rapid-fire culture will inevitably lead to sensory addictions, where the intensity and complexity of stimuli from an earlier generation will no longer satisfy the sensory needs of those of us growing up in late-twentieth-century America.[106]

Generation Rx

Was I bored? No I wasn't . . . bored. I'm never bored. That's
the trouble with everybody, you're all so bored. You've had
nature explained to you and you're bored with it; you've had
the living body explained to you and you're bored with it;
you've had the universe explained to you and you're bored
with it. So now you just want cheap thrills and like plenty of
them. And it don't matter how tawdry or vacuous as long as it's
new, as long as it's new, as long as it flashes and . . . bleeps in
forty . . . colors. Whatever else you can say about me, I'm not
. . . bored.

MIKE LEIGH
Naked

ALMOST everyone agrees that modern technology and American
individualism have opened up new freedoms for both past and present generations. What is less recognized, however, is that these two
developments have also unleashed a cascade of self-destructive
forces, forces that, through a circuitous route all their own, have
come to undermine many of these same hard-won freedoms. Borrowing from the coffers of popular culture, we might liken today's
hurried self to Dorothy of Kansas, a girl whose innocent desires tore
her from the slow and secure surroundings of home, dropping her
into a world full of dangerous illusions, with no road map of how to
get back home. So goes our present story, in which our wish for a
better, more prosperous life has led us to seize upon technology and

progress as the great agents of happiness, abandoning the social for the material, the secure for the sensational.

What has followed from these impulses has been very mixed indeed. We have greater wealth and more abundant resources than at any time before, and more of these than any other nation, yet we continue to pursue the same elusive dream that inspired us a century ago. We feel restless rather than relaxed. We feel anxious rather than secure. We feel distressed rather than contented. We feel psychologically empty rather than full. Out of this context of technological and economic progress, both the ADD syndrome and the Ritalin solution appeared suddenly on the American landscape, looking like derivatives of the same urges that drive the hurried society's overall race against time. Quick fixes, like soothing drugs and security systems, show our determination to master technology rather than ourselves. Endless bureaucratic "solutions," like suburbia, superhighways, and cellular phones, show our tendency to complicate matters rather than simplify them. In fact, all these offerings reveal an impressively stubborn attempt on our part to cope with our failed individualistic solutions with still more individualistic ones.

Meanwhile, using drugs and other technological "solutions" to deal with the unsettledness we feel from being stuck in time has resulted only in more virulent strains of psychological dysfunction, including *adult* ADD. By mastering technology rather than ourselves, and by reducing social phenomena to biological ones, our understanding of developmental problems—of how we become who we are and why we feel as we do—has been all but forgotten. To put it in the terms of the French sociologist Émile Durkheim, we've lost our sense of the priority of community, of how community, as the place where meaning and value rise out of durable social practices and traditions, shapes who we become as individuals.

Ironically and sadly, the portrayer of Dorothy of Kansas, Judy Garland, died of a drug overdose in 1969 after years of being addicted to the sedative Seconal and the stimulant Benzedrine, the latter of which was the first drug used to "calm" hyperactive children, in 1937.[1] As was fictionalized in Jacqueline Susann's best-seller *Valley of the Dolls*, Garland escaped the drudgery of homemaking only to become trapped in an empty shell of glitter and glamour. In Garland's life, her use and abuse of various psychostimulants were a futile attempt to counteract the hangover effects of the tranquilizers she took to put herself to sleep. It seems she was ahead of her time in real life as well as in her role as Dorothy, foreshadowing the dramatic rise of psychotropic drugs to "treat" the existential woes of the American self. Now, some three decades later, we Americans consume nearly as many psychotropic drugs as does the rest of the world combined, including about 80 percent of all the Ritalin in the world (five times more than any other nation) and a majority of all the Prozac.

With Ritalin as the exclusive treatment in about 90 percent of all cases of "ADD," the principal function of the ADD diagnosis now seems to be as gatekeeper to Ritalin. Indeed, when we consider the several hundred percent increase in Ritalin consumption in the United States since 1990, combined with the continued absence of evidence for any real medical disorder called ADD, we have to wonder whether the treatment was prompted by the disorder or the disorder prompted by the treatment.[2] Certainly the historical record will not rescue ADD since the use of stimulants to treat diagnosed children has been more stable than the diagnosis itself, which has changed repeatedly over the past few decades—and for no obvious reasons. As Peter Conrad argues in the journal *Social Problems*, because stimulant medication was available two decades prior to the labeling of hyperactive children, it appears likely that "ADD" and earlier categories of behavioral deviance were built around the discovery of behavior-controlling drugs.[3] One thing is surely true: Whether or not "ADD" is a real thing, the drug used on its behalf certainly is. Ritalin is a powerful psychostimulant drug that has biochemical effects very similar to those of amphetamines and even to cocaine.[4]

ON THE ROAD TO RITALIN

THE drug methylphenidate hydrochloride was brought to market under the trade name Ritalin in the early 1960s, replacing other psychostimulants like Benzedrine as the drug of choice for calming hyperactivity. Its approval for use in children notwithstanding, Ritalin remains a Schedule II drug, classified by the Drug Enforcement Administration (DEA) as a potent and potentially addictive substance, along with other abused drugs like morphine and cocaine. Despite the prevalence of its use and all the media gossip about its popularity, much of the public still has no understanding of Ritalin. Some believe it is some kind of tranquilizer used to calm children, whereas others think it is nothing more than a mild stimulant. This latter view is perpetuated by misinformation at the highest levels. For example, the maker of Ritalin, Novartis (formerly Ciba pharmaceuticals), describes it as "a mild central nervous system stimulant,"[5] as has the *New York Times*, which called it a "mild stimulant" that is "roughly [equivalent to] a jolt of strong coffee."[6]

Two historical events, well within living memory, led Ritalin to be classified as a drug with a high potential for abuse. In the late 1960s Sweden experienced an epidemic of street abuse of Ritalin, which led to its being banned there. Shortly thereafter the United States began experiencing its own rise in the popularity of stimulants, including amphetamines and cocaine.[7] Although this is rarely mentioned today, the Food and Drug Administration and the National Academy of Sciences both warned in the 1970s that Ritalin was developing a black-market value as a recreational stimulant. Since then the popularity of stimulants as recreational drugs has grown considerably. The cocaine and crack boom in the 1980s and 1990s; the emergence of popular hallucinogens with stimulant properties, like ecstasy; the apparent epidemic of methamphetamine ("meth") abuse in the southwestern United States; the spread of coffee bars in the 1990s; and the rise of the Ritalin solution—all these trends speak to the use of stimulants for faster living, their enduring popularity encouraged by the hurried society's rapid pace of life. Just consider this description of a methamphetamine craze that took place in 1996 in the small town of Newton, Iowa, reported on the front page of the *New York Times*: "'This is the most malignant addictive drug known to mankind,' said Dr. Michael Abrams of Broadlawn Medical Center in Des Moines, where more patients were admitted during the past year for abuse of methamphetamine than for alcoholism. 'It is often used by blue-collar workers, who feel under pressure to perform at a fast pace for long periods. And at first it works. It turns you into wonder person. You can do everything—for a while.' "[8]

Despite persistent efforts to play up ADD as a biological disorder while downplaying Ritalin as a powerful, mind-altering drug, we know that Ritalin is as powerful as any other stimulant, especially when crushed and snorted (or injected). As one journalist puts it, referring to the similarities between Ritalin and cocaine, "Americans would be horrified to learn that 2 million children across the nation are being given cocaine by their parents and doctors to make them behave better in school. It's also close to the truth that it takes a chemist to tell the difference."[9] We know of this similarity between these two drugs from both basic scientific studies and epidemiological reports. In the 1970s a reliable measure of a drug's potential for abuse indicated that Ritalin, when taken through the same route of administration as cocaine, has comparable reinforcing effects. This test, which consists of an animal model of drug taking, is used by scientists (and the FDA and the World Health Organization) as an assay for predicting a new compound's abuse liability. As a laboratory analogue of human drug taking, this procedure gained public attention in the 1970s and 1980s, when researchers reported that animals will work to self-administer the very same drugs that humans use and abuse recreationally, from prescription tranquilizers like Seconal and Valium to street drugs like PCP, cocaine, and THC (the pharmacological ingredient in marijuana).

Unfortunately, when cocaine use began capturing front-page headlines, some of these reports were used to exaggerate its dangers. For example, in 1989 in the journal *Science* we read, "Cocaine is the most powerful reinforcer known. . . . A variety of species from mice to monkeys will learn to self-administer cocaine faster than any other drug and will do it until they die"[10]; in 1992, in the *New York Times*, we read, "Cocaine addicts tend to go on binges, and monkeys hooked up intravenously will inject themselves repeatedly, rejecting food, sex and sleep until they die."[11]

The problem with these media claims is that they omit a number of crucial facts. For example, researchers who conducted these studies included in them other psychostimulants, which, under the same conditions, produced the very same toxic effects. In other words, despite what the media have encouraged us to believe, these studies did not show cocaine to be more dangerous than other stimulants, including Ritalin. Actually they showed just the opposite: The laboratory procedures that led to the *New York Times'* reporting that "monkeys hooked up intravenously will inject themselves [with cocaine] repeatedly, rejecting food, sex and sleep," also led to the finding, not reported in the *Times*, that lab animals given the choice to self-administer comparable doses of cocaine and Ritalin do not favor one over the other.[12] According to Charles R. Schuster, a former head of the National Institute on Drug Abuse, and his colleague, Chris E. Johanson, "when equal doses of cocaine and methylphenidate [Ritalin] were compared, no preference was shown."[13] A similar study showed monkeys would work in the same fashion for Ritalin as they would for cocaine.[14] These facts are not a deep dark secret of researchers buried away in some hideaway laboratory. In fact, Gene Haislip, a retired deputy assistant administrator of the DEA, has noted publicly: "We have become the only country in the world where children are prescribed such a vast quantity of stimulants that share virtually the same properties as cocaine."[15] With conclusions like this, the paradox of Ritalin seems not to be that stimulants "calm" hyperactive kids—which we know to be a false paradox—but rather that the children who take Ritalin do not actually become addicted to it.

How can we make sense of these findings? How can millions of children be taking a drug that is pharmacologically very similar to another drug, cocaine, that is not only considered dangerous and addictive, but whose buying, selling, and using are also considered criminal acts? If you are confused by this mix of findings, you are not alone. This confusion is widespread in both scientific and medical communities as well, as is summarized in the conclusions of a 1995 study comparing the neuropharmacology of cocaine and Ritalin, reported in the *Archives of General Psychiatry*: "Cocaine, which is one of the most reinforcing and addictive of the abused drugs, has pharmacological actions that are very similar to those of methylphenidate [Ritalin], which is the most commonly *prescribed* psychotropic medication for children in the United States."[16] By "pharmacological action," these authors mean that while the drug is not similar to cocaine in terms of its molecular structure, it has similar biochemical effects in the brain.

To make sense of these seemingly contradictory findings, the first thing to realize is that those who are *prescribed* Ritalin consume it orally. Oral consumption is not typically considered ideal for addiction since it weakens the acute experience of the drug by lengthening its duration of onset; it comes on more slowly and lasts longer. Indeed, those who use the drug recreationally get around this limitation by crushing up and snorting the drug (or injecting it in solution). Still, even oral use of a stimulant like Ritalin stands in contrast with psychiatric drugs that are not used recreationally, such as Prozac, which have psychological effects that begin only after several days or weeks.

Part of the confusion here stems from the fact that there is a tendency in our culture to view a psychoactive drug categorically, as either an angel (for example, Prozac) or a demon (for example, crack). The notable exception here is alcohol, which we deny altogether by trying to convince ourselves that it is not even a drug (as when we say "drugs and alcohol"). Because of this cultural prejudice of treating drugs as inherently good or bad, we do not realize that the nature of a drug can be greatly altered simply by changing the manner in which it is used. As we should know from the narcotics used to kill our pain in the hospital, whether a drug is an angel or demon is really more a question of context and personal perspective than one of pharmacological destiny. The route of administration is one example: Taking Ritalin orally blunts the nature of the psychological effect, eliminating the drug "high" and thus the way in which children perceive their use of the drug. A second example concerns the overall context of Ritalin's use: Children do not experience the same psychological effects from Ritalin as does a recreational user because the drug expectations and reasons for use are so divergent. We know this from various sources, including experimental and naturalistic studies showing that there are powerful psychological and social factors that determine drug experiences. We also know this from the regular users of powerful analgesics, like morphine, who take the drug because they are suffering from chronic pain. As was reported in a 1997 article in *Reason* magazine and on the TV newsmagazine *20/20*, there are hundreds of cases in which individuals regularly use what we often think of as inherently addictive narcotics yet never become addicted.

Regardless of how powerful the drug, its "mind-altering" effects depend as much on the person who uses it and the context of use as it does on the chemistry of the drug. This has been described in detail by psychologist Stanton Peele. In his book *The Meaning of Addiction*, Peele carefully documents how a variety of cultural, social, and psychological factors comes together to create the overall drug experience, thus determining whether or not an activity will come to dominate a person's life.[17] In the case of children taking Ritalin, the substance is not likely to be anything more than a "medication," since it is taken in a medical context for what has been defined as a medical problem. This does not change the fact that such children are ingesting a powerful, fast-acting drug that is commonly abused, but it does tell us why Ritalin can be very similar, pharmacologically, to the amphetamines and cocaine without appearing as such.

Meanwhile, the widespread availability of Ritalin encourages adolescent drug abuse, as when kids give their Ritalin away, have it stolen, or sell it. The article mentioned above from the *Archives of General Psychiatry*, which compared the pharmacology of cocaine and Ritalin, was part of a special issue focusing on ADD. The editors of this issue, psychiatrists Rachel Klein and Paul Wender, rebutted the reported similarities between cocaine and Ritalin, complaining that "Volkow et al. aver that the rationale for their study stems partly from concerns about methylphenidate [Ritalin] abuse based on widespread use in children with [ADD]. There is no basis for such concerns. There is a nearly total absence of methylphenidate abuse reported in methylphenidate-treated children and adolescents in spite of its very widespread application." These remarks are noteworthy in two respects. On the one hand, they express the accurate view that kids on Ritalin do not generally become "prototypical" drug addicts. They may have a psychological need for the drug, but they do not crave it in the manner that a recreational user might. On the other hand, these remarks are very misleading because the concern people have with Ritalin abuse is not so much that children taking it will become drug addicts as that some of the massive amount of Ritalin being infused into school systems around the country, including colleges, is clearly being diverted to recreational use.[18] In a recent survey at my college, for example, Ritalin was the number three drug of abuse, after marijuana and hallucinogens. Ritalin is also used recreationally during students' long hours of studying. A Harvard student confesses, "In all honesty, I haven't written a paper without Ritalin since my junior year in high school. I even wrote my Harvard essay on it. It keeps you up when you're tired, and makes you much more aware of what you're doing. Although there are certain risks involved, I think it's worth it."[19]

Ritalin's popularity as a "medication" increases the likelihood of its abuse in two ways. The more obvious way concerns its simple availability. Because Ritalin is a recreational stimulant that can be obtained with relative ease and with less risk of criminal charges, it stands out as a real option for many who are interested in having "a good time" with drugs. And, as greater numbers of children continue to take the drug in high school, greater quantities get into circulation.

What is equally serious but more subtle is the fact that the widespread use of Ritalin has a normalizing effect on kids' overall views of drugs and drug taking. Despite all the "just say no" slogans, the "just do it" manner in which children are now prescribed psychotropic drugs, from Prozac to Ritalin, greatly undermines the antidrug rhetoric of saying no. As a psychologist writing in the *Public Interest* observes, "There is something odd, if not downright ironic, about the picture of millions of American school children filing out of 'drug awareness' classes to line up in the school nurse's office for their midday dose of amphetamine."[20] Suggestive of this contradiction are the reports that have been surfacing saying that antidrug programs like D.A.R.E. are not curbing kids' drug use.[21] Antidrug rhetoric might be effective by itself, but it does little when it is overshadowed by what kids see and hear with regard to other drugs, including Ritalin. After all, do we really believe that the ADD child is convinced by our adult categories of "medication" and "drugs" once we tell him not to give his pills to other children who might want to use or sell them? When I was a kid, there were no "medicines" that other children wanted to sell, buy, and take just for the fun of it.

Everyone knows that what we do as adults is a more powerful source of education for children than what we say. This idea of setting a good example has even been extended to the drug-taking of parents, from drinking alcohol to smoking marijuana. What has not been realized, however, is the fact that once powerful psychoactive drugs come to be seen to be as harmless as vitamins, children lose the capacity to see a clear difference between appropriate and inappropriate use. A tragic example of this occurred on March 1, 1997, when fourteen Boston-area teenagers were hospitalized for overdosing on "handfuls" of the prescription muscle relaxant Baclofen.[22] Although none of the kids died from their overdose, their attitude toward prescription drugs — "just looking for an easy high" — is indicative of a larger problem in which drugs are being used, both medically and recreationally, in a very casual and reckless manner. With regard to Ritalin, if we as a society are having difficulty determining its appropriate use, we can hardly be surprised when children begin making poor drug-taking decisions themselves.

Meanwhile, although epidemiological studies on the abuse of Ritalin are sorely lacking, one need only search newspaper reports across the country to see that concerns of possible Ritalin abuse twenty years ago have become a reality (see the box "On the Ritalin Highway, from Coast to Coast"). Large numbers of children, adolescents, and adults, even teachers and school nurses have been linked to illicit use of Ritalin, with the drug being swallowed, snorted, and injected. (The DEA reported that Ritalin abuse in high school seniors increased from 3 to 16 percent from 1992 to 1995.)[23] To give an example of what can happen, one college student reports: "I know a girl in the freshman class who actually stole a script pad from the health center and faked her own prescription. She's an unbelievably smart girl, got a 1600 on her SAT, but is convinced she needs to snort Ritalin in order to do all her work. She's become an absolute speed freak — up all night and strung out all day. Ironically, she's failing two of her classes."[24]

In 1991 children between the ages of ten and fourteen were involved in only about twenty-five emergency room visits connected with Ritalin abuse. By 1995, just four years later, this number had climbed to more than four hundred visits, which, for this age-group, was about the same number of visits as for cocaine.[25] Summarizing the rising abuses of Ritalin, a 1995 *Newsweek* article, "A Risky Rx for Fun," notes that "the prescription drug Ritalin is now a popular high on campus—with some serious side effects."[26] Perhaps most distressing in this article was the acknowledgment that Ritalin abuse is a "white, upper-middle class phenomenon," since this uncovers a rather cruel double standard in our current drug policies: Although the majority of the illicit users of Ritalin are middle- and upper-class and white, the majority of the federal cocaine defendants are lower-class and black.

COSMETIC AND PROSTHETIC PHARMACOLOGY

JUST as the American outbreak of hyperactivity and attention deficits can be linked to the direct and indirect effects of life in the hurried society, so can the popularity of stimulant drugs. As we have seen, these two trends are pieces of the same puzzle: The sensory-addicted mind that produces impulsivity and short attention spans has a great appetite for stimulation, for which "stimulants" are of course perfectly suited. Paralleling these large cultural themes is a related trend to which the Ritalin solution also belongs. During this half century there has been a dramatic shift in the uses to which we are willing to put psychoactive drugs. Certainly the search for the magic bullet is nothing new. For example, even the pharmaceutical company Parke-Davis believed in the late nineteenth century that cocaine had the makings of a wonder drug that could cure all kinds of ailments, from fatigue to narcotic addiction.[27] What is new, however, is the vigor with which we now apply and embrace the spirit of "Better living through chemistry." This was reflected in a *Newsweek* cover story in 1994 entitled "Beyond Prozac," which declared that "Prozac to cheer you up and Ritalin to focus are merely the most prominent new mind drugs."[28] Nowhere has this mood been expressed more clearly, though, than in psychiatrist Peter

On the Ritalin Highway, from Coast to Coast

The following excerpts come from newspapers
throughout the United States

Rockville, DC: Joe, a student at Thomas S. Wootton High School in Rockville, usually waited until lunch before approaching a couple of buddies at school. When the time came he said, "Let's go to my office," and they'd steal away to a concrete stoop outside that Joe claimed as his own. He reached into his pocket for several tiny pills. The cigarette lighter came next, or his newly acquired driver's license, or anything else he could find to crush the pills into powder. Sometimes he used the heel of his shoe, grinding the tablets on the pavement before scooping up the powder with a rolled-up dollar bill. One snort gave Joe a jolt akin to drinking a quick cup of strong coffee. Two snorts, and "I thought I could do more work. I felt like going to class." From last April until late summer, Joe snorted his way to high several times daily. His drug of choice: **RITALIN**.[29]

New Orleans, LA: One death attributed to **RITALIN** abuse occurred in 1995 to a 19-year-old high school senior. The victim was not believed to be a chronic user, and was not prescribed the drug. He died 17 hours after being admitted to a hospital in Roanoke with adrenergic activity (adrenaline rush), heart arrhythmia (racing heart), fever and a racing pulse.[30]

Garden Grove, CA: Four suspects arrested in the breakup of an illicit drug lab Wednesday probably were going to package the powdered substance and sell it on the streets as "speed," officials alleged Thursday. Police said the drug—marketed by prescription under the brand name **RITALIN**—could have netted more than $1 million.[31]

Nashville, TN: A drug-addicted teacher who stole children's **RITALIN** from a middle school vault was fined $1,000 and ordered to spend 37 days in jail yesterday. James Smith, 35, is the second Grassland Middle School teacher convicted of stealing **RITALIN** from the vault.[32]

Grand Rapids, MI: Some youths are buying or stealing **RITALIN** from classmates prescribed the drug. They then crush the tablets and snort the powder like cocaine, said Muskego Detective Joe Tompson, who arrested a high school student last week on charges of selling the medication. Others cook the stimulant and inject it like heroin, he said.[33]

Los Angeles, CA: It began with pills, "reds" and "whites," when Ben Lawson was a sixth-grader in East Los Angeles. Marijuana, LSD, **RITALIN**, cocaine and heroin followed. Smith used virtually every drug for sale on city streets during a 22-year stint in the seamy subculture of chemical abuse and dependency.[34]

Washington, DC: One student at T. C. Williams High School in Alexandria remembers swallowing several times the normal amount of **RITALIN**, in a school bathroom last winter. "I was happy all weekend long," she recalls. The following Friday she took even more and regretted it by the time she arrived home. "I felt like I was going to die," she says. "I was shivering, my toes were tingling. I said, 'God, this sucks.'"[35]

North Charleston, SC: As a school bus sped toward Wando High School last October, a 14-year-old girl pulled out a bottle and passed around some pills. The girl who distributed the medicine on the bus was supposed to bring a bottle of pills every week to the school nurse, the girl's father said. The nurse was then supposed to dispense the pills on a daily basis. Instead, the girl kept the medicine. "But did the school ever call me and say 'we're not getting the drugs'? No, they didn't." In fact, even though the girl wasn't taking her medication, a teacher unwittingly told her parents that the child's attitude had improved since she had been on the **RITALIN**.[36]

Orange County, CA: State medical authorities are seeking to revoke the license of a former Fullerton doctor who has practiced for more than 30 years in Orange County and who, by his own admission, has been a drug addict for more than half that time. Joe Smith, 62, described as a respected, popular and kindly physician in court affidavits and interviews, is also facing

22 criminal counts of writing fraudulent or improper prescriptions to obtain the stimulant, RITALIN, for his own use.[37]

Allentown, NY: In October, a 13-year-old student at Eyer Junior High School was taking RITALIN only two days before school officials suspended him for distributing the medicine to another student. The boy said he started to doubt whether he really needed the medicine, so he decided not to take it. When the school nurse gave him the RITALIN pill, he drank the water, hid the pill, and then carried it out of the nurses' office. During class, he said, another student asked him for the drug so he handed it over.[38]

Jackson, MS: Traces of RITALIN have been found in the body of a former John Curtis Christian School model student who died in police custody last week after running nude into a Jackson, Miss., railroad yard. The dead youth, Joseph Fay, a former star athlete and top-notch student at Curtis, died early Saturday of a fractured skull. Police say he left his dorm room, disrobed, then wandered nude for 30 minutes through downtown Jackson before police arrived to arrest him in a rail yard. When RITALIN is snorted, people using it may exhibit superhuman strength and psychotic behavior, the Mississippi Medical Examiner stated.[39]

Washington, DC: At Episcopal High School, a boarding school in Alexandria, three students were expelled last spring after 25 students were discovered misusing the drug, according to school officials. The headmaster said four boys for whom RITALIN was prescribed shared the drug with other students who were hoping it would improve their concentration and help them make better grades on exams and papers.[40]

West Palm Beach, FL: Instead of swapping sandwiches and desserts at their lunchroom table, seventh-graders at the county's oldest Catholic school were dabbling in drugs, police said on Friday. Police said about a quarter of the 26 seventh-grade students at St. Ann's Catholic School were giving out or taking RITALIN.[41]

Raleigh, NC: A 15-year-old male was sentenced to a year's supervised probation Tuesday for distributing his prescription of the drug **RITALIN** to friends at Githens Middle School earlier this year. The teenager, whose name was not released because he is a juvenile, was convicted of a felony in February in connection with the incident. The drug was passed around to about a dozen students, who crushed it and sniffed it to get high.[42]

St. Louis, MO: Five students were suspended Tuesday from Parkway Northeast Middle School for possession and distribution of the prescription drug **RITALIN**. Two of the seventh- and eighth-graders gave five tablets to three other students. The students involved—two boys and three girls—were suspended for 10 days. After a district-level hearing, they may be suspended for up to 180 days or expelled.[43]

North Charleston, SC: It was way past midnight when the four Citadel cadets broke out the pills. They were in Joe Thomas' room on campus. A Citadel blanket covered the back window, and a black light glowed overhead. They were studying and sometimes playing dice, writing their scores in a spiral notebook. And they were grinding up the little white **RITALIN** pills, snorting the powder through the casing of a ball-point pen. It wasn't the first time they had used **RITALIN** to study or stay awake. Tom Clay had a current prescription, and Fred Kendrick had let his prescription expire a few weeks before. "It helps me focus," Kendrick explained. "I wasn't using an illegal drug." But the four cadets—Clay, Thomas, Kendrick, and John Brown—eventually were caught, and after a hearing last December, three were booted out of the Citadel for "using illegal drugs."[44]

North Charleston, SC: "There's a bunch of kids there who have prescriptions who don't even take it. They sell it," Brown said. "Firsthand, I've seen rank-holders go into somebody's room and say, 'Look I saw you doing this and this, and I'm going to pull (punish) you unless you give me some **RITALIN**.' I've seen people buy it."[45]

Salem, OR: Twenty-seven years ago, a military brat named Sam Conner was involuntarily drafted into America's first generation of **RITALIN** kids. Growing up in California in the late 1960's, Conner was given **RITALIN** at school to counter his unruly, hyperkinetic behavior. One drug led to another for Conner. He relentlessly medicated himself during a 17-year period by abusing prescription pills, marijuana, and other drugs.[46]

Dallas, TX: Last week, a dozen Barnett Junior High students admitted to using, selling or distributing the prescription drug **RITALIN**. The students were given three-day suspensions and placed in isolated classrooms to complete summer school. It marked the second incident this year in which Barnett students were involved in illegal distribution of **RITALIN**.[47]

Milwaukee, WI: A former Muskego elementary school teacher was charged Thursday with three counts of illegally possessing a prescription drug that authorities say he took from pupils. Douglas Smith, 44, stole **RITALIN** pills from pupils' prescription bottles stored in an office at Country Meadows Elementary School, early last year, according to the criminal complaint filed in Waukesha County Circuit Court.[48]

Washington, DC: Joanne, a junior last year at Seneca Valley High School in Germantown, said, "I could get **RITALIN** all the time. My mom was prescribed for it. She stopped taking it, and I'd take hers. My best friend's little brother had some, and I had two friends who had it prescribed." Joanne, now attending a county alternative school, says she used to snort **RITALIN** every day, usually at home or at her friend's house. "We were little perfectionists," she says of herself and her friend. "We'd use a mortar and pestle and grind it up real fine."[49]

Fulton County, GA: Ridgeview Middle School student Julia Solomon found that 10 percent of the more than 300 junior and senior high students she queried in an unscientific survey abused the drug **RITALIN**. And more than a quarter of the teens said they knew someone who abused the drug. Students who responded to the survey at Ridgeview Middle School and Riverwood High School indicated they think **RITALIN** is safe because it's prescribed to about 2 million American children, as well as adults to treat ADHD. "**RITALIN** is legal, so it is better than taking speed," one eighth-grader wrote.[50]

Fort Pierce, Fl: The Fort Pierce Central High School nurse who was at lunch last week when a student slipped into the infirmary and stole six bottles of **RITALIN** has been reassigned, officials said Friday. Another employee normally watches the clinic from her station while nurse Joanne Frank is at lunch. But that employee did not see the student enter or leave the infirmary. The 15-year-old student who took the medication last Wednesday tried to sell the drug, but when no one was interested, he took a handful of pills himself and started giving it away, sheriff's officials said last Friday. The boy was charged with sale and delivery of a controlled drug and petty theft. He has been suspended for 10 days and recommended for expulsion, in accord with the district's zero-tolerance policy for drugs and weapons on campus.[51]

New Orleans, LA: Tom, a 19-year-old student at a Virginia school, began behaving strangely a few months after he enrolled in college. At times he seemed overly anxious; at other times, the smallest thing set him off. Sometimes he was withdrawn and slept for hours on end. As the year wore on, Tom's symptoms worsened, and his parents' concern deepened. By spring of his freshman year, they hardly knew their son, and his parents insisted he withdraw from school so the family could help him get to the bottom of his bizarre personality problems. Tom, it turned out, was abusing the drug **RITALIN**. Like many of his college friends, he was using the drug recreationally, grinding the small tablets into a fine powder, then snorting it into his nasal passages.[52]

Garden Grove, CA: Roger Guevara, of the federal Drug Enforcement Administration, said that besides being abused, the drug, **RITALIN**, sometimes is purchased through illicit channels by people who qualify for prescriptions but are unable to obtain it because of shortages. "Due to the tendency of the drug being abused, there is a quota on its production imposed by the government," Guevara said. "As a result the supply, usually toward the end of the year, can be very limited. In fact, people with lawful prescriptions sometimes can't obtain it."[53]

Allentown, NY: Three students at Howard A. Eyer Junior High School pretended to be sick on a busy day in the nurse's office last spring. While the nurses were distracted, one of them stole a bottle of the prescription drug **RITALIN** from a cabinet. Four students were implicated in the case, including a teen-ager who had offered to buy some of the medicine from his classmates.[54]

Pittsburgh, PA: In America's hospitals, **RITALIN** is a medication that's kept under lock and key because the federal government fears its potential for abuse. Standard hospital policy dictates that at the beginning and end of every shift, two nurses check their unit's supply of **RITALIN** and other controlled drugs to make sure every dose in the narcotics cabinet is accounted for. Any shortage must be reported immediately to a supervisor. In contrast to that policy is how many schools handle **RITALIN**. One school nurse reported that her school used to keep **RITALIN** in a shoe box stored in an unlocked school office desk.[55]

Kramer's best-selling book *Listening to Prozac*.[56] Here Kramer coins the phrase "cosmetic pharmacology," which he uses in his inquiry into how we can now use psychotropic drugs to alter our psychological selves cosmetically. Cosmetic pharmacology is the notion of tinkering with our brain's biochemistry not because something's broken inside us but because if a drug can make us feel better, why not use it?

The idea of cosmetic pharmacology has clear relevance for Ritalin. Without considering the new laissez-faire attitudes we have developed toward prescription drugs, we are not going to understand how it has been possible that almost overnight millions of children could be put on a drug the government once considered a menace to society. American society has become so draconian about some kinds of drug use (for example, cocaine or marijuana) that it now imprisons more of its population per capita than any other nation in the world. What is so strange about our drug culture, though, is that we have simultaneously witnessed a great surge in the popularity of other kinds of psychoactive drug use (for example, with Ritalin and Prozac). Indeed, with plans to market a peppermint-flavored Prozac, its makers seem poised to capitalize on the growing "child" drug market created by the rush to Ritalin. Thus, one reason why stimulants are practically the lone treatment option for ADD is that any critique of this relaxed way of using powerful drugs would almost certainly shed a negative light on our overall appetite for psychiatric drugs.

Just how entrenched Ritalin is in the "treatment" of ADD was illustrated poignantly in the case of a 1996 government toxicology report showing that prolonged Ritalin use might cause cancer.[57] These studies, conducted by the U.S. Department of Health and Human Services, prompted the manufacturers of Ritalin to change the labeling of their product, warning users that animal studies have shown the drug to cause cancer when taken at doses beyond those recommended for therapeutic use (some problems occurred at doses that were only 2.5 times the recommended dose).[58] The authors of the study even went so far as to say that the drug should be avoided altogether. This finding is certainly not proof that Ritalin should be pulled off the market, at least not permanently, since the findings are only preliminary. Toxicologists note, for example, that although all carcinogens for humans are also carcinogens for rodents, the converse is not always true; Ritalin might cause cancer in rodents but not in humans.

This possibility notwithstanding, the immediacy with which advocates in the ADD industry dismissed these potentially serious findings, rather than suspend judgment (and use of Ritalin) until further studies were completed, is suggestive of why they cannot be trusted to make objective decisions on behalf of the current and potential consumers of this drug, most of them children. As the FDA stressed, these findings have significance partly because kids are now taking their use of Ritalin into adulthood. To use an all too real analogy, if all cigarette smokers quit in early adulthood, we know from epidemiological studies that cigarette smoking would no longer be a significant source of cancer; however, once people take up smoking as a lifetime activity, the risk of cancer balloons. The same could hold true for Ritalin. Thus, while further studies will most certainly clarify these findings, until they are completed, Ritalin should be kept under the light of scrutiny, not buried with fingers crossed under a blanket of fear and ignorance.

Another element of cosmetic pharmacology that illuminates our embrace of Ritalin has to do with its ability to "solve" everyday psychological problems parents and schools don't have time to deal with. Or worse, parents may see the ADD diagnosis as a positive advantage in a highly competitive world, feeding their children Ritalin, hoping it will give them an edge over other children. Both these scenarios fall in the category of cosmetic use, since Ritalin is functioning not as a treatment to resolve any real disorder but rather as a quick and easy pharmacological technique for managing (and masking) the child's behavior. One place where this debate is taking place is in academic and athletic competitions. Although the U.S. and International Olympic committees have banned Ritalin use in their competitions, there are many areas where Ritalin use is accepted as a "medication," despite its possible acute performance-enhancing effects.[59] These areas include academic settings, such as national entrance exams for graduate and law school, and athletic ones, including professional and collegiate organizations, such as the NBA and the NCAA. The problem of course is that while users of Ritalin (or their parents) want the drug to be considered a "medication," others see it first and foremost as a stimulant drug of abuse, with possible performance-enhancing effects.

Related to this is a kind of cosmetic drug use that is perhaps the most descriptive of Ritalin and might be called prosthetic pharmacology. This category covers most psychotropic drug use because it refers to all cases in which people incorporate drugs into their lives, not to solve their problems, but merely cope with stress, behavior problems, or negative psychological feelings. Given the known link between psychological problems and the desire to use and abuse drugs, prosthetic pharmacology also probably accounts for some of the use of street and store drugs (such as alcohol and cigarettes, or the "nicotine patch").[60] This possibility of self-medication was suggested by Ethan Nadelmann, a drug policy analyst, who wrote that "in many cases, the use of cocaine and heroin represents a form of self-medication against physical and emotional pain among people who do not have access to psychotherapy or Prozac."[61]

In the context of sensory addictions, prosthetic pharmacology means that the primary reason for Ritalin's use is as an artificial tool for soothing conscious minds in need of constant stimulation. It functions as a crutch that does not cure sensory-addicted persons but rather carries them over troubled waters. What are these troubled waters? They are the unavoidable slow spots in everyday life that would otherwise generate such behaviors as hyperactivity, impulsivity, forgetfulness, and withdrawal. For children, these slow spots include classroom situations (during classroom instruction), home situations (at the dinner table), or situations in public places (at the grocery store or church).

If someone loses a limb or an eye, a prosthetic device can protect him or her from potential discrimination and can even bring back partial function of the lost limb; in the case of something like a pair of crutches, the prosthetic has the function of ensuring a speedy recovery. In these cases, the prosthetic either fills in for something permanently lost or is used as an aid to full recovery. The trouble with prosthetic pharmacology, however, is that the use of drugs rarely has any of these positive consequences. Since many of the problems treated with psychotropic drugs will disappear during the course of one's life events, it would be a grave error to use these drugs as if something were permanently wrong with the person, as when physicians tell parents and children that the problem of ADD is biological and innate and will have to be treated as such. Moreover, although psychotropic drugs (including Ritalin and Prozac), are often said to serve as an aid in psychological recovery they also can stand in the way of it. Once parents (or teachers, or the children themselves) are led to believe that children's problems lie in their genes, the search for a permanent solution is abandoned. This then creates a self-fulfilling prophecy, since the failure to seek out a non-drug solution leaves these problems intact, making it appear that they are indeed unsolvable and constitutional.

Another problem with prosthetic pharmacology, one that operates at the societal level, is the way in which psychotropic drugs dull our experience of our increasingly impersonal and violent world. By making it easier to live under these unhealthy conditions, drugs reinforce the status quo, which allows a further deterioration in the psychological conditions that produced the urge for drugs in the first place. The fact that we Americans have the most psychological troubles and take most of the psychotropic medications is testimony to the fact that we are quickly becoming what author Robert Wright has described as a nation in despair.[62] The ADD diagnosis and the Ritalin solution are no exception. Opting for Ritalin, as if no other solution were possible, has only intensified the already fast, intense, and unstructured life experiences that saturate the child's formative years. This is partly why more use of Ritalin has not been correlated with an overall elimination, or concealment, of these problems at school and at home. To the contrary, we are finding that kids are staying on Ritalin longer and that more of them, both younger and older, are lining up for Ritalin.

A final reason why prosthetic pharmacology is problematic, and why most prescription drug use falls into this category, has to do with the simple fact that no drug in the psychiatrist's medicine cabinet is any kind of *cure* for psychological distress or illness. Prozac, Haldol, lithium, Xanax, Halcion, and Ritalin are not antibiotics of the mind, which rush in and wipe out some kind of brain bacteria. Nor do these drugs work simply by going in and returning the brain's biochemistry to balanced levels, as the public has been led to believe. For instance, Prozac elevates one's levels of the neurotransmitter serotonin after a single dosing, yet its therapeutic effects require several days or weeks of administration—and for reasons that are not at all understood. At best someone who is prescribed a psychiatric "medication" might recover from his or her psychological problem while taking one of these drugs, although sometimes this is either just a coincidence or an interaction of the drug with other ongoing cognitive and social factors. For instance, among the many contributing factors involved in the "successful" pharmacological treatment of psychological problems is the developmental process of natural remission, still the most common source of improved mental health in people's lives today.

It may well be the case, then, that the most beneficial way of using these drugs—that is, using them temporarily while changes are being made in the child's life circumstances—has been largely overlooked since our use of them tends to be in isolation. This possibility is consistent with the finding that nonpharmacological interventions (e.g., psychotherapy) can produce similar therapeutic outcomes as drugs and, at the biological level, the same biochemical or metabolic changes in the person's physiology. The difference of course is that the psychological manipulations actually affect and change the ecological context of the person's life and thus are more likely to persist over time after the removal of therapy. Related to this is the finding that since these drugs are typically used only in isolation, whatever effects they have may not be lasting; for example, even Prozac celebrity Peter Kramer has stated that Prozac's long-term utility seems overrated.[63]

Here again Ritalin is no exception. It is not a cure for problems of hyperactivity and inattention. To the contrary, the rise in its popularity has been correlated with a reduction in cases of natural remission, which have gone from being the rule to the exception. It seems that the more accepted Ritalin becomes, and the more it is used, the greater the likelihood that children will continue to have problems with impulsivity and inattention later in life. Without ever intending to, parents end up medicating the children's problems out of sight, thus leaving it to the children to address the deeper developmental roots of their problems once they become adults. Thus, rather than cure these problems, the Ritalin solution is, if anything, encouraging them. This, it turns out, is exactly what we would expect from the point of view of sensory addictions: *Adding more stimulation has robust behavioral effects, but by feeding the addiction rather than defusing it, Ritalin only worsens the problems in the long run.*

A CONSPIRACY OF IGNORANCE

IN the last chapter we saw that the ADD disorder is more the manufactured product of long-standing cultural biases than a discovery resulting from decades of painstaking medical research. We have seen in this chapter that Ritalin is more a generic psychostimulant drug that is often abused than it is a specialized medication. In light of these revelations, staunch advocates still in favor of the Ritalin solution are probably now standing at their last line of defense, declaring that whatever else is true, stimulant drugs are an effective treatment for the symptoms of hyperactivity and inattention, whereas nothing else is. As the cosmetic pharmacologist would say, Ritalin works, so why not use it? The problem of course is that it doesn't really work, at least not if what we mean by "work" is to improve the child's long-term prospects regarding academic achievement, psychological well-being, and prosocial behavior. In short, studies do not show the effects of Ritalin in ADD-diagnosed children to be paradoxical; we have long known that these "calming" effects occur in most children (and adults). Neither is Ritalin unique; other stimulants have these same effects. Finally, we know that Ritalin is in several important respects not an effective treatment; although it is true that it often makes the behavior of some children look more like the behavior of other children, studies have persistently failed to find evidence of any long-term benefits for academic performance. To the contrary, they suggest the Ritalin solution is undermining children's own psychological development, leaving them dependent on the daily administration of a powerful, mind-altering drug. Ritalin fails not only as a cure, but also as a reasonable interim solution.

Given these findings, how have advocates been able to maintain a hard-and-fast distinction between Ritalin as an effective "medication" and Ritalin as a dangerous "drug"? One explanation has to do with the fact that children's experiences on the drug seem to be unique since they do not fit the profile of an addictive drug. Advocates say, for example, that although Ritalin is like other psychostimulants, including cocaine, its effects on ADD-diagnosed children are uniquely therapeutic, with none of the side effects we might expect for what critics claim is a drug of abuse. The idea that Ritalin has these unique effects hinges on two understandable but nevertheless mistaken assumptions. The first is that because Ritalin is a powerful stimulant, it should have a stimulating effect on the behavior of "normal" kids, rather than the calming effects it has on children diagnosed with ADD; the second assumption we have already discussed: that because Ritalin is an addictive drug, it would produce withdrawal and dependence if these were "normal" kids.

Notice here that if these assumptions were in fact true, we would need only to give a child Ritalin and look at what happens to determine whether he or she did in fact have ADD. Psychologist Ken Livingston describes this very practice:

> . . . although many physicians use the drug as a diagnostic tool—in other words, if Ritalin seems to improve attention, the patient is assumed to have ADHD—an improvement in attentional control after taking a drug like Ritalin does not, in fact, establish the diagnosis of ADHD. Studies conducted during the mid seventies to early eighties by Judith Rapaport of the National Institutes of Mental Health clearly showed that stimulant drugs improve the performance of most people, regardless of whether they have a diagnosis of ADHD, on tasks requiring good attention. Indeed, this probably explains the high levels of "self-medication" around the world (stimulants like caffeine and nicotine, for example). Particularly interesting is the fact that cocaine, still reputed to be the illegal drug of choice in the world of the young, upwardly mobile, and highly focused crowd, has a psychopharmacology that is very similar to that of methylphenidate [Ritalin]. In short, even if you have never been diagnosed as having a problem paying attention, many of these drugs will improve your focus and attention. The fact that a child is more attentive while taking Ritalin doesn't mean that he has a documentable mental disorder.[64]

It is also because of this confusion over the meaning of Ritalin's effects that millions of parents have become convinced that their children have this thing called ADD. The process goes like this: Parents have their child "tested" for ADD and then, following an ADD diagnosis, put him or her on Ritalin; once the child is on it, the presenting symptoms of impulsivity, hyperactivity, or withdrawal decrease, thus affirming the diagnosis—"since a normal child would not be affected by the drug in this way." A case study in the book *Driven to Distraction* offers a good example: "'I came to see you and you started them on medication. And over a period of two weeks to a month their response to Ritalin was phenomenal. The teachers were amazed at the fact that these children, who had been so disruptive to the classroom, now could sit in their seats. David, who could not sit at his desk for longer than five minutes without flipping the desk over, well, all this sort of thing stopped. It all stopped.'"[65] Although only implicit, the tone of these remarks suggest how it is natural for parents to see Ritalin as having special "medicinal" effects and then conclude that they are evidence of their child's having ADD. This error of going from effect to cause rather than from cause to effect no doubt also functions as a common justification for choosing the Ritalin solution in the first place. Indeed, with Ritalin having become so popular, there is considerable pressure on parents today at least to "see what happens" when their child is put on it.

The idea that Ritalin's "therapeutic" effects are not unique or paradoxical is something we began exploring in earlier chapters. We tentatively concluded that no more should we expect Ritalin to induce hyperactivity in "normal" children than we should expect ADD-diagnosed children to become addicted to Ritalin after repeated use. At least since 1978, when psychiatrist Judith Rapaport and colleagues reported in the journal *Science* that psychostimulants decrease activity levels in most children, we have known that these effects are not paradoxical.[66] These drugs are for the most part stimulants, yes, but why do we assume a stimulant will increase our activity levels? Indeed, as we shall see below, once we realize that all of us actively regulate our incoming levels of stimulation, we will no longer be surprised that taking stimulants can actually decrease our sensory-seeking behavior. That is to say, by providing an artificial source of stimulation, the drug actually reduces our need to acquire stimulation through our own actions. After all, we see the same result, even in ADD-diagnosed children, from other "artificial" sources of stimulation, including television, movies, and video games. From this standpoint, Ritalin's effects turn out to be far more predictable than paradoxical.

Adding to this discovery is the fact that two decades prior to Rapaport and colleagues' report on psychostimulants, Peter Dews of Harvard Medical School, using animals, had already demonstrated something similar but even farther-reaching. Dews showed that the behavioral effects of drugs, including psychostimulants, could not be predicted by the drug alone. Instead, he found that whether or not a "stimulant" would increase activity and whether or not a "depressant" would decrease activity, even in animals, depended to a great extent upon the behavior of the organism prior to the drug's administration. If the animal's activity levels were relatively high, a "stimulant" would decrease them, and if the animal's activity levels were relatively low, a "depressant" would increase them.[67] Dews thus showed that not only the magnitude of a drug effect but even the direction of its effect ("stimulating" or "depressing") are as dependent on psychological and behavioral factors as they are on pharmacological ones.[68] This adds to the later discovery by Rapaport et al. by telling us that while a "stimulant" will typically decrease sensation-seeking behavior in the child, it can also produce "hyperactive" behavior in children whose levels of activity—and overall need for stimulation—are low.

Included in the controversy over Ritalin's paradoxical effects is a related claim sometimes made by physicians and ADD advocates, which is that Ritalin is not paradoxical because we now know it works by stimulating areas of the brain that have an inhibitory function for behavior. According to this claim, children diagnosed with ADD benefit from stimulants because the drug triggers the part of their brain that should keep their behavior in balance (such as the caudate nucleus) but doesn't. Even if there were scientific evidence for this, and there is not, the criticism above would still apply: Since Ritalin's effects are not unique in children diagnosed with ADD, its effects in the ADD-diagnosed child cannot be due to any such brain abnormality. If they were, we would once again expect different effects when "normal" children took the drug since the normal inhibitory functioning of their brains would then be overstimulated.

What does the manufacturer of Ritalin, Novartis, have to say about all this? Not only does it acknowledge that Ritalin's effects are not understood scientifically, it also concedes that there is no known connection between the drug's effects on behavior and any kind of brain abnormality in the child who uses it. Instead, it simply makes the claim that Ritalin is a drug that acts on anyone and everyone as a central nervous system (CNS) stimulant. In the *Physicians' Desk Reference* Novartis reports: "The mode of action in man is not completely understood, but Ritalin presumably activates the brain stem arousal system and cortex to produce its stimulant effect. There is neither specific evidence which clearly establishes the mechanisms whereby Ritalin produces its mental and behavioral effects in children, nor conclusive evidence regarding how these effects relate to the condition of the central nervous system."[69]

GIVEN how long we have known the truth about Ritalin's behavioral effects, it is disappointing to see how many in the ADD industry (and the media) continue to use these notions to set it apart as some kind of special medication. We saw the same thing in our investigation of the scientific basis of ADD: The gap between what the public knows and what science says is dangerously wide. In this case even the distance between what physicians believe, what the manufacturer of Ritalin claims, and what science supports is quite vast. As we should know from looking at the scientific evidence for ADD as a medical disorder, anyone who assumes that medical practice and public policy are the pure products of science is in for a big surprise. It's fairer to say that science lives only in the shadows of what we are led to believe about our human nature, handmaiden to larger cultural forces that shine a light only on the facts that conform to prevailing prejudices.

In the case of Ritalin, the cultural prejudice has been to interpret the evidence so as to make it appear that it is unique when in fact it is not. Included in this bias is the belief that Ritalin has long-term positive effects on children's academic performance and psychological well-being. While advocates of Ritalin point to certain studies and say yes, it's effective, researchers themselves look at the evidence and consistently conclude that no, it is not. The point here is not that there is confusion and debate over what the studies show. There have been many studies, many reviews, and even reviews of the reviews, and there is, outside of the ADD establishment, a clear consensus that for the great majority of children, taking Ritalin has very few benefits beyond simply masking their problems and controlling their behavior. And even these effects disappear as soon as the drug wears off.

Just as there was a study in 1978 reporting that Ritalin's effects on hyperactivity are not paradoxical, so another prominent study published that year showed that Ritalin does not improve the academic performance of hyperactive children.[70] This study by Russell Barkley and Charles Cunningham reported that while teachers often believe Ritalin facilitates student achievement, studies using more objective measures have not been able to demonstrate this. Instead, these researchers concluded that there has often been a failure to distinguish between the effects Ritalin has on students' manageability from its effects on their cognitive/intellectual abilities, thus leading to false generalizations about its long-term efficacy. Another review of these early studies concluded:

> The traditional reviews show a surprising consensus about the actual effects of stimulant medication on children with ADD. First, they agreed that in a majority (about 75%) of cases, treatment with stimulant medication produces immediate and dramatic positive changes in parent and teacher perception . . . [of] performance on tests requiring concentration and attention. Second, they acknowledged that placebo and expectancy effects, as well as pharmacological effects, contribute to the perceived positive effects of stimulants on children. Third, the reviews agreed that the short-term perceived positive change [i.e., who appears better] cannot be predicted by premedication physiological or psychological profiles of the children being treated. *Fourth, they agreed that the documented effects of stimulant medication on long-term adjustment (academic achievement or prosocial behavior) are negligible.*[71]

Negative findings similar to these and the 1978 report were also made in another study three years prior to the 1978 study. In this study researchers looked at the experiences of hyperactive children in the classroom over an extended period of time, when they were and were not taking Ritalin.[72] What they found was that the drug reduced behavior to more acceptable levels but that this came at the expense of dimming students' cognitive abilities. This study is especially interesting because the researchers also compared Ritalin's effectiveness with a nondrug alternative "treatment" regimen that encouraged higher academic performance by linking it with classroom rewards and privileges. This behavioral procedure lowered the hyperactivity to the same levels as Ritalin, but it also improved rather than impaired the students' cognitive abilities. As one observer noted about this study, "there would seem to be the choice between very quiet children who do not learn or children who are quiet because they are involved in learning. The first effect is reliably and easily produced by drugs, but there is little doubt that the second approach, though requiring more effort and more attention to individual requirements, is preferable."[73]

These reports are early ones, admittedly, and it is fair to ask whether studies since have confirmed these findings. Among newer reports, one study stands out as the most comprehensive. This is a "review of reviews" by James M. Swanson and colleagues on the "effect of stimulant medication on children with attention deficit disorder," published in the journal *Exceptional Children*.[74] Because this study is highly thorough, examining studies from 1937 to 1993, its conclusions are worth detailing. Fortunately, this can be done easily, since the authors summarized their findings in a table that listed what should and should not be expected to occur as a result of "treating" a child diagnosed with ADD with Ritalin.

First, in terms of what should be expected, this report lists two areas of improvement. One is the "temporary management of diagnostic symptoms," including "overactivity (improved ability to modulate motor behavior), inattention (increased concentration or effort on tasks), [and] impulsivity (improved self-regulation)"; the second is the "temporary improvement of associated features," including "deportment (increased compliance and effort) [and] aggression (decrease in physical and verbal hostility)." These are the only areas of improvement the authors consistently found in the literature.

In terms of what should *not* be expected, they reported on five areas: First, a "paradoxical response," finding instead that "responses of normal children are in same directions, responses of normal adults are in same directions, [and] responses of affected adults and children are similar"; second, a "prediction of response, not by neurological signs, not by physiological measures, [and] not by biochemical markers"; third, an "absence of side effects," finding instead "infrequent appearance or increase in tics, frequent problems with eating and sleeping, [and] possible psychological effects on cognition and attribution"; fourth, "large effects on skills or higher order processes," finding instead "no significant improvement of reading skills, no significant improvement of athletic or game skills, no significant improvement of positive social skills, [and] improvement on learning/achievement less than improvement in behavior/attention"; and fifth, "improvement in long-term adjustment," including "no improvement in academic achievement [and] no reduction in antisocial behavior or arrest rate." In short, we should not expect much beyond better management of behavioral symptoms.

In a 1996 Newsweek cover story, "Ritalin: Are We Overmedicating Our Children?," Ritalin was described by a Columbia University professor of medicine as "one of the raving successes in psychiatry."[75] As just noted, however, the literature on the efficacy of Ritalin suggests something quite different. This can be summarized using a statement scientist Ronald Gots made about MCS; if we modify his statement for ADD, it reads: ". . . the diagnosis of [ADD] begins a downward spiral of fruitless treatments . . . condemning the sufferer to a life of misery and disability. This is a phenomenon in which the diagnosis is far more disabling than the symptoms."[76] There is, after all, only one significant reason why Ritalin could possibly be so popular, and this is not because it is a raving success, not at least for the children taking it. Rather, it is because Ritalin is a powerful reinforcer for those who deal directly with children and thus benefit from its effects on their sensory-addictive behavior. This, as we just saw, includes lowered activity levels, greater attention, less aggression, and increased compliance and productivity. For those who actually take the drug, however, the overall picture is much less promising, since again, this includes added problems with eating and sleeping, possible impairment of cognition and attribution, no improvement in reading skills, no improvement in social skills, no improvement in academic achievement, and no clear reduction in antisocial behaviors.[77]

What is going on here is, however, more complicated than just a bunch of kids being so out of control, or so withdrawn, that parents and teachers need a powerful drug to bring them back to reality. While it's true that those who supervise Ritalin's use benefit more from it more than do children, especially when we look at the long-term consequences of taking the drug, it would be overly cynical for us to think that parents and teachers realize this or that they knowingly participate in such a failed solution. I think it is much more accurate to say that by assuming that better behavior and attention necessarily translate into better performance and, over time, a better life, parents and teachers (and physicians) have failed to scrutinize what is actually going on. What is actually going on is that because Ritalin has fast-acting behavioral effects, we have been fooled into thinking that we are treating these children in an informed, rational, and effective manner, even though we're not.

Supporting the view that parents and teachers fail to grasp fully what is taking place in the case of ADD and Ritalin is an interesting line of research showing that people are in fact quite poor at evaluating changes in performance, including changes in their own performance.[78] What this means here is that parents and teachers are not likely to be accurate in their evaluations of Ritalin's therapeutic effects. This would also hold for children prescribed the drug and their estimations of Ritalin's usefulness. Indeed, this is exactly what has been reported in outcome studies of Ritalin (and for the effects of placebos on parents' and teachers' ratings of Ritalin's effects), in which adults have been shown to be unconsciously biased in favor of Ritalin. The following conclusion, taken from a psychological report on biases in performance evaluations, is easily applied to the Ritalin solution: "Health professionals . . . often realize that patients may feel compelled to report that a treatment is helpful even when they know it is not. . . .We are saying something different, however. *Patients may well believe their reports of self-improvement, yet be wrong.* The best reminder of this is the history of medicine, as it is replete with examples of miracle cures that turn out to be nothing more than placebo effects. . . . Many of these cures were evaluated solely on the basis of patients' self-reports. When self-reports are a primary indicant of improvement, a conspiracy of ignorance may emerge in which the helper and helped each erroneously believe in the achievement of their common goal."[79]

IN SEARCH OF OPTIMAL STIMULATION

BY now we have examined in some detail the idea that hyperactivity and attention deficits represent developmental problems—problems that stem from the direct and indirect effects of life in a hurried society. Rapid-fire culture has transformed the American mind, partly by promoting sensory adaptations in a world of constant sensory consumption and partly because of the loss of external structure in the daily lives of children. With this alternative account in hand, we are now ready to put this theory to the full test by exploring two interlocking questions: Are the problems of the ADD child well described by the notion of sensory addictions? If so, might it be that Ritalin suppresses these problems, gratifying these sensory needs, and does so by providing a backdrop of constant stimulation? The answers to these questions have importance beyond those whose lives are directly affected by children diagnosed with ADD, however, since the consciousness of all Americans have been influenced by life in the hurried society. Thus the ADD child is not the *only* representative of sensory addictions, but rather the *best* representative. Looking at their lives can inform us about our own lives and the society in which we live.

Any scientific theory worth considering should lead to predictions that can be tested empirically and the theory of sensory addictions is no exception. We have already applied this standard to the theory of ADD and have found it wanting. We have also applied it to the idea that Ritalin has unique effects in the ADD child, and it has fared no better. In the particular case of sensory addictions versus the theory of ADD, we are able to put these theories to the test because viewing hyperactivity and inattention as culture-based developmental problems—sensory addictions—leads to different predictions about what we will find when we look closely at the "ADD child" than does the biological ADD approach. In other words, it is not possible that both accounts will explain the ADD child equally well.

Consider, for example, the common belief that children diagnosed with ADD are characterized as having poor concentration and high distractability. The idea of sensory addictions does not predict this since it views these children as characterized by high sensory needs, which will lead to problems of impulsivity, attention, or distractability *only* under certain slow circumstances. In other words, the theory of sensory addictions predicts that when needed levels of stimulation are present, the ADD child will not differ in distractibility from the "normal" child. In fact, since sensory addictions have nothing to do with a child's overall intelligence or competence, we should not be surprised when the ADD child outperforms the "normal" child, as often happens, especially if the sensory needs of both are being met. In short, the present account offers the alternative prediction that these two groups will be indistinguishable when the levels of sensory stimulation are high. As the levels of stimulation drop, however, the two groups will begin to come apart: To cope with the loss of needed external stimulation, the children with the greatest sensory needs will begin to fade out; they either will fade out altogether and become withdrawn, or they will begin to behave in a manner that increases their levels of stimulation by engaging in self-stimulatory behaviors.

Underlying this prediction is the notion, central to the idea of sensory addictions, that all of us avoid and engage in sensory-seeking behaviors in order to maintain a desired level of stimulation. This idea, which we began examining in Chapter 4 in terms of people's (and animals') adaptation to, and pursuit of, more complex stimuli, has been called the *theory of optimal stimulation*.[80] I've noticed this myself, for example, on my drives cross-country. When I enter a metropolitan area where traffic becomes hectic, I turn off my car stereo, then turn it back on only when I leave the area. Even though these are different sources of stimulation, together they can easily create stimulus overload, which I have learned to avoid by turning the stereo on and off as necessary.

This notion of optimal stimulation is the third of three core ideas that define sensory addictions. The first of these concerns how our attempts to excite our conscious minds quickly lead to long-lasting, neurologically based sensory adaptations, thereby neutralizing the initial, excitatory experience of more intense stimulus events. Not only does each of us have our own ways of maintaining a satisfying level of stimulation, but we also have different overall sensory needs, compared to one another and to people who lived in different times. As we've seen with the history of television and video games, plugged-in sources of stimulation that are awe-inspiring at one time quickly become outdated and boring later on. They are then replaced by new, "more" exciting experiences; of course these also fall quickly into obsolescence, at which time the whole cycle starts all over. This adaptation process is normal and unavoidable, but it sets the stage for sensory addictions when two other historical conditions are met: first, culturally, there must be the underlying psychological urge to do more and to go faster (that is, the urge to collapse the future into the present), which we have seen to be true throughout our history in the United States; second, technologically, we have to develop the capacity to keep this inflationary practice going, as has also been especially true in our nation's history.

This capacity to transform human consciousness was unleashed first in the industrial age but has since exploded in today's so-called information age. Combined with the urge to do more in less time, these developments have meant that a growing number of people now live with transformed states of consciousness. Such consciousness is characterized by two qualities: a compressed experience of time and heightened sensory expectations. The sense of protracted duration that results when time seems to slow down under conditions of slowness represents the second key aspect of sensory addictions. Because our sense of time is determined by the pace and structure of life, our sense of time has become compressed, creating an aversion to situations of low intensity. First come sensory adaptations, followed immediately by rising sensory expectations.

The problems produced by these sensory expectations are anticipated by the third aspect of sensory addictions, the search for optimal stimulation. Although we all make decisions each day both to slow down and to increase incoming levels of stimulation, our over-all sensory needs can become so great that sometimes there is no way to satisfy them. Moreover, the greater our sensory expectations, the more we suffer from the unavoidable slow spots in our environment. The number of slow spots may even be on the rise for us and our children since with our growing sense of temporal compression there are more situations that are experienced as too slow, from waiting in the checkout line at the market to using the dial on the rotary phone. At this point the child or adult will become more impatient, and his or her decision making will increasingly be influenced by the need to sustain a greater level of stimulation. When a television program becomes slow or boring, we start flipping through the channels; when what someone is saying doesn't seem interesting or important, we interrupt or fade out of the conversation altogether; when we stop at a streetlight, we crawl toward the intersection in a desperate attempt to maintain some sense of motion; when we sit down to read a book, we get antsy and look for something else to distract us; when we get stuck in traffic, we get anxious and frustrated and perhaps even hostile; when our kids are making slow progress in a game, work, or homework, we just do it for them, rather than work with them to help them solve the problem on their own; when nothing is jumping out at us to do at home, we get on the phone, jump in the car and go shopping, or go rent a movie; when advertisers or TV producers feel our attention span has sunk to a new low, they crank up the intensity or put more ticker tape across the screen.

As we live life faster, we adapt to the intensity of the stimuli around us. This adaptation leads to heightened sensory expectations, and these expectations send us searching for a steadier stream of stimulation, which only leads us back to the beginning of this process, adapting to even more intense stimuli. With this process of sensory addictions in mind, we can now apply it to the poster child of sensory addictions, the ADD child. If it is true that this child's consciousness has been transformed by a hurried, unstructured life, such that he or she now suffers psychological discomfort when things slow down, we should see at least three things. We should see that these children look identical to other children under stimulus conditions of their choosing but not when levels of stimulation are slow for them; we should find that when we look at the hallmark symptoms of ADD, these symptoms look invariably like a child in search of optimal stimulation; and finally, we should find that the stimulus effects provided by Ritalin are functionally equivalent to external sources of stimulation such that Ritalin is merely a substitute for them.

The popular idea that individuals diagnosed with ADD have innate problems with impulse control and attention is inherent in the diagnosis itself. Nothing in the diagnosis states anything about these problems' being specific only to certain situations or certain contexts; the attention deficit or hyperactive child is thought to be consumed by these problems. Yet when we take a close look at these children, we find case after case in which the disorder momentarily vanishes on its own, independent of any medication. For instance, ADD children have been shown to perform average or better in attention tasks when allowed to choose their own activities, when they receive individual attention, when they are paid to do activities, and when they are given novel or stimulating tasks to do. In one study ADD-diagnosed children were shown to respond poorly compared with normal controls on an attention task, suggesting they had a clear attention deficit. Yet when they were excited by the opportunity to earn money for responding quickly and accurately, their poor responses suddenly vanished, making them indistinguishable from the controls.[81] A variety of empirical studies have examined the context specificity of these problems, with much the same results: A study examining hyperactive kids using a different attention task reported that "there was no evidence indicating that a hyperactive group could be distinguished in terms of a sustained attention deficit"[82]; another study concluded: "ADHD children are not abnormally distractable"[83]; yet another study examined hyperactivity in both a formal, traditional classroom setting and in an informal setting and concluded that "there were significant differences between the hyperactive and control groups in the Formal but not in the Informal setting"[84]; finally, a study examining these problems under conditions of "free" and "restricted" play showed that "in the 'free play' conditions, hyperactive children were rated similarly to the nonhyperactive children. In a situation which made few demands for attention and self-control, both groups were relatively comparable across a broad range of behavior ratings. However, as the situation became more restrictive . . . the two groups became increasingly distinguishable."[85]

This influence of context, where prevailing levels of stimulation determine the levels of attention and hyperactivity in the sensory-addicted child, suggests why children are more often than not mistaken as "normal" children at the doctor's office and in all other contexts that offer a high degree of novelty or attention.[86] For many of these kids, television, where most can sit for hours without showing any sign of hyperactivity or distractibility, is the next best drug for ADD. As one study concludes, "children, like their normal counterparts, are active and strategic viewers of television."[87] This also applies, as suggested above, to the behavior of these children at school, where the ADD child melds into the classroom when activities are, from the child's point of view, highly engaging. Once again, in making this point, I am not suggesting that we need to intensify our homes and schools to meet these sensory needs. Doing so can only perpetuate the sensory addiction. As we shall see in the following chapter, we need to do just the opposite: bring structure and slowness back into the lives of children.

If the ADD child's problems disappear under stimulating circumstances, we should also expect the inverse to hold true: that signs of sensory addictions will appear most under conditions of slowness. One study of sustained attention in different classroom settings reports, for example, that "settings of relatively low stimulation or structure precipitated the more deviant variant of off-task behavior."[88] Indeed, when we look at the current diagnostic criteria for ADD, not only do we find the problems to be specific to conditions of slowness, but we also find that these "symptoms" of ADD fit the image of a child (and often adult) in search of constant sensory stimulation. To meet the diagnostic criteria for today's ADHD, based on the *Diagnostic and Statistical Manual*, vol. IV, you must fulfill either six of the symptoms for inattention or six of the symptoms for hyperactivity, all of which have to have existed for at least six months.[89] Let us consider each of these separately, starting with the diagnostic symptoms of inattention, followed by the diagnostic symptoms of hyperactivity. Note that these diagnostic criteria are, from the point of view of sensory addictions, redundant since they all reflect various examples of the same basic process of searching for optimal stimulation.

This table displays the symptoms we have to choose from in making an ADD diagnosis. But as it shows, these symptoms also paint a rather vivid picture of someone who has developed heightened sensory needs and tries to escape from them, either through withdrawal or by acting out.[90] This alternative interpretation, combined with the knowledge that these problems tend to decrease or disappear under more optimal sensory circumstances, suggests that these problems may indeed be more representative of an adaptive consciousness searching for optimal stimulation than a biologically imbalanced consciousness that drives the individual to misbehave. As one review of the theory of optimal stimulation points out, "Reported observations of hyperactive children have noted that under conditions which would be labeled highly stimulating, hyperactive behaviors actually appear to decrease. The results of an increasing number of studies suggest that hyperactive behaviors function to increase stimulation under conditions where stimulation is not sufficiently high . . . the motor activity seen in hyperactive children under conditions of low stimulation (e.g., waiting) may [therefore] function to reduce the effects of stimulus deprivation by increasing visual, auditory, kinesthetic, and proprioceptive stimulation."[91]

DSM SYMPTOM	WHEN VIEWED AS A SENSORY ADDICTION
Symptoms of Inattention	
Often fails to give close attention to details or makes careless mistakes in schoolwork, work, or other activities.	Paying attention to detail requires an ability to cope with slowness and to concentrate until a project is completed, that the sensory-addicted individual has trouble summoning.

DSM Symptom	When Viewed as a Sensory Addiction
Often has difficulty sustaining attention in tasks or play activities.	The longer one has to pay attention, the more boring or taxing the task becomes, especially for the sensory-addicted individual.
Often does not seem to listen when spoken to directly.	If the sensory-addicted individual is "spoken to" rather than involved in the conversation, the level of sensory input will be low and the individual will lose concentration.
Often does not follow through on instructions and fails to finish schoolwork, chores, or duties in the workplace.	As one continues with a required task, its novelty fades, the sensory-addicted individual loses interest, and the mind begins to wander.
Often has difficulty organizing tasks and activities.	Such problems of organization offer little in terms of stimulus excitement, and thus the sensory-addicted individual has difficulty staying on task.
Often avoids, dislikes, or is reluctant to engage in tasks that require sustained mental effort.	As with organizing tasks and staying on task, difficult tasks, such as a game of chess, may not offer enough moment-to-moment stimulation to maintain the attention of the sensory-addicted individual.
Often loses things necessary for tasks or activities.	Losing things is a product of being easily distracted, which follows from the fact that the sensory-addicted individual often

DSM Symptom	When Viewed as a Sensory Addiction
	switches from one activity to another, trying to maintain a constant flow of stimulation.
Is often easily distracted by extraneous stimuli.	By definition, extraneous stimuli are novel and thus have an immediate attractiveness for the mind searching for optimal stimulation.
Is often forgetful in daily activities.	Again, forgetfulness is a by-product of being easily distracted by extraneous stimuli.

Symptoms of Hyperactivity

Often fidgets with hands or feet or squirms in a seat.	These are simple, sensory-seeking behaviors for increasing overall sensory input.
Often leaves a seat early in a classroom or in other situations.	Again, this is behavior prompted by the search for optimal stimulation.
Often runs about or climbs excessively at inappropriate times.	Although an adult would engage in more appropriate behavior, the sensory-addicted child is simply behaving to increase incoming stimulation.
Often has difficulty playing or engaging in leisure activities quietly.	Play activities in the sensory-addicted child may be done more intensely in order to elevate levels of stimulation.

DSM Symptom	When Viewed as a Sensory Addiction
Is often "on the go" or acts as if "driven by a motor."	This is a classic description of someone in search of optimal stimulation, as is found in many young individuals when "sitting still."
Often talks excessively.	This is a common self-stimulatory and sensory-seeking behavior, readily available to the sensory-addicted individual.
Often blurts out answers before questions have been completed.	Listening is usually a waiting situation that provides a low-level of stimulation; hence, there is a tendency not to pay attention or to interrupt.
Often has difficulty awaiting a turn.	Again, because waiting is a low-sensory situation, the sensory-addicted individual has trouble waiting.
Often interrupts or intrudes on others.	Again, waiting is a low-sensory situation, prompting sensory-seeking behaviors that will increase incoming stimulation.

We have seen that the problems of the ADD-diagnosed child are situation specific, as is predicted by the notion of sensory addictions. We have also seen that these symptoms are the same ones that are used as the diagnostic criteria for ADD. In other words, the behaviors identified in making the diagnosis of ADD are the very ones we would expect to find based on the idea of sensory addictions. With this knowledge in hand, we can now turn to the third and final step in our investigation into sensory addictions, which looks at Ritalin's effectiveness as a sensory stimulus. That is to say, is it possible that a drug stimulus can substitute for an external source of stimulation, thereby explaining Ritalin's apparent therapeutic effect in these individuals?

The nature of the stimulus effects of psychoactive drugs has been explored in detail, especially in animals, and it is clear from these studies that the psychological nature of drug-induced stimuli is not different from the environmental stimuli we find in our everyday surroundings. For several decades, animals (even humans) have been trained under laboratory conditons to respond to the stimulus effects of drugs. The principal purpose of this research is pharmacological. Because animals are especially precise in their discriminations between drugs having different biochemical effects, animals that are properly trained can report on the pharmacology of a new compound—that is, by telling the difference between the stimulus effects of one psychoactive drug and those of another, they can tell us something about the therapeutic potentials of the drugs. There has long been a need for such research since one cannot simply look at the chemical structure of a substance and know its psychoactive effects; instead, the drug's effects must be examined in a living organism.

In one study rats were trained to discriminate between a drug that made them anxious (an anxiogenic drug) and a placebo.[92] In order for the animal to earn food, it had to respond on a different button depending upon which "drug" it received, using the stimulus effects alone to determine on which of the two buttons to respond. It is as if a red light told the animal to respond on the left button and a blue light told it to respond on the right button, except that here the stimuli are interoceptive drug stimuli instead of exteroceptive visual stimuli.

This particular study also had a feature with special relevance for us. Once the researchers had trained the animals to discriminate reliably between these two drugs (to press the correct button for each drug), they replaced the anxiety-producing drug with a visual/olfactory stimulus: a cat dowsed in catnip. When the rats were presented with the "cat" stimulus, they did not run and hide; rather, they immediately turned to the anxiety button and began pressing it, thereby telling the researchers that they were experiencing what we would call anxiety. This study thus showed that regardless of whether the stimulus came from the drug or from an environmental source, it was for all intents and purposes the same stimulus. This finding, that a drug can function as a stimulus and alter one's behavior in the same manner as an environmental stimulus, has been replicated in numerous studies, including studies with humans. Most significant for us, these findings suggest that the stimulus effects produced by the oral Ritalin consumption could indeed be used to satisfy the stimulus needs of the sensory-addicted individual, just as they can function as a substitute for the stimulus effects produced by his or her troubled search for optimal stimulation.

Having examined the vast but neglected literature on Ritalin, we have come to the end of our investigation into the origins of Generation Rx. Our main conclusion is that Ritalin is no more an effective medical treatment than ADD is a valid medical disorder. It seems the growing number of cases of ADD are best described instead as cases of sensory addictions, with Ritalin as the treatment drug of choice. The problem of course is that as with all addictions, consuming more of the substance that produced the addiction is no way to solve it. No one would ever expect to cure the drug addict by giving him or her a cheap and efficient source of the drug (as we know from the use of methadone in the treatment of opiate addiction), but this is exactly what has been done in the case of the ADD syndrome and the Ritalin solution. Consequently, the problems of impulsive sensory-seeking behavior and shrunken attention spans are only becoming worse. More children are developing sensory addictions, more parents are choosing the Ritalin solution, and more are deciding to continue taking the drug later on in life. Why has all this been allowed to take place? The best explanation, especially in light of how little the medical and pharmaceutical establishment has learned from the scientific literature on ADD and Ritalin, is that a conspiracy of ignorance has been under way for some time. Because pharmaceutical companies have benefited enormously, and physicians, teachers, and parents perceive children as having benefited some, this willful state of ignorance has been allowed to continue. Children, however, have not benefited from this ignorance. That is why we must give it up and turn to the crucially important task of finding real solutions for these developmental problems, which millions of American families now face.

Deliberate Living: Because Patience Comes to Those Who Wait

> *Deliberate Living:* Conscious attention to the basics of life, and a constant attention to your immediate environment and its concerns, example ➤ A job, a task, a book; anything requiring efficient concentration (*Circumstance* has no value. It is how one relates to a situation that has value. All true meaning resides in the personal relationship to the phenomenon, what it means to you).
>
> *From the journal of*
> CHRISTOPHER J. MCCANDLESS, 1968–1992[1]

MORE than a century ago John Stuart Mill wrote that there is "a common tendency among mankind to consider all power which is not visibly the effect of practice, all skill which is not capable of being reduced to mechanical rules, as the result of a particular gift."[2] This tendency, still very much alive, also operates in the other direction. Just as exceptional abilities today are being reduced to the level of biological destiny, so are exceptional traits of a less popular sort. Depression, criminal deviance, and the problems that concern us here — impulsivity, inattention, and hyperactivity — all have been reinterpreted as problems that start and finish within the skin of the individual. With this as the assumed origin of the problem, so is this the level at which the solution is aimed: We treat the child diagnosed with ADD with powerful mind-altering drugs because drugs are the individual-based "solution" for what we now consider strictly a biomedical problem.

In their acclaimed book *Meaningful Differences in the Everyday Experience of Young American Children*, developmental psychologists Betty Hart and Todd Risley give us a striking example of what John Stuart Mill had in mind as the real source of exceptional behavior.[3] This was an extensive, federally funded research project that studied the verbal experiences of children across forty-two families. By focusing on families of different social classes—welfare families, working-class families, and professional families—Hart and Risley investigated the developmental hypothesis that children of less advantaged families would have radically different verbal experiences from children of well-to-do families and that these differences would translate into measurable developmental differences in children's verbal skills. And that is exactly what they found. As they note in their book, "It took 6 years of painstaking effort [and] we were astonished [with the results]."

First, there was no doubt that children's language abilities were linked directly to the type of access they had to a verbal community. In terms of the raw amount of language heard by the child from age one to three, children were exposed to an average of about twenty million words. There were alarming differences in the exposure across the different social classes, however. By age three children's experiences varied from about ten million words for the children of welfare families to about thirty million words for children of professional families (working-class children fell between the two). Thus, although the amount of exposure to language was great, the difference in exposure as a function of social class was equally great. Hart and Risley also measured what portion of this language exposure was directed toward the children either positively or negatively. Here they found that welfare children received considerably more discouragement (twice as many discouraging words as for professional children), whereas the professional children received considerably more encouragement (five times that for children from welfare families).

These differences in the daily experiences of young children, living in what is ostensibly the same society, are astounding. Their developmental significance can be seen, however, only when we correlate them with children's actual language learning. Hart and

Risley, in assessing vocabulary development at age three, found that children of professional families had mastery of about one thousand words, whereas the vocabulary of children from welfare families was below five hundred—i.e., one-half the size. Can there be any doubt that these differences in language acquisition show the dramatic cumulative effects of systematic disparities in the everyday experiences of these forty-two families? I do not think so, although it may be tempting for some to think that the children from welfare backgrounds may have had less inherited intelligence than professional children or may even have been more from black and Hispanic families than from white families. Biological and racial interpretations of this sort do not make any sense, however, given the strong correlation found between language exposure and language learning. That is, the size of a child's vocabulary was almost perfectly correlated with the number of words he or she had heard earlier in life. From this we can only conclude that had the poor child been adopted by a wealthier family, his or her vocabulary would have been significantly larger. In fact, this research found that these differences in language acquisition were not correlated with the race (or birth order) of the children. When the researchers looked at children within the same social class, there was no connection between what the children learned and their race.

John Stuart Mill would almost certainly have been pleased by these results. Not only do they show how complex skills derive from daily life experiences, but they also show why we should be concerned that psychological phenomena that are "not visibly the effect of practice" may be just that, the effect of simple life experiences happening day in and day out in the lives of children. It should not be difficult to see the implications of these results for the problem at hand: sensory addictions and the diagnosing of children with ADD. First of all, the fact that behavioral traits develop gradually over time makes it easier for us to conclude that ADD has nothing to do with psychology and society and everything to do with biology and genetics. The impact of a day's events will rarely be noticeable at the end of the day, giving us the sense that these events have no lasting or cumulative effect. In reality, though, development is more like watching the minute hand of a clock: At no time do we see any movement, yet the hand moves—just as the child changes—right before our eyes.

Hart and Risley's study thus reminds us that the family, nestled within the forces of culture, is the immediate source of the individual differences that arise during child development. The family shapes the psychological makeup of the child, often without ever realizing that this is happening or just how it is happening. In the case of the ADD child, sensory addictions emerge as part of the evolution of the self, in much the same way as does the child's speaking of English. The only difference between learning to speak English and becoming a hyperactive child is that all families in the United States provide at least the minimal conditions for learning the language, whereas only some families provide, albeit unintentionally, the conditions for encouraging a hyperactive or inattentive child. Stressing this obvious fact, that the family is a powerful force for child development, also raises an important point about the danger today of viewing everything as genetic and biological, whether it's criminal deviance, alcoholism, hyperactivity, intelligence, emotionality, depression, drug addiction, sexual preference, personality, religiosity, or divorce.[4] Once we as parents and as public citizens lose the ability to think abstractly about how daily life gradually molds the mind of the child, we also fail to take the necessary steps to safeguard children during their critical developmental years. Indeed, knowing the societal pressures that define today's culture of neglect, combined with our knowledge of how the child's brain is transformed from age zero to three, the zeitgeist of "My genes made me do it" goes a long way toward explaining why children are having so many problems.

Still, this is not as simple as saying there are no biological or genetic factors involved in child development. The problems identified as ADD certainly have a biological component, which has to do with the lasting neurophysiological changes that result from living a life of constant sensory consumption. They also have a genetic component, which no doubt explains in part why some children with similarly unstructured, sensory-laden lifestyles are much worse off than others. Genetics is not the only explanation for these differences, though. We know from looking at identical twins raised together, as most are, that they will often turn out quite differently from each other. Indeed, I know of "identical" cases in which one twin is seen as having ADD or some other "childhood disorder," whereas the other is not. As noted in Chapter 1, the concordance rate for such twins and ADD is well below 50 percent, meaning that when one twin has been diagnosed with ADD, there is less than a favorable chance that the other will also.

Having underscored the importance of psychological development, we can now turn to our final task, which is the search for real solutions to the problems of sensory addictions. If the rise of ADD is largely the result of a culture-derived disorder of human consciousness, then we must look for ways to reverse the effects of chronic exposure to an increasingly impulsive, sensory-charged way of life. Fortunately the solution may well be easier and less painful than expected, since returning ourselves to a slower realm of life yields its own benefits, beyond those having to do with sensory addictions. This is true not only for those children and adults who have been diagnosed with ADD but for all of us who are caught up in the hurried society and suffer to some degree from sensory addictions. After all, parents of the ADD child often show many of the same symptoms, which means that we are going to have to deal with our own addictive lifestyles if we are going to deal with theirs.

STEP ONE: BREAKING THE SENSORY ADDICTION

IT might seem as though the solution to the problems children (and adults) are developing with attention and hyperactivity should be obvious, at least in terms of preventing these problems. All adults need to do, if they haven't done so already, is slow down their lives, rethink what is truly important, and exert more thoughtful control over the direction of their children's psychosocial development. This is basically true except for one problem: If people already know this, why haven't they already begun to make changes?

The problem is that the hurried society is structured in such a way that once someone has gradually learned hurried ways of thinking and behaving, there never seems to be an opportunity to go back and question them or to defuse them. Rapid-fire culture has a way of locking us into a certain "on the run" routine that does not easily let go. Moreover, for the ADD-diagnosed child, there is every reason to believe that breaking the sensory addiction will not be easy; of course this is why many have wrongly concluded that these problems are part of the constitution of the child. As the notion of "addictions" tells us, just because something is difficult to overcome does not mean that it is not a developmental problem. Solving our sensory habits will not be easy, and that is why we should try to prevent them in the first place. But it does not mean we shouldn't also try to solve them.

Consider, for example, the habit of cigarette smoking, which is often considered the most difficult addiction to overcome. Despite this perception, half of all living Americans who have ever smoked regularly have actually quit (about 1.3 million Americans quit each year). Now if more than a million people can quit smoking each year, there is no reason why a child should not be able to develop out of his or her ADD-related problems, provided that active steps are taken—i.e., steps that halt the problem of sensory addictions by bringing a predictable structure to the child's life and by leading him or her into a slower pace of activities.

In summary, then, because problems that develop under chronic conditions can be solved only by living under *different* chronic conditions, there is a need to look beyond commonsense solutions for overcoming the symptoms of ADD. That is, we must first find ways to close the gap between knowing that things need changing and actually accomplishing these changes. We may know we need to break from the insidious routine that frames our lives and determines how our children are growing up but nevertheless find it almost impossible to achieve this. This is partly because we think we lack the resources—"we don't have the time"—partly because we are conservative about change—we lack the faith that making lifestyle changes will pay off for ourselves or our families—and partly because we are confused about our priorities and thus are hesitant about abandoning whatever pole position we have achieved thus far in our rat race with time. But the stakes are high. We really don't want children to grow up having psychological problems. This is why we must resist the idea that is so popular today in the

ADD literature, that these problems cannot be fixed. After all, there is a whole earlier generation of children who had the ADD diagnosis but have since overcome them. The difference between then and now is that we no longer expect these problems to go away, and thus we no longer take the steps necessary to turn these expectations into certainty.

IF *you have an ADD child, avoid making excuses, even if the excuses are in many ways legitimate. Find resolve in the idea that children deserve a better life, and then work to break him or her from overload and sensory addictions. Do this by creating a slower pace of life that over time will transform human consciousness and, as a consequence, transform your child.*

STEP TWO: CHALLENGING THE DOMINANT PARADIGM OF WORK, WORK, WORK

IN rapid-fire culture we are of course more rushed than ever before. Rushing comes from cramming more into our daily lives and then trying to get it all done. Rushing comes from a state of hurried consciousness that, by soothing our immediate sensory needs, deepens our habits of impulsivity. Rushing also comes from our future-directed consciousness, in which the present moment is overlooked because of an obsession with anticipated future events; this obsession may be either a worrisome one, in which we dwell on the need to get things done, or an optimistic one, in which we anticipate better things to come. As was noted earlier, a majority of Americans now report "feeling always rushed." The word "feeling" here is key because being rushed is as much a state of mind as it is a state of being. Indeed, we know from biographies, history, and research studies such as those on flow that keeping busy and being fully engaged in meaningful activities do not *necessarily* have anything to do with being hurried, just as sitting around all day engaged in passive activities, such as TV or the Internet, doesn't necessarily mean we don't feel rushed. At the same time, this also does not mean that engagement in our culture of work will ensure a culture of happiness. The work most of us do is either highly stressful or inanely repetitive, or both, not the conditions that induce the state of consciousness called flow.

If rushing is the first curse of the hurried society, the second curse is how, by wanting too much, we have become conflicted in our everyday priorities. As a headline reads in a 1998 issue of *Barron's* magazine, "Glutted with goods, Americans increasingly want 'feel-goods'—cruises, makeovers, golf lessons, and the biggest luxury of all, free time."[5] In a kind of existential mathematics, doing more tends to diminish the quality of lived experience, and thus having more shows up in the psychological column as having less. There may be no more striking an illustration of this than the contrast provided by groups like the Amish. The Amish live their lives steeped in sacred tradition, meaningful work, and community. They create a purposeful life in the present that, although consistent with the tenets of flow, is inconsistent with mainstream American ambitions. The Amish avoid insecurity by rejecting the adventures of individualism in favor of a devotion to community; they avoid social problems such as poverty, alienation, and psychological illness by sharing abundance and by ignoring both the cult of competition and the cult of material happiness that lie behind our selfish pursuits of fortune and fame; they also avoid childhood problems like inattention, hyperactivity, impulsivity, and aggression by incorporating children into the center of community life, rather than ushering them off to the margins, where technology takes care of them.

Still, we are not going to become a nation of Amish. One thing we can learn from them, though, is that although the pleasures of slowness may have disappeared in our society, this does not mean they no longer exist. To the contrary, rediscovering these pleasures requires little more than making different choices about how we spend our time. Of course we have to remember that to achieve these pleasures, we may first have to endure a period of discomfort as we readapt our minds and unwind our sensory addictions. Author Bernard McGrane writes that "it is easier to shorten attention spans and increase distractibility than to lengthen attention spans, increase concentration, and calm, quiet and still the mind. There is an old Zen analogy that the way to calm, clear and quiet the mind is similar to the way to clear a muddy pool—not by action, by doing, by stirring it up, but by stillness, by letting it be, by letting it settle itself."[6]

The Amish example also reminds us of an earlier point regarding simplicity. Just as being fully engaged in meaningful activities does not *necessarily* have anything to do with being hurried, living a simple life does not *necessarily* have anything to do with living a boring one. As was often stressed to me while I was writing this book, there is a rich and wondrous world out there that we miss when we speed right by it. We saw an example of this in the passage by Noelle Oxenhandler, where "those trains that can whip from Paris to Provence in a matter of four hours" turn the trees and the villages "into a blinking pattern."[7] Another notable example of this came when a powerful ice storm hit northern Vermont, New York, and parts of Canada in the winter of 1998. Because the ice storm knocked out the power for hundreds of thousands of people, it generated stories about coping with the unplugged world, including several I heard about people's rediscovery of slowness. Especially striking were stories about children who awoke from their television slumber, and began playing together, inventing new games, and discovering new skills like making light without electricity. Most encouraging was the fact that many children were at least a little sorry to see the power come back on. Again, simplicity does not mean boredom; in fact, boredom may be more likely under conditions of rapid-fire culture, which produce an insensitivity to the richness around us.

One place where we can see how conflicted our priorities are is in the debate about work versus family. Work is necessary to support oneself and one's family, obviously, so it's easy to assume the more the better. However, because we have become a society of work—because there are now so many two-career households, with each parent working long hours—some have begun to ask whether the growing world of work is a threat to the family. For example, family scholar Urie Bronfenbrenner, who has examined the research findings on this subject, concludes that stress from work clearly contributes to the stress and instability at home and in the lives of children.[8] There is even evidence, he suggests, that the biggest problems come from the father since he is much more likely than the mother to be insensitive to the effects of work on the family. Worst of all, there seems to be a trend, again especially for fathers, in taking refuge from the disarray at home by spending more time at work.[9] We now live in a time when, as David Elkind has shown, the neglected member of the family has shifted from the mother to the child.

This raises the following question: Can we sustain equal opportunities for women and still nourish the developmental needs of children? The only way to accomplish this seems to be for parents to realize that in a world of finite resources mothers cannot have these equal opportunities if fathers are unwilling, as they have been, to take up their own responsibilities at home. A father must claim his natural right to work inside the house when the mother assumes her own natural right to work outside the house. This was the conclusion of Sharon Hays's *The Cultural Contradictions of Motherhood*, which, much like Elkind's account, shows that mothers now face a situation of "intensive mothering," torn between the nurturing demands of motherhood and the competitive demands of the workplace.[10] Part of the problem here lies in how the structure of work in American society encourages our culture of neglect. For example, as Bronfenbrenner has suggested, we need more flexible work schedules, we need to begin encouraging part-time work over full-time work by changing the all or none practice of employment benefits, and we need to establish more resources and organizations at work that concern themselves explicitly with the impact work has on family life. In the meantime we also need to ensure that child care and school programs are encouraging long-term healthy development in our kids.

When contemplating needed changes in our relationship to work, we must consider as well the problems that stem from the fact that the fastest-growing segment of our society is the single-parent family. This is an equally complicated social phenomenon, to be sure, but there can be no doubt that this breakup of the nuclear family results from our conflicted priorities, just as much as it contributes to them. The failure to do the work required of a marital relationship, for example, and the desire to enter continually into new ones are not just questions of people's personal lives; these trends are also occurring because of a shift that has taken place in our cultural priorities. If you reflect on how you regard members of your family, for example, you will no doubt find a bond that you take for granted: that family is family, blood is blood. Yet there was a time not too long ago when this sense of belonging was just as applicable to family membership through marriage, as it still is for some groups in our society. Men and women understood vows like "until death do us part" not as a prediction about how lasting their love would be but rather as a lifelong commitment to another person, to someone who within moments was to become a true family member. By contrast, many today understand marriage as merely a legal arrangement, with little or no connection to a lifelong commitment. To see how much of a shift has taken place in the tradition of marriage, consider the number of conservative politicians who, while ranting and raving about family values, have gone on to leave their first wives for younger ones. Among others on this dubious list are Bob Dole, Phil Gramm, and Newt Gingrich.[11]

Barbara Dafoe Whitehead, in *The Divorce Culture*, calls this shift in cultural values the divorce ethic:

[It has] radically changed established ideas about the social and moral obligations associated with divorce. In the past Americans assumed that there were multiple stakeholders in the unhappy business of marital dissolution: the other spouse, the children, relatives, and the larger society. All these stakeholders held an interest in the marital partnership as the source of certain goods, goods that were put at risk each time a marriage dissolved. At particular risk were children, who were the most likely to experience severe losses as a consequence of divorce, especially the loss of the steady support and sponsorship of a father. . . . However, the notion of divorce as the working out of an inner life experience cast it in far more individualistic terms than in the past. Because divorce originated in an inner sense of dissatisfaction, it acknowledged no other stakeholders. Leaving a marriage was a personal decision, prompted by a set of needs and feelings that were not subject to external interests or claims. Expressive divorce reduced the number of legitimate stakeholders in divorce to one, the individual adult.[12]

As our divorce culture suggests, we still harbor dreams about marriage, family, and perhaps even everlasting love, but we have trouble holding on to these dreams as they collide with a whole host of other, individualistic priorities.

Connected to our hurried lives and our conflicted priorities is the third curse of the hurried society, which is that our lives are increasingly dictated by an economic attachment to the bottom line. This doesn't have to do only with our working more; it also has to do with our losing the ability to weigh questions of quantity (of income and wealth) against questions of quality (of life). Bottom-line thinking exists whenever someone bases his or her decisions, knowingly or unknowingly, solely on the question of maximum financial gain. If I have to rent an office for my business, then I know that the more hours I work, the less overhead I have; if I have a promising career or a valuable education, I cannot waste it at home with my children; if I'm offered a full-time position or extra work responsibilities, I must take them, for otherwise I might lose future opportunities; if I have clients willing to pay fifty dollars (or five hundred dollars) per hour, I must take all the business I can get. As in all these hypotheticals, bottom-line thinking means that there is no attempt to place a value on the hidden family costs of always making a bottom-line decision. If I work a few more hours, I see the direct economic result, but the personal and family results of this decision—which may eventually lead to depression, divorce, or psychological problems in my children—are harder to see, like the motion of the clock, and thus easier to ignore.

To give a real-life example, I know a family in which one parent is paid so handsomely that the whole family can live off just two days of her work per week. In almost all cases like this, the parent works tirelessly and the family has, by worldly standards, a grand lifestyle. In this particular family, however, the "working" parent has in fact chosen to work only these two days. The rest of the week the family has a relaxed pace of life, although this is by psychological standards and not material ones. The adults enjoy each other's company, take the time to pursue their leisure interests, and teach their children interesting and important things. Meanwhile, we all know of many families in which *both* parents make very handsome incomes. Even in these cases, though, either because of their dedication to their careers, restrictions on part-time work, or because the money is just "too good," most of them cling to the idea that both parents must work in order to earn as much as possible.

Another example that strikes me as bottom-line thinking is that of middle-class parents who work themselves silly, thinking they must earn extra income to save for their children's college education. As someone with three college degrees, I'm hardly in the position to say that a college education is useless (although I see no reason why parents should have to pay for it), but as someone who teaches at the college level, I also know that no education is more important and lasting (and free) than the day-to-day education that children and teenagers receive at home. A teacher at any level can do little with a student who is very immature and lacks all seriousness about his or her education and perhaps his or her own life. But where does she come from, the sincere, moral individual who shows up in my classes ready to challenge and be challenged by what she learns? Today everyone's looking at the past and fretting about the dysfunctional family from which he was thrown, yet no one is looking to the future to see what kind of dysfunctional family he is cultivating for his own children. After all, parents have to take responsibility for their children's turning out poorly if they want to take responsibility for their children's turning out well. Hence, it seems that rather than "save" for the future by working all the time, it would be much wiser if parents stole back their time from work and then used it to ensure that their children's development is not being left up to the winds of chance.

REDEFINE *the bottom line. Spend less time at work; parent more and parent better. Learn more effective life skills, and pass them on to your children. Do these things by being less worn out, stressed out, and distracted by the perceived necessity of material wealth.*

STEP THREE: RETURN THE SENSES BACK TO A NATURAL SPEED AND RHYTHM

THE critical remarks above won't apply equally well to everyone, I realize. You may be a struggling single parent, or you may not even have a family. Still, for many of us, this is more or less how we currently find our lives: too hurried, too materialistic, and too confused and conflicted about what's important to us. As a result, we are also finding that the conscious interiors of our lives are being transformed by the exterior world, and in much the same way as have the minds of children diagnosed with ADD: We are restless, anxious, and even depressed. Hence, whether or not we have children whose lives are stressed because of how our lives are stressed, the problem of how to recover a rewarding sense of experience is the same. We must free ourselves from the clenching jaws of the hurried society by returning ourselves to slowness and a more intentional way of life. To see what this means in concrete terms, let us begin with a lesson that comes from an area of psychological research that may appear, at first glance, to have nothing to do with our topic. This is the study of expert performance.

It is commonly believed that the loss of fine motor skills in elderly people is a natural process of old age, an idea that conflicts with a growing literature on human performance. In 1996 Anders Ericsson, a psychologist at Florida State University, and a colleague looked at this assumption. Four groups of pianists were examined. Two groups consisted of amateur pianists, one of individuals who were relatively young and the other elderly; the other two groups were also divided by age, but these pianists were professionals. Looking only at their fine motor skills in the context of everyday tasks, the researchers found what we would expect: that the older pianists had lost a significant amount of their motor control compared with the younger pianists, regardless of whether they were amateurs or professionals. When they looked at their actual playing of the piano, however, the two groups of older pianists did in fact differ. While both human and computer evaluations of the piano performances could easily distinguish between the performances of younger and older amateurs (under blind conditions), this was not true for the professional pianists, despite the differences that existed between them when doing everyday tasks. This is exactly what Ericsson had hypothesized on the basis of earlier findings: Elderly professional pianists would not lose their fine piano skills in old age because they would continue to engage in a special mode of practice that would keep this from happening. This mode of practice is called *deliberate practice*.

According to the research on expert performance, there are few, if any, documented cases in which individuals develop into elite performers without several years of deliberate practice of one sort or another: not Einstein, not Mozart, not Hemingway. Echoing John Stuart Mill, Ericsson and another colleague, Neil Charness, wrote in the *American Psychologist*, "Counter to the common belief that expert performance reflects innate abilities and capacities, recent research in different domains of expertise has shown that expert performance is predominantely mediated by acquired complex skills . . . For elite performers, supervised practice starts at very young ages and is maintained at high daily levels for more than a decade."[13]

Deliberate practice means more than just a steady diet of practice. As Ericsson and colleagues have demonstrated for a wide array of cognitive, athletic, and artistic abilities, to become an elite performer, you must engage in a form of practice that focuses constant attention on assessing current levels of performance and comparing them with clearly specified goals. Ericsson and Charness write: "[D]eliberate practice is an effortful activity motivated by the goal of improving performance. Unlike play, deliberate practice is not inherently motivating; and unlike work, it does not lead to immediate social and monetary rewards."[14] Indeed, research shows that practice will not lead to an increase in performance unless one has both an expectation of improved performance and a clear means of achieving it. This can be seen in Ericsson's elderly professional pianists. Their piano playing did not succumb to the predicted decrepitude of old age for the simple reason that despite social expectations about old age, the pianists maintained a set of objectifiable criteria and then arranged their lives to meet or sustain them.

Deliberate practice also tells us something about how to escape from the decidedly nondeliberate ways of living that characterize life in the hurried society. Everyone has a basic idea of what it means to live, just as everyone has a basic idea of what it means to practice. But there is a world of difference between living and deliberate living, and it is much the same difference as exists between practice and deliberate practice. To see this, consider the passages above, revised for deliberate living: *Deliberate living is not immediately motivating, and unlike work, it does not lead to immediate social and monetary rewards. . . . Living today will not lead to an increase in life satisfaction unless one has both an expectation of improved living and a means of achieving it.* By being deliberate, we can orchestrate the course of our lives and raise them to a higher level, rather than have our expectations and choices defined a priori by the toxic standards of the hurried society and its culture of neglect. Deliberate living thus differs from everyday living in that we begin to contemplate seriously the real consequences of our choices, freeing ourselves and our children from our usual bumbling through the world, where we are pushed and pulled by the powerful external forces of our individualistic, materialistic, image-oriented society. In Christopher McCandless's description above, deliberate living has to do with "Conscious attention to the basics of life, and a constant attention to your immediate environment and its concerns." That is to say, when we fail to direct our attention to our everyday present experiences and notice their connection to the way we have chosen to live our lives, we end up unconsciously conforming to societal impulses that in these times have little to do with creating a meaningful, contented life.

The dangers of blind social conformity in a world that fills our heads with rising expectations about the future are ultimately greatest for children, since they are blind to the ulterior motives of market culture. Take cigarette smoking, for example. The desire to self-fashion a life of "cool" by smoking turns out to be very much in line with "corporate cool." It can hardly be a coincidence that kid-friendly characters like Joe Camel stand behind one of the best-selling products of the cancer industry. As child and adolescent smoking suggests, children are the ones least capable of reflecting on their experiences and using them to steer their development toward building sustainable, healthy selves. These are selves that don't need a cartoon camel to reinforce their own sense of worth, don't need prosthetic drugs like Ritalin or Prozac to prop them up, day in and out, and don't need a constant flow of newness or change.

Kids are not the only ones, however, who fool themselves into thinking they have deliberately authored their own (disastrous) lifestyle choices. Although it is natural for all people to internalize the social norms and beliefs of their dominant culture or subculture, we live in a time when these forces serve an array of conflicting interests, only some of which are good for us and for society as a whole. Cigarette advertising makes this clear, as do the messages that come from the billions of dollars spent each year on television commericals. As can be seen in examples like the Amish, local communities once controlled the social beliefs or mores that governed their expectations and actions. The social forces operating in contemporary society still serve those who promote them; the problem is that those who promote them are no longer members of the local community. As social psychologist Bernard Guerin tells us:

> . . . the sources of control have changed from smaller cohesive communities to a more general and widespread control. A problem with modern information media such as television is that they can support the creation of counterfactual social representations even in the absence of a social group. . . . This means that there is great potential for counterfactual knowledge being maintained in modern society because behavior is becoming more frequently verbal, because the controls on verbal behavior are becoming more easily detached from nonsocial environmental controls, and because mass media can maintain counterfactual verbal behaviors that previously could only be controlled by communities.[15]

It is because of our absorption into the worlds of counterfactual knowledge—with their perfect personalities, perfect bodies, perfect cars, perfect pills, and perfect love—that deliberate living takes on such significance today. Take, for example, the common belief that the more you earn, the more you need to earn, or the notion that once you earn more, your lifestyle always expands to absorb the extra income. If you are like the hundreds of thousands of other people with the 2.4 children, the two-car garage, and Prozac in the medicine cabinet, then the reverse logic might be well worth considering. That is, we might just as well earn less, scale down the conspicuous consumption that compensates us for living lives of perpetual work, and then take this freedom and pursue life on a slower, more human scale. Yes, if we are single and fulfilled by our love of work, then work we will do. But if we have many other interests and other responsibilities, then the question of being deliberate becomes crucial, especially for the lives of our children.

BE *deliberate and restrict yourself to a greater quality of experience instead of a greater quantity of it. Then live your life knowing that the decisions you made each day constitute the entirety of your life and determine how you feel while being caught in the middle of it. When this is done, the isolation and loneliness in your and your children's lives will begin to disappear, replaced by greater meaning and contentment.*

STEP FOUR: RETURN CONSCIOUSNESS TO REAL EXPERIENCE IN REAL TIME

A whole generation of youth has now taken a trek down Ritalin road and never come back. Instead, they just kept going, and they took Ritalin with them. The Ritalin solution is like reacting to a blazing house fire by building quick additions on the back of the house; at some point this solution has to break down when the demand for real change becomes undeniable. At that point, a deliberate approach to living can help. Being deliberate means slowing down, and slowing down means gradually decompressing our and our children's conscious minds. Living in the present also means slowing down so that time no longer rushes through our lives, leaving us empty handed. To give an example, each summer I do pretty much the same things I do during the rest of the year, except I no longer have, in addition, a full-time teaching load. Hence, when the slowness of summer comes to an end and I'm thrown back into my hectic teaching schedule, I go nuts. It is at this point that I become fully aware of just how much having a free summer has slowed time down and has unwound my hurried consciousness. Unwinding is always a gradual process, but being thrust back into things can happen so suddenly that it seems too much to take. Eventually my consciousness adapts, however, the contrast fades, and at least until next summer I once again find the hurried life to be the norm.

Living deliberately means, then, that not only will we begin to make more rational decisions about how to improve the quality of our life and the lives of those around us, but we will also begin changing the everyday rhythm of our lives. Since conscious experience merely reflects the acute and chronic conditions of one's life, slowing down will gradually alter our inner experience. We saw this with the two children whose hyperactivity (and serotonin levels) went up and down as the conditions of their lives changed (this was discussed in Chapter 4). We also saw this in Chapter 3 in studies on flow. When researchers investigated the conditions that cultivated a harmonious state of mind, they found that these were situations that produced an absorption in the here and now. The problem of course is that conditions of flow are just the opposite of the conditions cultivated by the hurried society, which is once again the reason why deliberate living has become so crucial in modern times.

In changing the everyday structure of our lives, we need to do more than just slow down. We also need to awaken from our growing absorption in simulated worlds of passive entertainment. This means more hands on, more televisions off. Thomas Armstrong, in *The Myth of the ADD Child*, applies this philosophy to television:

> Television and video games also negatively affect children's behavior by taking them away from activities that are more active, multisensory, and intellectually, socially, and emotionally nourishing. Social critic Jerry Mander, author of *Four Arguments for the Elimination of Television*, writes, "It is bizarre and frightening . . . that many parents use television as a means of calming hyperactive children. It would be far better to calm them with physical exercise, sports, wrestling, hugging, bathing, and a lot of direct attention that gives them wide-ranging sensory and intellectual stimulation. . . . The worst thing one can do for a hyperactive child is to put him or her in front of a television set. Television activates the child at the same time that it cuts the child . . . off from real sensory stimulation and the opportunity for resolution."[16]

Sensory addictions emerge as part and parcel of a hurried life, to be sure, but we must remember that for many the hurried life also unfolds within a world that is greatly amplified by artificial means. Sometimes this engrossment in sensory consumption comes to us unsolicited, when stimulation shouts from all directions. But more often than not we bring it upon ourselves. It is our failure to find fulfillment in our future-directed pursuits that seems to be encouraging this search for fulfillment in the alternative worlds of virtual reality. Take as a simple example genres of film: action, adventure, drama, comedy, romance. These categories of experience, which we can rent each day at the corner video store, symbolize the way in which our lives have become entangled in a web woven of both reality and illusion. This is a world in which our brains are being soaked in virtual reality at one instant and then plunged into real life the next. What is more, because simulated reality has become so increasingly realistic, the problem of what is real and what is artificial has become for many confused, as when an adolescent commits a heinous crime and then says he got the idea from watching television. Sure, we know when the show is over, but the emotions, ideas, and images of artificial life nevertheless creep into our subconscious minds, first as we're growing up and then as "free" adults. Not unlike Freud's unconscious desires, the relentless impressions of virtual reality eventually show up in our and our children's expectations about how life works, undermining our ability to cope with the facticity that remains for us in everyday life.

This culture of rising expectations can explain how it is possible that we live in an age of both affluence and rampant discontent. First, the more sophisticated, gripping, jarring, and violent the virtual experience of artificial reality, the more unsettling the contrast becomes between the magnified images and emotions of artificial worlds and what real life has to offer. Beginning in childhood, we move to and from the worlds of cinema, television, and video, each time returning to reality with a more inflated (and accelerated) sense of real life. Hence, by letting our children run freely through virtual worlds, we are not only encouraging heightened sensory needs, but also encouraging the development of crippling expectations about the meaning of life. Because these heightened needs are so unrealistic and thus unobtainable in one's own life, they bring us full circle, as adults, by encouraging lifestyles that lead to even greater expectations. Herein lies the vicious cycle behind the rat race of modern society: As we become more engrossed in high-tech, simulated worlds and our brains begin to move in sync with them, we find our lived experience in the unplugged world to be increasingly impoverished, thus pushing us even deeper into the worlds on sale for the sensory-addicted person.

To give a detailed example, in December 1997, the most expensive film ever in cinema history, *Titanic*, came to the movie theater. The film consists of a fictional love story superimposed on the actual events of the *Titanic*, which sank under dark, clear skies four hundred miles south of Newfoundland in 1912. The man behind the film, director and screenwriter James Cameron, spent two hundred million dollars in production costs alone, with a total film budget from Fox and Paramount, including advertising and other marketing costs, projected to be somewhere between three and four hundred million dollars.

To make the film, Cameron had the two central ingredients of the story built, the *Titanic* itself and the ocean in which it sank.[17] The filmed ship was a 775-foot replica, 90 percent the size of the original, created and sunk solely for Cameron's purposes. Inside the football field–size ship was the same decor, created with the same materials of that period and with the same attention to detail. Along with the faux furnishings of the actual *Titanic* there were also about seventy miles of power cable, forty-five hundred lights, forty thousand amps of power, and fifty electricians. Outside the ship was a twenty-five-million-dollar, forty-acre complex, also built to Cameron's lavish specifications. Within the complex was a "believe it or not" seventeen-million-gallon water tank that housed the twice-fated ship. As one journalist describs it, "Cameron spent months sinking a 775-foot-long replica of the doomed ship in a massive water tank, pitching hundreds of extras and stuntpeople into freezing waters."[18] In addition to these costly production features, Cameron took advantage of advanced technology to do two other things. He joined with American and Russian submarine expeditions to film, using robotic cameras, deep-sea footage of specific sites inside and outside the *Titanic*, which he then used throughout the film to help project the audience back and forth across the eighty-five years spanning 1912 and the present. He also used state-of-the-art digital technology to create about 550 computer-generated shots (*Jurassic Park* had only 80). For example, 40 special effect shots were used to show survivors exhaling frozen air into Cameron's fictional Newfoundland night.

To say that these are extravagant means for a rather trivial end goes beyond understatement. All this time, energy, creativity, and money are dedicated to re-creating one of the most horrific moments in world history, just for a few hours of mere titillation. Even this was not enough. Cameron also had to impose upon history his make-believe love story to ensure that the titillation factor would be great enough to ensure a profitable film, as of course it was. To get a sense of the proportions of *Titanic*, consider that at about the same time that the film was opening at theaters, the Getty Center was opening in Los Angeles. While the Getty's cost was about threefold that of *Titanic*, the Getty Center is a massive complex of several buildings, considered by some to be one of the great architectural achievements of the twentieth century. Whereas the former holds our attention for a mere few hours, the latter will remain a part of Los Angeles's cultural life for decades, perhaps even centuries to come. These two projects are also strikingly different in another way. The center of attraction of the Getty Museum is ultimately its international art collection, which could not be more different in its visual content from what we find in a big-budget romance thriller like *Titanic*. This is exactly the point. Hundreds of millions of dollars are spent by those watching one film for one simple reason: It can submerge us into a world far, far away from our own. Although the fine art shown on the walls of the Getty Museum could do the same, it does for only a few. For although viewing fine art is an active, authentic experience, it cannot compete with the passive, pulsating experience that comes from the limitless worlds of virtual reality. Indeed, when we look at the trajectory of the technological revolution of the past century, we might wonder, as has natural historian Stephen Jay Gould, whether there even is an enduring human need for authenticity.[19] Are future generations destined to live out their search for perfection in separate artificial worlds, leaving behind the annoying imperfections of the natural world we all share?

THE alternative to simulated reality is the hands-on reality of real, lived experience. Partly because of the lure of simulated worlds and partly because of the laissez-faire conditions in which children are growing up, children are often not developing the basic skills that allow them to engage the real world. This applies to solitary activities, such as making things, and social activities, where the experience is a collective one, requiring certain social skills, such as cooperation and patience. These activities have two crucial qualities. First, they are low-tech, meaning that the intensity of the activity does not greatly exceed the intensity of other everyday situations, such as in the classroom, doing homework, or at the dinner table. Second, they are active, meaning that the children are learning how to live in the world in the same way that research tells us is necessary for a harmonious state of mind to emerge. By getting lost in interesting but also slow activities, children learn to use their own skills to occupy themselves, which is very useful when slowness arrives. The virtues of having children experience the world in this way were articulated in Rousseau's story of Émile. As historian Peter Gay describes it, for Rousseau childhood is "the age when the senses are keen and the body is vigorous; this is the time when one should train the first through observation and the second through exercise. The child must not study geography out of books: he should wander in the fields, across streams and hills . . . Émile is being educated in the only way that education can work: by making his experience his own."[20] As Rousseau himself put it: not "words, more words, still more words," but "things, things!"[21]

SOLVE *children's sensory problems, and prevent them in the first place, by acknowledging the role of daily experience in shaping the child's mind. Then act deliberately to ensure the child is developing into a healthy, thoughtful person.*

STEP FIVE: OVERCOME CYNICISM
THROUGH HOPE AND ACTION

As we hurry toward our own self-defined, uninterrupted worlds of simulated perfection, the problem remains of how we are going to cope in the meantime with the constraints and imperfections of the real world. So far the solution has been to label those as ill who cannot cope with the stresses of modern life. This is the tendency to interpret all psychosocial problems in a way that locates the source within the individual, forgetting that psychological problems are often the embodiment of social problems. As in our comparison between the syndrome of multiple chemical sensitivity (MCS) and the syndrome of ADD, the idea of linking the psychological crises of our time to larger, external causes has fallen out of the realm of common sense. MCS and ADD are psychiatric concerns, it is said, not cultural ones.

Even when there has been some appreciation of the fact that ADD is on the rise because of the hurried society, there has also been a tendency to treat it as normal. Just as George Beard praised "American nervousness" more than a century ago, suggesting it proved our status as the world's most modern nation, so increasing numbers today view sensory addictions and the problems they produce as acceptable side effects of our new postmodern existence in a global information age. When several hundred kids in Japan were hospitalized because of a visually toxic cartoon episode, for example, journalists and public officials (both in Japan and in the United States) placed the blame on the kids, saying they suffered from mild cases of epilepsy, triggered by the cartoon. When millions more children in the United States began bouncing off the walls with hyperactivity or could no longer pay attention, we once again blamed it on the children, saying their genes made them do it. It is true that some kids may be genetically more prone to epilepsy or hyperactivity than others, but it's certainly not the genes that are responsible for these outbreaks; rather, it's the toxicity of the changing environment with which children (and their genes) are having to cope.

When we try to understand our failure to grasp this societal crisis, the question arises of why the family is so quick to turn away from a cultural/developmental understanding and succumb to a cynical view about what can be done to improve the lives of children. Consider the example of the "myth" of quality time. With the economic prosperity of our nation, an outsider might think there should be an abundance of time and resources for children. Instead, we have lowered our standards to the point that we believe the best we can do for them is to give them fifteen minutes of focused attention after dinner. Clearly, much of this cynicism over "what is possible" has to do with the hurried society and its culture of neglect. It also is connected, however, to the larger sense of hopelessness that has trickled down from our society, into the family, and now into the world of the developing child. Psychologist Paul Goodman has described this in a 1977 essay entitled "The Psychology of Being Powerless": "People believe that the great background conditions of modern life are beyond our power to influence. The proliferation of technology is autonomous and cannot be checked. The galloping urbanization is going to gallop on. Our overcentralized administration, both of things and men, is impossibly cumbersome and costly, but we cannot cut it down to size. . . . *Our psychology, in brief, is that history is out of control.*"[22]

The notion that the future is out of control is among the ideas that have crept into our subconscious, undermining our capacity to live deliberately. We may still believe in economic and technological progress, but most of us feel as though our own future is both uncertain and out of our hands. Once hopelessness sets in, the prospect of working for a better life for ourselves and our children is replaced by a myopic sense of economic survival, of "hanging in there" or "just getting by." Under these conditions of perceived scarcity, not only do families turn their backs on their community, but even family members themselves begin to see a conflict of interest between one another. Nowhere is this hopelessness more clear than in the case of ADD and the Ritalin solution. Two decades ago there was outrage at the idea that massive numbers of children would be drugged indefinitely. The fact that today we can rationalize this individualized "solution" for as many as 10 percent of all kids shows just how diminished our standards have become. We have been compromised by our conflicting priorities, and we have rationalized our pseudosolutions for making our children's lives better, saying they are the best we can do. Although I could write here that we must *D.A.R.E.* to take our kids off Ritalin or keep them off it, the reality is that most families with children on Ritalin believe even with the drug, they are barely holding things together. Just consider how many exhausted parents out there are saying, to borrow a quote from *Time*, "it was going to be a very long day without the help of Ritalin."[23]

When we speak with groups and individuals about ADD, it is easy to see the consequences of this sense of hopelessness. For children, this has to do with the fact that they are not receiving the appropriate attention for their problems. Even if their parents refuse to have them on medication, they and their parents are still left alone to deal with the problems, since the assumption is that they are medical problems, not developmental or social ones. No wonder most parents in our hurried society turn to physicians for a way out. Of course physicians also deal with problems only on an individual basis, so they are in no better position to solve this problem than is the overworked parent who, losing hope, clings to the status quo.

For adults diagnosed with ADD, the picture is equally complex. For example, students at my college sometimes come to me with serious questions and concerns about the dreadful prospect of a life of ADD and Ritalin. Fortunately they resist the idea that their problems can be treated but not solved. Still, even in adults, hopelessness has clearly affected their lives, as can be seen in the relief they feel when they receive the diagnosis of ADD. I hear statements like "Being diagnosed with ADD gave me my life back" or "At last my problem has a name and it's not my fault."[24] At first this kind of thinking struck me as bizarre, and not just because they saw ADD as an explanation (rather than a description) of their psychological problems. I wondered why anyone would be relieved to be diagnosed with what they view as a neurological disorder. But then I realized that much of this has to do with their own sense of isolation in our individualistic society. With everyone having to make it on his or her own, people often feel a tremendous relief when they lose responsibility for their problems—or their children's problems. In the case of ADD, they look to a medical disorder and a medical quick fix to take up the burden of what we as a society have defined as "their" or "their children's" problems.

Today this tendency to treat life as an illness and childhood as a disease may be the single greatest obstacle in overcoming the psychological problems associated with ADD. Think of the thousands of kids who just can't sit still, who fidget when they are at their best and disrupt everything around them when they are at their worst. Or consider the growing number of stories about kids who seem unable to lock their attention on the matter at hand, whose attention seems somehow trapped in a fog between them and reality. We look upon these children and feel as though we have a clear, intuitive understanding of how the ADD disorder lurks inside them, undermining their sincere desire to be good. But this intuition is wrong. As in the example above of the young children learning to speak English, it would be a very distorted perception indeed to attribute their different speaking abilities to some innate capacity. In these children as well as in the ADD-diagnosed children, the developmental circumstances that gradually produce these differences may be subtle, but they do exist. Like the forces that carve out mountain walls and river beds, the forces that shape the child reveal the power of history, and these are the very forces we are overlooking in our rush to Ritalin.

This is no abstract matter. As long as we continue reducing the causes of children's difficulties to the individual level, we will continue searching only for individualized solutions to fix them. Whether it's Ritalin for ADD, Xanax for angst and anxiety, or Prozac for malaise and depression, there is overwhelming evidence that these prosthetic solutions are always going to fail in the end. They fail because they lead us to overlook the real causes of our problems and thus the possibility of building lasting solutions. As is often said, the devil's in the details, and so we must reject convenient excuses for why children cannot sit still or cannot pay attention and create a new, deliberate structure of living that will, over time, take them to, or return them to, a healthy state of mind.

The psychological consequences of the lack of structure in children's lives, the inconsistency of child care, and the habit of constant sensory consumption have not been well appreciated, as we have seen. The benefits that would come from reversing these trends also have not been appreciated. But we could discover these benefits ourselves if we increased the structure of the child's daily life by creating a slow, regular schedule that minimizes high-intensity, passive, artificial experiences. To ensure this restructuring, we need to return our highest priorities to parenting by spending "significant time" rather than "quality time" with our children. Parenting is about creating a social, moral, and emotional environment that encourages children to be thoughtful and deliberate in their ways. When they are not developing this way, it is the parents who must keep the developmental train on its tracks.

My earliest experience with this kind of deliberate structuring of a child's life came as an undergraduate, when I was serving for a summer as an educational aide for an autistic child. Relying on books and published articles, the mother of the child first developed her own ideas about what was possible. She then sought out the resources to make sure what was possible in the abstract was in fact possible for him. Finally, she used these resources to create a world that was not overwhelming for her child but that nevertheless encouraged him to grow. It was in this third stage that I came along, unsuspectingly. I had little experience working with autistic children, but I was nevertheless quickly absorbed into his daily life, encouraged as I was by the tireless efforts of his mother. This type of deliberate action I now know is common in the lives of developmentally disabled children. There is also, I think, a lot these parents could teach us about how to bring children diagnosed with ADD back to normal, healthy lives.

Not surprisingly, when discussing with parents and teachers the issue of solving rather than accepting a child's "disability," I have often found the realm of possibilities imagined to be narrow. More important, the frame of reference for these problems is also narrow, since parents, teachers, administrators, and physicians have been encouraged to believe that the structure of the child's life is not related to these problems. For example, parents often seem willing to consider only options that fall within the current structure of their hectic lives. There is a very concrete reason for this narrowness, however, which has to do with the fact that the question "What should I do?" can be answered on two different levels.

On the one hand, within the contingencies of my hectic day-to-day life, it may be rational to have my child on Ritalin. First, he acts better and he gets into less trouble. Second, my child's school may have little tolerance for him when he's off Ritalin. Third, the compromise of Ritalin may seem to me much better than having to rearrange everyone's lives just to deal with "his" problems, especially if I have no faith that this "rearranging" will do any good. Finally, it may be that the Ritalin solution is encouraged in my life by the contingencies of the pharmaceutical-medical establishment since the diagnosis and treatment of ADD are defined medically and thus are likely to be covered by my medical insurance.

On the other hand, if we want our children really to overcome their problems, then the ADD-Ritalin approach is not at all rational. Given that Ritalin does not in fact promote well-being or academic performance in the long run, there is the looming question of why we consider it anything more than a stopgap measure. But because Ritalin and the ADD diagnosis have been packaged together as a medical success story, they make it harder for us to see the need to take direct action in restructuring the way we and our children live.

Some of these solutions are suggested in studies we have examined above, that look directly at the evolution of hyperactivity and inattention. We saw how infants in certain types of "overstimulating" households grow up to be distractible, hyperactive kids. We saw how children diagnosed with ADD (and their parents) tend to watch more television than do other children, including those with other developmental problems. We saw how children learn the slow-paced or fast-paced problem-solving styles of their first-grader teachers.[25] We saw how nondrug "treatment" approaches in the classroom could produce markedly lower levels of hyperactivity while encouraging high academic performance.[26] We also saw how children's levels of hyperactivity (and brain states) can change as a function of the chronic environmental conditions in which they live. Studies such as these make it clear that changing the nature of childhood will indeed have powerful psychological effects.

These examples also suggest the various locations in which changes can and need to be made. The emphasis here has been on making changes in the hurried life of the family, with its lack of structure and its absorption into passive entertainment, but this does not mean that activities at school and with peers are not also significant. Indeed, because it's the cumulative interaction of these factors that ultimately determines the course of child development, parents must be involved in a deliberate way in all these realms.

SOLVING *and preventing sensory addictions lie primarily in deliberately slowing down the pace of children's lives. Gradually decrease the intensity of their everyday experiences by taking the time to teach them new interests and modes of being engaged in the world. This takes time, so make time by cutting back on the demands made on your own adult life.*

CONCLUSION: LIVING DELIBERATELY MEANS LOCATING ONE'S PLACE IN HISTORY

LET us conclude with some remarks about life in the hurried society. Because I know the ideas presented here are controversial, since they call into question a widespread practice in mainstream society, I feel it's necessary to restate something I note in the Preface. I did not write this book because I have an agenda beyond the message itself. The goal was to provide the public with a broader, scientifically based account of what is going on in the minds and lives of children. In reading this, you have been bombarded with facts and theories from a variety of disciplines, including history, psychology, neuroscience, genetics, sociology, biology, philosophy, geography, and anthropology. The meaning of these facts and theories can be understood, however, only within the context of a third realm, which is your own lived experience. As I often suggest to my students, think about what you have heard and read, and apply it with an open mind to your own personal experiences; be skeptical of what you hear and see that tells you to reject your own experience of what is right and wrong. Of course the danger here lies in the possibility that we will confuse our own experiences with what we have been led to believe from other sources of influence, such as the mass media or professional organizations. As in the case of my students, sometimes we are too quick to accept or reject an idea on the basis of what else we have been told, rather than take the time to reflect on the relationship between new ideas and our own firsthand experiences.

The following letter to the editor exchange, taken from the ADD advocacy magazine *Attention!*, illustrates just how crucial the need has become for parents to question the gentle persuasion they receive about what is best for their children:

> I am a fourteen-year-old girl who needs some advice. My mother is a member of CH.A.D.D. because both of my older brothers who are fifteen and seventeen have ADD. I have read your column in the newsletter and hope you can give me some advice. I don't think my mother notices the trouble I am having because she's so busy with all the stunts my brothers are always pulling. They aren't such bad guys but they are always in trouble cutting up in school or climbing the town water tower. At home they are a disaster wrestling for fun and they have even broken furniture. They call me the "baby" and tease some but aren't too bad. What is my trouble is that I think I'm getting ADD too. I'm not anything like my brothers, but I have a lot of trouble getting my work done for school and take longer to finish tests than other kids in my classes. Now that I am in high school, I have noticed that the problem is worse. I tried to talk to the school counselor, but she just said that it's because I have such a disorganized home but I don't think so because I'm used to that. Math has always been very hard for me and this year freshman algebra is really tough. No one seems to care. What should I do?

To this the editor replies:

> Girls with ADD often do not have the behavioral problems that your brothers show, but mainly have the kinds of trouble you describe with getting things done and staying organized. Since ADD is an inherited disorder, the fact that your brothers have ADD increases the likelihood that you may also have ADD. For

many people, ADD doesn't get in the way of their life until they get to middle or high school when teachers demand more effort, organization, and sustained concentration; this might explain why you are now noticing your difficulties. As you have correctly noted, it is easy for your family to overlook your situation when your brothers are such troublemakers. It is also easy for people like your counselor to explain away your problems by saying that they are the result of a chaotic environment. People can have chaotic environments and also have ADD. . . .

The point here is not that this young teenager has no problems but rather that they should be interpreted as part of the unfolding drama of her life. After all, this is not an ordinary life. This girl and millions like her were born at a unique time and in a unique place, and the drama of her life cannot be grasped outside this historical context. Modern American life is highly unstructured, stressful, indulgent, conflicted, and frenetic, and this experience leaves many children bewildered about themselves, the world, and the future that confronts them. In the 1992 edition of Dr. Spock's highly influential *Baby and Child Care* one finds an explicit warning about this culture of neglect.[27] In the section "Raising Children in a Troubled Society," we read, "American society in the 1990s is extraordinarily stressful. Normal family tensions are heightened in many ways: Our society is excessively competitive and materialistic; many working parents find less satisfaction and pleasure at their jobs while the good day care they depend on becomes harder to find; there is less spiritual and moral direction compared to the past; the traditional supports of the extended family and community are breaking up; and a growing number of people are concerned about the deterioration of the environment and international relations."

By ignoring the "troubled society" in which this girl's development is unfolding, and by treating her life as an illness instead, we are removing her from the greatest possible source of well-being— that is, her own capacity for self-understanding. Without this, she will not succeed in drawing the connections between the life she lives and how it impacts on her and those around her. Moreover, if she fails as an agent of change in her own life, how can we expect her, and millions of kids like her, to be positive agents of change in the world in which we all must live? In the end parents should not be demanding that their kids to be treated as legitimately disabled. No one should have to accept such low standards that he or she ends up fighting for the right to remain ill. Instead, we should be fighting for a world that is no longer so toxic that millions of kids will become psychologically sick just because they happen to live in it.

Notes

CHAPTER ONE. THE HURRIED SOCIETY AND ITS EXPERIENCE

1. January–February 1991. The *Utne Reader* followed up this issue with a similar one (March–April 1997) with the cover title "Slow down: Finding your natural rhythm in a speed-crazed world."
2. M. Kundera (1996). *Slowness*. New York: HarperCollins.
3. B. Russell (October 1932). In Praise of Idleness. *Harper's*; 49.
4. Other psychostimulants in use for ADD include Dexedrine and Cylert.
5. The following was taken from CH.A.D.D.'s mission statement at its Web site (March 1998): "Today, children and adults with ADD have CH.A.D.D., the national organization with over 32,000 members and more than 500 chapters nationwide, to provide that support and information. Thanks in large part to the efforts of CH.A.D.D., ADD is now recognized as a treatable, yet potentially serious disorder, that affects up to 2.6 million school-aged children between the ages of 5 and 18, and an estimated 2–5 million adults. Today, children with ADD can receive special education services or accommodations within the regular classroom when needed, and adults with ADD may be eligible for accommodations within the regular workplace under the Americans with Disabilities Act of 1990 guidelines issued by the Equal Employment Opportunity Commission in 1997.

CH.A.D.D. is a success story, inspired by the desire of countless parents to see their children with ADD succeed. From one parent support group in Florida, the organization grew dramatically from year to year to its present status as the leading non-profit national organization for children and adults with ADD. CH.A.D.D.'s first annual conference in 1989 attracted 300 attendees. The fourth annual conference, held in Chicago in 1992, drew over 2,500 people."

6. (September 22, 1996). From What Teachers Check For. *Wisconsin State Journal*; 4G.

7. E. M. Hallowell (May–June 1997). What I've Learned from ADD. *Psychology Today*; 41–44.

8. James Gleick writes in the *New York Times Magazine*, "No matter how fast a movie goes these days—or a situation comedy, newscast, a music video or a television commercial—it is not fast enough. Vehicles race, plunge and fly faster; cameras pan and shake faster, and scenes cut faster from one shot to the next. Some people don't like this." J. Gleick (September 28, 1997). Technology Makes Us Faster; Addicted to Speed. *New York Times Magazine*; 54.

9. (January–February 1996). Social Science and the Citizen. *Society*; Vol. 33, 2.

10. D. Elkind (1981, 1988). *The Hurried Child: Growing Up Too Fast Too Soon*. Reading, Mass: Addison-Wesley Publishing Company; 3.

11. J. M. Healy (1990). *Endangered Minds: Why Our Children Don't Think*. New York: Simon & Schuster; 171.

12. R. Sweet (November 19, 1997). News Quirks. *Seven Days* (a weekly newspaper in Burlington, Vermont).

13. R. McIlwraith, R. S. Jacobvitz, R. Kubey, and A. Alexander (1991). Television Addiction. *American Behavioral Scientist*, Vol. 35; 104-21.

14. The ball must be thrown within twelve seconds after the batter enters the batter's box, which is a change from an older, unenforced rule of throwing within twenty seconds. The problem is not just that people demand a faster pace for America's pastime, but that they also are too busy to spend four hours watching a game on television or at the ballpark. See, for example, J. Falls (March 19, 1998). Baseball's 12-Second Rule Not Enough to Speed Up Game. *Detroit News*; F1.

15. My thanks go to Mark Nelson for this example.

16. R. G. Jacob, K. D. O'Leary, and C. Rosenblad (1978). Formal and Informal Classroom Settings: Effects on Hyperactivity. *Journal of Abnormal Child Psychology*, Vol. 6, 47–59.

17. R. L. Spitzer, M. Gibbon, A. E. Skodol, J. B. W. Williams, and M. C. First (eds.) (1989). Into Everything. *DSM III-R Case Book*. Washington, D.C.: APA Books; 315–16. I chose to use this particular case study because it also suggests the new "strains" of behaviors that teachers are having to cope with today in their classrooms.

18. While there are any number of reasons why a child might be acting out in class, including attention-seeking behaviors that result from emotional problems and problems of self-esteem, a classic sign of sensory addictions is those behaviors, such as fidgeting and restlessness, that occur independent of social reinforcement.

19. D. Ackerman (1990). *A Natural History of the Senses*. New York: Random House; 304–05.

20. In *Amusing Ourselves to Death*, Neil Postman gives some striking examples of the changes that have taken place in people's attention spans during American history. Describing the famous (and lengthy!) debates between Abraham Lincoln and Stephen A. Douglas in 1858, he writes, "Is there any audience of Americans today who could endure seven hours of talk? or five? or three? Especially without pictures of any kind? Second, these audiences must have had an equally extraordinary capacity to comprehend lengthy and complex sentences aurally. In Douglas' Ottowa speech he included in his one-hour address three long, legally phrased resolutions of the Abolition platform. Lincoln, in his reply, read even longer passages from a published speech he had delivered on a previous occasion." N. Postman (1985). *Amusing Ourselves to Death: Public Discourse in the Age of Show Business*. New York: Penguin; 45–46.

21. R. M. Yando and J. Kagan (1968). The Effects of Teacher Tempo on the Child. *Child Development*; Vol 39; 27–34.

22. E. A. Carlson, D. Jacobvitz, and L. A. Sroufe (1995). A Developmental Investigation of Inattentiveness and Hyperactivity, *Child Development*; Vol. 66, 37–54; 42.

23. Ibid.

24. American Psychiatric Association (1994). *Diagnostic and Statistical Manual of Mental Disorders*, 4th ed. Washington D. C.: American Psychiatric Association.

25. The best evidence of this bias is the fact that a few poorly conducted studies with marginal results have been taken as proof that ADD is biological and innate (see Chapter 4), while dozens of studies (and reviews of studies) concluding that its treatment with Ritalin has few or no long-term positive effects have led to the mere conclusion that "it is not clear whether they produce long-term benefits" (see Chapter 5). In other words, the standing assumption is that ADD is biological until proved otherwise, but it's doubtful that any amount of evidence will be capable of disproving otherwise. The quote is from T. F. Oltmanns and R. E. Emery (1998). *Abnormal Psychology*, 2d ed. Upper Saddle River, N.J.: Prentice-Hall; 602.

26. I. J. Knopf (1979). *Child Psychopathology: A Developmental Approach*. Englewood Cliffs, N.J.: Prentice Hall.

27. A. Geggis (January 24, 1997). Reading, Writing and Ritalin. *Burlington Free Press*; 1A, 4A. Armondo Vilaseca, a principal in a Vermont high school, was a grade school teacher for ten years.

28. T. Achenbach and C. Howell (1989). Are American Children's Problems Getting Worse? A 13-year Comparison. *Journal of American*

Academy of Child and Adolescent Psychiatry, Vol. 32, 1145–51.

29. L. Shapiro (May 12, 1997). The Myth of Quality Time. *Newsweek*; 62–68.
30. M. Rutter (1978) Diagnostic Vaildity in Child Psychiatry. *Advances in Biological Psychiatry*, Vol. 12, 2–22; 3.
31. G. Bignami (1982). Disease Models and Reductionist Thinking in the Bio-medical Sciences. In S. Rose (ed.). *Against Biological Determinism*, 94–110. London. Allison & Busby. See also A. Pam, (1990). A Critique of the Scientific Status of Biological Psychiatry. *Acta Psychiatrica Scandinavica, Supplemental*, Vol. 362, 1–35.
32. Pam. op.cit.
33. C. VanDyke and R. Byck (March 1982). Cocaine. *Scientific American*; 128–141.
34. D. Blankenhorn, S. Bayme, and J. B. Elshtain (1991). Discovering What Families Do. *Rebuilding the Nest: A New Commitment to the American Family*. Milwaukee: Family Services; 35.
35. D. Elkind (1994). *Ties That Stress: The New Family Imbalance*. Cambridge: Harvard University Press.
36. Ibid. 1.
37. Blankenhorn et al., op.cit.; xiv.
38. Elkind, op.cit.; 4.
39. Shapiro, op.cit.; 64.
40. J. Schor (1991). *The Overworked American: The Unexpected Decline of Leisure*. New York: Basic Books; 165.
41. Elkind, op.cit.; 40.
42. Shapiro, op.cit.
43. Ibid.
44. Healy, op.cit.; 172.

CHAPTER TWO. GREAT MISADVENTURES IN TIME

1. An important difference between the alternative view and the nature/nurture approach is the fact that the newer view breaks from the traditional quest for certainty and the search for absolute knowledge. The nature/nurture approach has been very much the stuff of encyclopedic science, in which nothing less than complete knowledge is acceptable. By contrast, the alternative approach represents a search for a broader understanding that flows with the intricacies, uncertainties, and dynamics that characterize the history of life on earth, from dinosaurs to people. This is not a quest for certainty but rather an attempt to appreciate the full complexity of life, without reducing it to parts that don't add up to make the whole that we see around us. This is a choice between the dialectical over the dichotomous. As evolu-

tionary biologists have taught us, the products of nature have a contingent quality that makes their full understanding practically impossible. As Darwin knew all too well, any attempt to trace the origins of what nature and history combine to produce is apt to be a bewildering experience, which is just as applicable to the evolution of species as it is to the psychosocial evolution of a human being.

2. J. M. Nash (February 3, 1997). Fertile Minds. *Time*; 49.

3. G. M. Edelman (1992). *Bright Air, Brilliant Fire*. New York: Basic Books; 65.

4. R. J. Cadoret, E. Troughton, L. M. Merchant, and A. Whitters (1990). Early Life Psychosocial Events and Adults Affective Symptoms. In L. Robins and M. Rutter (eds.). *Straight and Devious Pathways from Childhood to Adulthood*; 300–13. Cambridge, U.K.: Cambridge University Press. Note that interactions can also be negative, where two or more variables have less than an additive effect when combined. Whether the interaction is negative or positive, however, the variability associated with the interaction is partitioned out as separate from the variability associated with each independent variable.

5. C. Geertz (1973). The Impact of the Concept of Culture on the Concept of Man. In *The Interpretation of Cultures* (33–54). New York: Basic Books; 49.

6. See Edelman, op.cit.

7. Just as an either/or approach to understanding Ritalin Nation will do us little good, we also want to stay clear of a related problem, the "naturalistic fallacy." This term, taken from the philosophy of science, refers to the temptation to see the way things are as the way they must be. Black slaves were viewed as intellectually inferior because they couldn't read; women were viewed as suited only for homemaking because they worked at home. The naturalistic fallacy can also be seen in the way American doctors understand and treat hyperactivity and inattention as incurable medical diseases. Because the symptoms of ADD do not easily disappear (something that was actually less true in the 1970s and 1980s), we assume that they cannot. Thus ADD becomes identified as a biological problem in need of a biomedical solution. Confusing historical facts for natural ones can cause us to overlook the unique historical forces that, hiding behind the mask of time, shape us and the world in which we live.

8. M. Nemethy (February 1997). Attention Deficit/Hyperactivity Disorder. *ADVANCE for Nurse Practitioners*; 22–29.

9. This is described well in J. W. McKearney (Autumn 1977). Asking Questions About Behavior. *Perspectives in Biology and Medicine*; 109–18.

10. R. Plomin (1990). The Role of Inheritance in Behavior. *Science*, Vol. 248; 183–88. Psychiatrist Alvin Pam has shown as recently as 1990 that the scientific basis for claiming that schizophrenia or alcoholism is genetic remains tenuous. A. Pam (1990). A Critique of the Scientific Status of Psychiatry. *Acta Psychiatrica Scandinavica*, Supplementum, 362; 1–35.

11. T. G. Wilson, K. D. O'Leary, and P. Nathan (1992). *Abnormal Psychology*. Englewood Cliffs, N.J.: Prentice Hall; 305.

12. This is a recessive condition rather than a dominant condition, the latter of which requires a copy from only one parent; the influence of genes on behavior is neither dominant nor recessive because the effect is a composite of multiple genes rather than just one. That is, multiple genes combine with life experiences (including diet and injury) to produce effects. In regard to malaria, some estimate that it has been the leading cause of death in the history of human existence; see G. Taubes (March 1998). Malarial Dreams. *Discover*; 108.

13. For this example and others like it, see R. Hubbard and E. Wald (1993). *Exploding the Gene Myth*. Boston: Beacon Press; 24.

14. A. I. Gurevich (1985). *Categories of Medieval Culture*. London: Routledge and Kegan Paul; 94.

15. J. Tierney (July 20, 1997). Some Like It Fast. *New York Times Magazine*; 16.

16. Theorists and historians have investigated this in detail. What I'm referring to is the need to bring this scholarship into public view, which requires some added clarification and simplification.

17. Quote taken from J. A. Wheeler (1990). *A Journey into Gravity and Spacetime*. New York: Scientific American Library; 3.

18. M. Ende (1985). *Momo*. Garden City, N.Y.: Doubleday & Co.; 47

19. D. Harvey (1996). *Justice, Nature and the Geography of Difference*. Oxford: Blackwell; 212.

20. Quote is from Oswald Spengler.

21. Gurevich, op.cit., 147.

22. G. M. Beard (1881). *American Nervousness*. New York; 103.

23. J. Rifkin (1987). *Time Wars*. New York: Henry Holt; 55.

24. While for Einstein's general theory of relativity there are as many "times" as there are bodies in motion, for us earthlings there are about as many times as there are distinct historical periods. As Oswald Spengler writes in *The Decline of the West*, "For primitive man time can have no meaning. All of us are conscious as being "aware" of space only, and not of time. Time is a discovery which is only made by thinking. We create it as an idea and do not begin till much later to suspect that we ourselves are Time, inasmuch as we live." Spengler, op.cit., 77.

25. G. Basalla (1988). *The Evolution of Technology*. Cambridge, U. K.: Cambridge University Press; 8.
26. Ibid.
27. Gurevich op.cit., 148–49.
28. For this and similar examples, see Chapter 3 in Rifkin, op.cit.
29. There are other examples of what can happen without a sense of external time. In some nonindustrialized nations, for instance, the number of days that make up a week can vary across cultures, lasting from as few as three days to ten days. Even the objective length of an hour has been found in certain places to vary throughout the day, with daytime hours treated as longer or shorter than nighttime hours, depending upon the season. As suggested by the subtitle of Robert Levine's 1997 book *The Geography of Time: How Every Culture Keeps Time Just a Little Bit Differently* (New York: Basic Books), the march toward a universal, objective time has been both slow and uneven.
30. Taken from J. Walljasper (March–April 1997). The Speed Trap. *Utne Reader*; 41–7.
31. S. Kern (1983). *The Culture of Time and Space; 1880–1918*. Cambridge, Mass.: Harvard University Press; 15.
32. Quote taken from Gurevich, op.cit., 148–49, 121.
33. Among other problems resulting from our future-directed consciousness is the rise of insomnia, in which obsessing about the impending future is a significant factor in keeping us awake. A Canadian article suggests, for example, that each of us wastes, on average, about five hundred more hours per year trying to fall asleep today than we did fifty years ago. L. Gendron (April 15, 1997). Les Secrets du Sommeil. *L'Actualité*; 16–25.
34. This quote and a more general discussion of this can be found in S. Pinker (1997). *How the Mind Works*. New York: Norton; 392.
35. J. Whitelegg (July–August 1993). Time Pollution. *The Ecologist*, Vol. 4; 131–34; quote is from Ende op.cit. 47.
36. J. Gélis (1989). The Child: From Anonymity to Individuality. In R. Chartier (ed.). *A History of Private Life*, Vol. 3, *Passions of the Renaissance*, 309–26. Cambridge, Mass.: Belknap Press of Harvard University Press.
37. R. Wright (August 1995). The Evolution of Despair. *Time*; 50–57.
38. C. Geertz (1983). "From the Native's Point of View": On the Nature of Anthropological Understanding. In *Local Knowledge* (55–70). New York: Basic Books; 59.
39. Gurevich, op.cit. The only example that strikes me as similar today is the drive-in theater, where the show begins at "dusk."
40. Harvey op. cit, 214. The quote at the end is from Gurevich, op.cit.,

29. Ideas of salvation, which then promoted a greater sense of linear time, actually go back centuries to the Judaic conception of time, which, interestingly enough, was itself a break from Greek and Eastern notions of cyclical time.

41. The rise of modernity was of course gradual, varying dramatically across the regions and countries of Europe. In twelfth century France, for example, there were already clear signs of change, which included new ideas or attitudes toward money, private ownership, earned income, entrepreneurial activities, and migrations to larger, more urban areas. See G. Duby (1988). Solitude: Eleventh to Thirteenth Century. In G. Duby (ed.). A History of Private Life, Vol. 2, Revelations of the Medieval World, 509–34. Cambridge, Mass.: Belknap Press of Harvard University Press.

42. M. Berman (1988). All That Is Solid Melts into Air: The Experience of Modernity. New York: Penguin Books; 15.

43. Kern, op.cit., 94.

44. J. Lukacs (1970). The Passing of the Modern Age. New York: Harper & Row.

45. M. Kundera (1992). Immortality. New York: HarperPerennial; 76.

46. P. R. Saunders (1981). Social Theory and the Urban Question. New York: Holmes & Meier Publishers; 87.

47. An interesting example of the new self-awareness of modernity was the rise of the autobiography: "Some writers have held that truly unfettered autobiography did not exist until the modern age, when, they say, a new mode of self-narration was invented and autobiography finally distinguished itself from history and apologetics. Man, discovering himself at the center of the universe, between two infinities, exulted to find that God had given him the faculty to develop his potential; autobiography proclaimed the individuality of destiny." Quote from P. Braunstein (1988). Toward Intimacy: The Fourteenth and Fifteenth Centuries. In G. Duby (ed.). A History of Private Life, Vol. 2: Revelations of the Medieval World 535–630. Cambridge, Mass.: Belknap Press of Harvard University Press. 540.

48. L. C. Simpson (1995). Technology, Time and the Conversations of Modernity. New York: Routledge; 50.

49. N. Postman (1993). Technopoly. New York: Vintage; 45.

50. H. Nowotny (1994). Time: The Modern and Postmodern Experience. Cambridge, U.K.: Polity Press; 26.

51. E. F. Schumacher (1973). Small Is Beautiful. New York: Harper & Row.

52. A. Toffler (1971). Future Shock. New York: Bantam; 39–40.

CHAPTER THREE. SPEED AND ITS TRANS-FORMATION OF HUMAN CONSCIOUSNESS

1. G. Eliot (1907). *Felix Holt, the Radical.* Boston and New York: Hougton Mifflin and Company; 2.
2. N. Oxenhandler (June 6, 1997). Fall from Grace: How Modern Life Has Made Waiting a Desperate Act. *The New Yorker,* 65–78; here 66.
3. As Neil Postman makes clear in *Amusing Ourselves to Death,* this has much to do with the technological transformations that have taken place in human culture and human affairs:

   To be unaware that a technology comes equipped with a program for social change, to maintain that technology is neutral, to make the assumption that technology is always a friend to culture is, at this late hour, stupidity plain and simple. Moreover, we have seen enough by now to know that technological changes in our modes of communication are even more ideology-laden than changes in our modes or transportation. Introduce the alphabet to a culture and you change its cognitive habits, its social relations, its notion of community, history and religion. Introduce the printing press with movable type, and you do the same. Introduce speed-of-light transmission of images and you make a cultural revolution.

   N. Postman (1985). *Amusing Ourselves to Death: Public Discourse in the Age of Show Business.* New York: Penguin; 157.
4. K. J. Gergen (1996). Technology and the Self: From the Essential to the Sublime. In D. Grodin and T. R. Lindoff (eds.). *Constructing the Self in a Mediated World,* 127–140. Thousand Oaks, Calif.: Sage Publishing; 131–32.
5. J. M. Sbert. (1992). Progress. In *The Development Dictionary* (192–205). London: Zed Books; 192, 195.
6. In *Technopoly,* Neil Postman links the American obsession with progress to a love of technology, asking:

   Why did Technopoly—the submission of all forms of cultural life to the sovereignty of technique and technology—find fertile ground on American soil? . . . The first [reason] concerns what is usually called the American character, the relevant aspect of which Tocqueville described in the early nineteenth century. "The American lives in a land of wonder," he wrote; "every movement seems an advance. Consequently, in his mind the idea of newness is closely linked with that of improvement. Nowhere does he see any limit placed by nature to human endeavor; in his eyes something that does not exist is just something that has not been tried." . . . Second, and inexorably related to the first, is the genius and audacity of American capitalists, men who were quicker and more focused than those of other nations in exploiting the economic possibilities of new technologies. . . . Third, the success of twentieth-century technology in providing Americans with convenience, comfort, speed, hygiene, and abundance was so obvious and promising that there seemed no reason to look for any other sources of fulfillment or creativity or purpose. To every Old World belief, habit, or tradition, there was and still is a technological alternative.

N. Postman (1993). *Technopoly*. New York: Vintage; 52–54. The quote is from A. de Tocqueville (1969). *Democracy in America*. New York: Anchor Books.

7. R. Dowthwaite (1993). *The Growth Illusion*. Tulsa: Council Oak Books.

8. S. Kern (1983). *The Culture of Time and Space: 1880–1918*. Cambridge, Mass.: Harvard University Press; 1–2.

9. For a look at how the *Titanic* disaster has been interpreted socially and morally over the years, see S. Biel (1996). *A Cultural History of the Titanic Disaster*. New York: Norton.

10. W. Lord (1986). *The Night Lives On*. New York: William Morrow and Co.; 65–66.

11. Ibid.

12. Ibid.

13. Similar stories have surfaced with regard to commercial aviation. For example, the Valujet crash into the Florida Everglades on May 11, 1996, was as similarly horrifying a spectacle as the *Titanic*, and it too was found to be directly linked to the priority of speed. As was noted in a *USA Today* article titled "Valujet Probe: Workers Were Rushed" (November 19, 1996), the plane's downfall was the result of two oversights, both of which were tracked to employees' rushing.

14. D. Abram (1996). *The Spell of the Sensuous*. New York: Vintage; 40.

15. A. J. Palmer (1956). *Riding High: The Story of the Bicycle*. New York: E. P. Dutton & Co.

16. Quote is from L. Bertz (1931). *Das Volkauto: Rettung oder Untergang der deutschen Automobilindustrie*. Stuttgart. Cited in W. Sachs (1992). *For Love of the Automobile*. Berkeley: University of California Press; 103.

17. Sachs, Ibid.

18. Kern op.cit., 110.

19. P. Adam (1907). *La Morale des sports*. Paris: La Librarie mondiale; 449–50. Cited in Kern, op.cit., 110. In full, Adam writes, *"Exalté par le cycle, le culte de la vitesse et du voyage décupla, moins du voyage que de la vitesse. On voulut vaincre l'espace et le temps."*

20. Sachs, op.cit., 106. In terms of the automobile and its connection to individualism, the automobile, cinema, and telephone illustrate how technology allowed for a more immediate and thus impulsive lifestyle, where the whim to transport oneself to a different place and time could now be satisfied with ease. In the case of the automobile, Sachs writes, "Automobiles promised the old independence of self-propelled vehicles, to help individual authority regain its own, for they offered emancipation from the inconveniences of the railway; the regimentation of the timetable, the compulsion of the unwavering rails, and—not least—the perspiration of the crowd"; 94.
21. Kern, op.cit., 113.
22. Ibid., 129.
23. Sachs, op.cit., vii–viii.
24. J. Baudrillard (1968). *Le Système des objets*. Paris: Gallimard; 4; cited in K. Ross (1995). *Fast Cars, Clean Bodies*. Cambridge, Mass.: MIT Press; 21.
25. E. Panofsky (1970). Style and Medium in the Motion Pictures. In D. Talbot (ed.). *Film: An Anthology*. Berkeley: University of California Press; 15.
26. M. Quigley, Jr. (1948). *Magic Shows: The Story of the Origin of Motion Pictures*. Washington, D.C.: Georgetown University Press.
27. Cited ibid., 36.
28. If the real Bill Miner did in fact see a motion picture just after his release, as this movie suggests, it wasn't Edwin S. Porter's *The Great Train Robbery*, for it came out in 1903, two years after Miner's release.
29. A. B. Carson (September 19, 1928), cited in R. Marchand (1985). *Advertising and the American Dream*. Berkeley: University of California Press; 3.
30. A. Kleinman and A. Cohen (March 1997). Psychiatry's Global Challenge. *Scientific American*; 86–89.
31. F. T. Marinetti (May 11, 1916). The New Religion-Morality of Speed. Published in the *First Number of L'Italia Futurista*. Reprinted in R. W. Flint (1972). *Marinetti: Selected Writings*. New York: Farrar, Straus and Giroux.
32. This is not as absurd as it may sound. For example, the late Terry Sanford, when governor of North Carolina from 1960 to 1964, employed a novelist to aid him in his development of new social and educational programs.
33. C. E. Ayres in the 1962 foreword to his 1944 book *The Theory of Economic Progress* gives an example of the assumptions common in the West regarding progress:

   Since the technological revolution is itself irresistible, the arbitrary authority and irrational values of pre-scientific, pre-industrial cultures are doomed. Three alternatives confront the partisans of tribal values and beliefs. Resistance, if sufficiently effective, though it cannot save the tribal values, can bring on total revolution. Or ineffective resistance may lead to sequestration like that of the American Indians. The only remaining alternative is that of intelligent, voluntary acceptance of the industrial way of life and the values that go with it.

We need make no apology for recommending such a course. Industrial society is the most successful way of life mankind has ever known. Not only do our people eat better, sleep better, live in more comfortable dwellings, get around more and in far greater comfort, and . . . live longer than men have ever done before. In addition to listening to radio and watching television, they read more books, see more pictures, and hear more music than any previous generation or any other people ever have. At the height of the technological revolution we are now living in a golden age of scientific enlightenment and artistic achievement.

For all who achieve economic development, profound cultural change is inevitable. But the rewards are considerable.

34. G. Wallas (1928). *The Great Society: A Psychological Analysis*. New York: Macmillan Company; ix; italics added.
35. Sbert op.cit., 197.
36. M. Csikszentmihalyi (1990). *Flow: The Psychology of Optimal Experience*. New York: HarperPerennial; 10.
37. Taken from T. Lutz (1991) *American Nervousnesss, 1903*. Ithaca: Cornell University Press; 3.
38. G. M. Beard (1881). *American Nervousness: Its Causes and Consequences*. New York: G. P. Putnam's Sons.
39. Taken from Kern, op.cit., 125.
40. First published in Germany in 1895, M. Nordau (1968). *Degeneration*. New York: Howard Fertig.
41. Lutz, op.cit., 6.
42. P. Cushman (1990). Why the Self Is Empty: Toward a Historically Situated Psychology. *American Psychologist*, Vol. 45, 599–611; 600.
43. For a general discussion of these matters, see R. Wright (August 28, 1995). The Evolution of Despair. *Time*; 50–57.
44. Csikszentmihalyi, op.cit.
45. Ibid., 10.
46. Ibid., 74.
47. R. Kubey and M. Csikszentmihalyi (1990). *Television and the Quality of Life*. Hillsdale, N.J.: Lawrence Erlbaum Associates, Publishers.
48. Quoted Ibid., p. 23.
49. Csikszentmihalyi op.cit., 83.

50. S. Zweig (1943). *The World of Yesterday.* New York: Viking Press; 26.
51. In the film *The Wonderful, Horrible Life of Leni Riefenstahl,* the ninety year-old German filmmaker recounts her experience living with two traditional African tribes. What most surprised her during this period was the high level of contentment—the optimal experience—that she experienced on a daily basis. Riefenstahl knew the tribal world would be primitive in a material sense, but she was nevertheless struck by how highly enriched their lives were socially and culturally. As José María Sbert points out, "Paradoxically, this unacknowledged faith, this false consciousness—often labeled materialistic or even hedonistic—flagrantly contradicts true attachment to the world. It is a desperate search for transcendence that, again and again, annihilates the world as it is and substitutes for any real sense of place, rhythm, duration and culture a world of abstractions, a nonworld—of homogeneous space, linear time, science and money." Sbert, op.cit., 192, 195.
52 This and the above accounts were taken from R. Sweet. New Quirks. *Seven Days* (Burlington, Vermont).
53. Kern, op.cit.,130.
54. A. Toffler (1971). *Future Shock.* New York: Bantam; 42.
55. R. A. Berkley, K. R. Murphy, and D. Kwasnik (1996). Motor Vehicles Driving Competencies and Risks In Teens and Young Adults with Attention Deficit Hyperactivity Disorder. *Pediatrics;* Vol. 98, 1089–95.

CHAPTER FOUR. SENSORY ADDICTIONS: HOW CULTURE MANUFACTURES DISEASE

1. Letter (April 1976). *American Journal of Psychiatry;* 457.
2. M. Fumento (June 1996). Sick of it All. *Reason,* 20–26.
3. J. Stossel and B. Walters (August 22, 1997). Allergic to the World. ABC News, 20/20.
4. Fumento, op.cit.
5. Ibid., p. 20.
6. See C. E. Sleeter (1986). Learning Disabilities: The Social Construction of a Special Education Category. *Exceptional Children;* Vol. 53, 46–54.
7. See T. Armstrong (February 1996). ADD: Does It Really Exist? *Phi Delta Kappa;* 424–28. R. Reid, J. W. Maag, and S. F. Vasa (1993). Attention Deficit Hyperactivity Disorder as a Disability Category: A Critique. *Exceptional Children,* Vol. 60, 198–214; L. A. Sroufe and M. A. Stewart (1973). Treating Problem Children with Stimulant Drugs. *New England Journal of Medicine,* Vol. 289, 407–412.
8. Fumento, op.cit., 21.
9. Quoted ibid.

10. E. Taylor (1989). On the Epidemiology of Hyperactivity. In *Attention Deficit Disorder: Clinical and Basic Research.* Hillsdale, N.J.: Lawrence Erlbaum Associates; 31–52, 31.

11. J. Stossel and B. Walters (August 22, 1997). Allergic to the World. ABC 20/20. Quote is from John Stossel.

12. J. Talan (January 21, 1997). Allergic to Everything. *Newsday.*

13. American Academy of Pediatrics (1994). Understanding the ADHD Child. Elk Grove Village, Ill.: American Academy of Pediatrics Division of Publications.

14. E. M. Hallowell and J. J. Ratey (1995). *Driven to Distraction.* New York: Pantheon; 41.

15. Cited in A. Kohn (1989). Suffer the Restless Children. *Atlantic Monthly*; 90.

16. The diagnosis can be based on the same evidence because of the use of videotapes, written descriptions, or simultaneous observation.

17. E. M. Mann et al. (1992). Cross-cultural differences in rating hyperactive-disruptive behaviors in children. *American Journal of Psychiatry*, Vol. 149, 1539–42; 1539.

18. Taylor, op.cit., 31–52.

19. Kohn, op.cit., 90–94.

20. B. Fish (1971). The "One Child, One Drug" Myth of Stimulants in Hyperkinesis. *Archives of General Psychiatry*, Vol. 25, 193–201.

21. Hallowell and Ratey, op.cit.

22. D. L. Rosenhan (1973). On Being Sane in Insane Places. *Science*, Vol. 179, 250–58.

23. S. Peele (1989). *The Diseasing of America.* Lexington, Mass.: Lexington Books.

24. For example, one of the most comprehensive assessments of changing rates of depression around the world found that although the rate of depression varied across cultures, there was nevertheless a measurable increase in the risk of depression from each generation to the next in all but one of the nations studied. Also, in the United States, according to psychiatric epdemiologist Myrna Weissman, Americans born before 1905 had only a 1 percent rate of depression by the age of seventy-five. For Americans born a half century later, 6 percent had become depressed by the age of twenty-four. Similarly, while the average age of onset for manic depression was thirty-two years in the mid-1960s, its average onset today is about nineteen. See Cross-National Collaborative Group (1992). The Changing Rate of Major Depression: Cross-national Comparision. *JAMA*, Vol. 21, 3098–3105; S. Peele and R. J. DeGrandpre (July–August 1995). My Genes Made Me Do It. *Psychology Today*; 50–53, 62, 64, 66, 68.

25. Fumento, op.cit., 22.

26. Ibid., 24.
27. Stossel and Walters, op.cit.
28. C. Horswell (June 9, 1997). Something in the Air. *Houston Chronicle.*
29. K. Tyson (1991). Childhood Hyperactivity. *Smith College Studies in Social Work*, Vol. 61, 133–60; 139.
30. See G. F. Still (April 1902). Some Abnormal Psychical Conditions in Children. *Lancet*, 1008–12, 1077–82, 1163–68; P. M. Levin (1957). Restlessness in Children. *Archives of Neurology and Psychiatry*, 764–70; M. W. Laufer, E. Denhoff, and G. Solomons (1957). Hyperkinetic Impulse Disorder in Children's Behavior Problems. *Psychosomatic Medicine*, Vol. 19, 38–49.
31. See Levin, op.cit., 769.
32. Tyson, op.cit.,139; 136.
33. Kohn, op.cit., 95–96.
34. The rising prevalence of adult ADD was described in D. J. Morrow (September 2, 1997). Attention Deficit Disorder Is Found in Growing Numbers of Adults. *New York Times*; D1, D4
35. American Academy of Pediatrics, op.cit.
36. Hallowell and Ratey, op.cit., 269.
37. Zametkin, op.cit.
38. Reid et al., op.cit.; Tyson, op.cit.
39. P. Elmer-De Witt (November 26, 1990). Why Junior Won't Sit Still. *Time*, 59. A. J. Zametkin et al. (1990). Cerebral Glucose Metabolism in Adults with Hyperactivity of Childhood Onset. *New England Journal of Medicine*, Vol. 323, 1361–66.
40. Each adult had both a history of hyperactivity and at least one hyperactive child. None of the adults had any history of treatment with psychostimulants.
41. As quoted in G. Kolata (November 15, 1990). Hyperactivity Is Linked to Brain Abnormality. *New York Times*; A1.
42. As is discussed in the main text, Zametkin and colleagues themselves have completed several follow-up studies, none of which suggested that the 1990 report was a valid one.
43. See R. Reid, J. W. Maag, and S. F. Vasa (1993). Attention Deficit Hyperactivity Disorder as a Disability Category: A Critique. *Exceptional Children*, Vol. 6, 198–214.
44. The same criticism applies to another popular study in the ADD literature by H. C. Lou and colleagues. This study reported anomalies in the cerebral blood flow in children with hyperactivity. H. Lou, L. Henriksen, P. Bruhn, H. Borner, and J. Nielsen (1989). Striatal Dysfunction in Attention Deficit and Hyperkinetic Disorder. Archives of Neurology, Vol. 46, 48–52. For these and other criticisms, see K.

Tyson (1991). Childhood Hyperactivity. *Smith College Studies in Social Work*, Vol. 61, 133–60; Reid et al, op.cit.

45. L. R. Baxter et al. (1992). Caudate Glucose Metabolic Rate Changes with Both Drug and Behavior Therapy for Obsessive-Compulsive Disorder. *Archives of General Psychiatry*, Vol. 49, 681–89.

46. In *Newsweek* (December 3, 1990), Zametkin is quoted as saying, "This shows this is not the result of bad parenting. . . .This is a medical problem." As far as evidence of a bias in the *New England Journal of Medicine*, it published another of Zametkin's studies (with D. Hauser) in 1993 showing a mere correlation between hyperactivity and a rare thyroid condition. The logic of this study was analogous to the idea that because some rare form of brain cancer produced headaches, perhaps all headaches should be treated as an illness. It is also worth noting that many of the researchers studying the neurobiology of ADD have persistently searched for biological evidence to advocate their fervent belief that ADD is innate; as was noted in a letter to the editor of the *Jupiter Courier* (August 17, 1997), "[Judith] Rapport received funding by the makers of Ritalin to conduct studies that would show a 'biological' component of 'ADD,' thus justifying drug 'treatment.' Zametkin's brain imaging studies, which have been criticized by a former NIMH psychiatrist, are used as 'proof' that the brains of 'ADD' children are different than 'normal' children. Although Rapport reported that one study showed 'clear differences,' she followed by saying that 'a radiologist would not read these scans as abnormal.'"

47. These studies are discussed in the main text.

48. This is also discussed in T. Armstrong (1995). *The Myth of the A.D.D. Child*. New York: Dutton.

49. Elmer-De Witt, op.cit.; Kolata, op.cit.; S. Squires (November 15, 1990). Brain Function Yields Physical Clue That Could Help Pinpoint Hyperactivity. *Washington Post*, A18; (December 3, 1990). A New View on Hyperactivity. *Newsweek*, 61A.

50. Hallowell and Ratey, op.cit., 71, 275.

51. A. J. Zametkin et al. (1991). Brain Metabolism in Teenagers with Attention-Deficit Disorder. *Archives of General Psychiatry*, Vol. 50, 333–40.

52. J. A. Matochik et al. (1994). Cerebral Glucose Metabolism in Adults with Attention Deficit Hyperactivity Disorder after Chronic Stimulant Treatment. *American Journal of Psychiatry*, Vol. 151, 658–64.

53. Tyson, op.cit.

54. C. Pert (November 5, 1997). Capitol Hill Hearing Testimony House. Appropriations, Labor, Health, and Human Services.

55. This fact becomes obvious when we realize that these specific con-

nections will be different in each child anyway; this can be seen, for instance, in the cloning of simple insects, where the same neural development looks considerably different, yet has the same behavioral function. See G. M. Edleman (1987). *Neural Darwinism: The Theory of Neuronal Group Selection.* New York: Basic Books; (1992) *Bright Air, Brilliant Fire: On the Matter of the Mind.* New York: Basic Books.

56. M. Coleman (1971). Serotonin Concentrations in Whole Blood of Hyperactive Children. *Journal of Pediatrics*, Vol. 78, 985–90.

57. These ideas are developed more fully in R. J. DeGrandpre (1996). The impact of socially constructed knowledge on drug policy. In W. Bickel and R. J. DeGrandpre, eds. *Drug Policy and Human Nature.* New York: Plenum.

58. J. M. Golding, R. Smith, Jr., and M. Kashner (1991). Does Somatization Disorder Occur in Men? *Archives of General Psychiatry*, Vol. 48, 231–35.

59. N. Angier (July 24, 1994). The Debilitating Malady Called Boyhood. *New York Times*; 1, 16.

60. As cited in G. Weiss et al. (1979). Hyperactive as Young Adults, *Archives of General Psychiatry*, Vol. 36, 675–81; here 675.

61. D. C. Howell and H. R. Huesy (1981). A 14-Year Follow-up of Hyperkinetic Behavior. In M. Gittelman, ed. *Strategic Interventions for Hyperactive Children.* Armonk, N.Y.: M. E. Sharp, Inc.

62. E. M. Hallowell (May–June,1997). What I've Learned from ADD. *Psychology Today*; 41.

63. J. L. Rapoport et al (1978). *Science*, Vol. 199, 560–63.

64. From J. Lang. (June 10, 1997). Did Great Minds Need Ritalin? *Rocky Mountain News*, 3A.

65. P. Schrag and D. Divoky (1975). *The Myth of the Hyperactive Child.* New York: Pantheon; xvii.

66. M. Nash (February 3, 1997). Fertile Minds. *Time*, 50–56; *Newsweek* (Spring–Summer, 1997). Special edition: Your child, (April 28, 1997). *I Am Your Child.* ABC.

67. S. Begley (Spring–Summer, 1997). How to Build a Baby's Brain. *Newsweek*, 28–32; 28.

68. Edelman, *Bright Air, Brilliant Fire*, loc.cit.

69. S. J. Ceci (1990). *On Intelligence . . . More or Less.* Englewood Cliffs, N.J.: Prentice Hall; 12.

70. To imagine this developmental process taking place, you might think of a tree growing in a forest. We know that the tree is genetically programmed to grow tall and branch out with needles or leaves, but we also know the particular way in which the tree grows will depend — and must depend — on the particular conditions in which it finds

itself. If the forest floor is dense, the tree will shoot upward, leaving few branches at its stem; if the floor is open, however, the tree will be broad rather than tall. Similarly, if a tree is nestled up against another tree or wall, the tree will develop in a way that reflects these circumstances, taking advantage of the space it is provided. In other words, using this metaphor, we should not be surprised that given its great capacity for learning, the human brain is an adaptive organ that uses developmental experiences to steer its course.

71. See G. M. Edelman (1987). *Neural Darwinism: The Theory of Neuronal Group Selection.* New York: Basic Books. Edelman *Bright Air, Brilliant Fire:* loc.cit.

72. Nash, op.cit.

73. Just such a conclusion was offered in Jane Healy's *Endangered Minds: Why Our Children Don't Think,* in which she describes how if children "are being attracted to different types of stimuli, both [the] structure and function [of their brains] could be altered." J. Healy (1990). *Endangered Minds: Why Our Children Don't Think.* New York: Simon & Schuster; 52.

74. American Psychiatric Association (1994). *DSM IV.* Washington, D.C.: American Psychiatric Association.

75. E. A. Carlson, D. Jacobvitz, and L. A. Sroufe (1995). A Developmental Investigation of Inattentiveness and Hyperactivity, *Child Development,* Vol. 66, 37–54.

76. Ibid.

77. Ibid., p. 37.

78. D. Elkind (1994). *Ties That Stress.* Cambridge: Harvard University Press; 4.

79. J. Shanahan and M. Morgan (1989). Television as a Diagnostic Indicator in Child Therapy: An Exploratory Study. *Child and Adolescent Social Work,* Vol. 6, 175–91; 181.

80. M. Gordon (1991). *ADHD/Hyperactivity: A Consumer's Guide.* DeWitt, N.Y.: DSI Publications; 24.

81. Ibid., 23.

82. See Chapter 12 in L. A. Sroufe (1996). *Emotional Development: The Organization of Emotional Life in the Early Years.* New York: Cambridge University Press.

83. Gordon, op.cit.

84. Carlson, Jabobvitz, and Sroufe, op.cit.

85. Statistics from the Britain's Department of Health, cited in R. Dobson (October 12, 1997). More Children Given "Chemical Cosh". *Independent* (London).

86. For a detailed account of the changes taking place in the United States, see D. Blankenhorn, S. Bayme, and J. Bethke Elshtain (eds.)

(1991). *Rebuilding the Nest: A New Commitment to the American Family*. Milwaukee: Family Services America.

87. This statement is especially applicable when we compare racial and ethnic groups within the same social class. In the late 1960s and 1970s there were even charges that stimulants were being used to suppress the behavior of black children.

88. Hallowell and Ratey, op.cit., 191.

89. T. Achenbach and C. Howell (1989). Are American Children's Problems Getting Worse? A 13-Year Comparison. *Journal of the American Academy of Children and Adolescent Psychiatry*, Vol. 32, 1145–51.

90. P. R. Nader (ed.) (1993). *School Health: Policy and Practice*. Elk Grove Village, Ill.: American Academy of Pediatrics; 140. Cited in Elkind op.cit., 8.

91. D. Goldman (1995). *Emotional Intelligence*. New York: Bantam, 232.

92. S. E. Taylor (1989). *Positive Illusions*. New York: Basic Books; 21, 23.

93. P. A. Russell (1983). Psychological Studies of Exploration in Animals: A Reappraisal. In J. Archer and L. Birke (eds.). *Exploration in Animals and Humans*, 22–54. Cambridge, England: Van Nostrand Reinhold.

94. H. Fowler (1965). *Curiosity and Exploratory Behavior*. New York: Macmillan.

95. W. N. Dember, R. W. Earl, and N. Paradise (1957). Response by Rats to Differential Stimulus Complexity. *Journal of Comparative Physiological Psychology*, Vol. 50, 514–18. For a review of such studies, see Fowler, op.cit.

96. R. A. Butler, (1957). The Effect of Deprivation of Visual Incentives on Visual Exploration Motivation in Monkeys. *Journal of Comparative and Physiological Psychology*, Vol. 50, 177–79. See also J. M. Stahl, R. A. O'Brien, and P. Hanford (1973). Visual Exploratory Behavior in the Pigeon. *Bulletin of the Psychonomic Society*, Vol. 1, 35–36.

97. Russell, op.cit.

98. D. E. Berlyne (1960). *Conflict, Arousal, and Curiosity*. New York: McGraw-Hill.

99. H. Helson. (1964). *Adaptation-Level Theory*. New York: Harper & Row; 369.

100. D. G. Myers (1996). *Social Psychology*, 5th ed. New York: McGraw Hill; 446.

101. P. Brickman, D. Coates, and R. J. Janoff-Bulman (1978). Lottery winners and Accidental Victims: Is Happiness Relative? *Journal of Personality and Social Psychology*, Vol. 36, 917–27.

102. See Edelman *Neural Darwinism*, op.cit.

103. R. Desimone (1996). Neural Mechanisms for Visual Memory and Their Role in Attention. *Proceedings of the National Academy of Sciences*, Vol. 93, 13494–99; 13494.

104. From T. Beardsley (February 1995). Commanding Attention. *Scientific American*; 16.

105. Desimone, op.cit., 13494.

106. ADD critic John Rosemond drew a similar conclusion: "The picture on a television screen changes, or flickers, every three to four seconds. A child watching a 30-minute TV program, therefore, isn't paying attention to any one image for longer than a few seconds. Multiply that by 5,000 hours of watching (one-fourth of the child's waking time!) during the years most crucial to brain development, and it is hardly far-fetched to suppose that the attention span of the child in question will be compromised." Note the similarity to the observations of physician Matthew Dumont, writing in 1976: "I suggest that the hyperactive child is attempting to recapture the dynamic quality of the television screen by rapidly changing his perceptual orientation. I also wonder if it is possible that amphetamines control his behavior by producing a subjective experience comparable to the fleeting worlds of television." J. Rosemond (July 10, 1997). New Suspect in ADD Sits in Our Houses—TV. *Dallas Morning News*, 6c; letter (April 1976) *American Journal of Psychiatry*.

CHAPTER FIVE. GENERATION RX

1. C. Bradley (1937). The Behavior of Children Receiving Benzedrine. *American Journal of Psychiatry*, Vol. 94, 577–85.

2. Prior to the 1960s, when Ritalin use began to grow exponentially, the primary method of treatment for hyperactivity was not drug treatment, but rather psychotherapy.

3. P. Conrad (1976). The Discovery of Hyperkinesis: Notes on the Medicalization of Deviant Behavior. *Social Problems*, Vol. 23, 12–21.

4. It is important to stress that just because a drug has powerful mind-altering effects, it does not mean that the specific nature of these effects are actually built into the drug itself. As noted in Chapter 2, such a coming together of nature and nurture produces an interaction that, although dependent upon the variables themselves, is not at all reducible to them. For example, MacAndrew and Edgerton showed in their classic study of drunken comportment that alcohol has powerful psychological and behavioral effects, but these effects observed historically and cross-culturally cannot be predicted by the consumption of alcohol alone. C. MacAndrews and R. B. Edgerton (1969). *Drunken Comportment: A Social Explanation*. Chicago: Adline Publishing Company; see also R. J. DeGrandpre and E.

White (1996). Drugs: In the Care of the Self. *Common Knowledge*, Vol. 4, 27–48; R. J. DeGrandpre and E. White (1996). Drug Dialectics. *Arena*, Vol. 7, 41–64

5. *Physicians Desk Reference* (1998), 52nd ed.; 848.
6. See L. H. Diller (1997). Does Attention Deficit Disorder Really Exist? (letter). *New York Times*, section 4; 16.
7. Ibid. (March 1996). The Run to Ritalin: Attention Deficit Disorder and Stimulant Treatment in the 1990s. *Hastings Center Report*.
8. D. Johnson (February 22, 1996). Good People Go Bad in Iowa, and a Drug is Being Blamed. *New York Times*, A1.
9. J. Lang (June 9, 1997). Ritalin: Helpful or Harmful? *Rocky Mountain News*; 3A.
10. C. Holde (1989). Street-wise Cocaine Research. *Science*, Vol. 246, 1378–81; 1378.
11. D. G. McNeil, Jr. (June 14, 1992). Why There's No Methadone for Crack. *New York Times*; section 4, 7.
12. C. E. Johanson and C. R. Schuster (1975). A Choice Procedure for Drug Reinforcers: Cocaine and Methylphenidate in the Rhesus Monkey. *Journal of Pharmacology and Experimental Therapeutics*, Vol. 193, 676–88.
13. Ibid., 676.
14. J. Bergman et al. (1989). Effects of Cocaine and Related Drugs in Nonhuman Primates, III, Self-administration by Squirrel Monkeys. *Journal of Pharmacology and Experimental Therapeutics*, Vol. 251, 150–155. While studies with human participants have reported more ambiguous results, these studies are hindered by the fact that they examine oral administration of these drugs, since they are typically abused via the intranasal and intravenous routes.
15. Cited in Lang, op.cit.
16. N. D. Volkow et al. (1995). Is Methylphenidate like Cocaine? *Archives of General Psychiatry*, Vol. 52, 456–62.
17. S. Peele (1985). *The Meaning of Addiction: Compulsive Experience and its Interpretation*. Lexington, Mass.: Lexington Books. See Chapter 5.
18. See, for example, R. Chacón (February 12, 1998). On Campus, Ritalin. Getting Attention as a "Good Buzz." *Boston Globe*; A1, A10. R. Klein and P. Wender (1995). The Role of Methylphenidate in Psychiatry. *Archives of General Psychiatry*, Vol. 52, 429–33; 431.
19. Quoted in C. Tennant (1997). The Ritalin Racket. *Student.Com* (Internet).
20. K. Livingston (March 1997). Ritalin: Miracle Drug or Cop-out? *Public Interest*.
21. See, for example, D. Sneider (March 24, 1997). As Teen Drug Use Climbs, Schools Seek New Answers. *Christian Science Monitor*, 3; and E. Texeira (October 21, 1995). Study Assails School-Based Drug

Programs; Education: Attempts to Discourage Use Are Largely Ineffective, Researchers Say. *Los Angles Times*; B1.

22. C. M. Sennott and F. Latour (March 2, 1997). 14 Youths 'Lucky' to Live after Overdoses. *Boston Globe*; B1, B5.

23. Data were provided in the letter to the editor (August 17, 1997), Drugs Not the Answer for ADD in Children. *Jupiter Courier*; 4A.

24. Quoted in Tennant, op.cit.

25. Lang, op.cit.

26. J. Leland (October 30, 1995). A Risky Rx for Fun. *Newsweek*; 74.

27. Parke Davis and Company (1885). *Coca Erythroxylon and Its Derivatives*. Detroit and New York: Parke Davis and Co. Cited in L. Grinspoon and J. B. Bakalar (1985). *Cocaine: A Drug and Its Social Evolution*. New York: Basic Books.

28. (February 7, 1994). Beyond Prozac. *Newsweek*; 37.

29. *Washington Post*, February 5, 1996.

30. *New Orleans Times-Picayune*, November 17, 1997.

31. *Orange County* (California*) Register*, July 24, 1987.

32. *Nashville Tennessean*, October 12, 1995.

33. *Phoenix Gazette*, March 14, 1995.

34. *Los Angeles Times*, October 19, 1986.

35. *Washington Post*, February 5, 1996

36. *Charleston Post and Courier*, December 11, 1995.

37. *Los Angeles Times*, June 28, 1990.

38. *Allentown Morning Call*, December 18, 1995.

39. *New Orleans Times-Picayune*, March 30, 1995.

40. *Washington Post*, February 5, 1996.

41. *Fort Lauderdale Sun-Sentinel*, April 1, 1995.

42. *Raleigh News and Observer*, March 14, 1996.

43. *St. Louis Post-Dispatch*, March 14, 1996.

44. *Charleston Post and Courier*, March 24, 1996

45. *Charleston Post and Courier*, March 24, 1996.

46. *Salem* (Oregon) *Statesman Journal*, March 31, 1996.

47. *Dallas Morning News*, July 24, 1996.

48. *Milwaukee Journal Sentinel*, January 24, 1997.

49. *Washington Post*, February 5, 1996.

50. *Atlanta Journal and Constitution*, May 11, 1997.

51. *Fort Pierce News*, October 3, 1997.

52. *New Orleans Times-Picayune*, November 17, 1997.

53. *Orange County* (California) *Register*, July 24, 1987.

54. *Allentown Morning Call*, December 18, 1995

55. *Pittsburgh Post-Gazette*, August 3, 1997.

56. P. Kramer (1993). *Listening to Prozac*. New York: Pantheon.

57. Studies such as this are being done now because when Ritalin came

on the market, tests of carcinogenicity were not required.

58. See K. Rodgers (1996). Sorting Out Relevant Data on Rodent Carcinogenicity. *Drug Topics*, Vol. 3, 53.

59. M. Bass (1997). Athletes' Use of Stimulant Debated by Sports Officials. *Rocky Mountain News*, 3A.

60. See R. J. DeGrandpre and E. White (1996). Drugs: In the Care of the Self. *Common Knowledge*, Vol. 4, 27–48.

61. From the collective article The War on Drugs Is Lost (February 12, 1996). *National Review*; 39.

62. R. Wright (August 28, 1995). The Evolution of Despair. *Time*, 50–57.

63. Interview with Terry Gross (September 8, 1997). *Fresh Air*. National Public Radio.

64. Livingston op.cit.

65. E. J. Hallowell and J. J. Ratey (1995). *Driven to Distraction*. New York: Simon & Schuster; 57.

66. J. L. Rapaport et al. (1978). Dextriamphetamine: Cognitive and Behavioral Effects in Normal Prepubescent Boys. *Science*, Vol. 199, 560–63.

67. An exception applies at very high doses, where most psychoactive drugs tend to have depressant effects.

68. See P. B. Dews (1955). Studies on Behavior, I, Differential Sensitivity to Pentobarbital of Pecking Performance in Pigeons Depending on the Schedule of Reward. *Journal of Pharmacology and Experimental Therapeutics*, Vol. 113, 393–401; R. E. Hicks, J. P. Mayo, and C. J. Clayton (1989). Differential Psychopharmacology of Methylphenidate and the Neuropsychology of Childhood Hyperactivity. *International Journal of Neuroscience*, Vol. 45, 7–32; K. Weber (1985). Methylphenidate: Rate-Dependent Drug Effects in Hyperactive Boys. *Psychopharmacology*, Vol. 85, 231–35.

69. *Physicians Desk Reference*; p. 848

70. R. A. Barkley, and C. E. Cunningham (1978). Do Stimulant Drugs Improve the Academic Performance of Hyperkinetic children. *Clinical Pediatrics*, Vol. 17, 85–92.

71. J. M. Swanson et al. (1993). Effect of Stimulant Medication on Children with Attention Deficit Disorder. *Exceptional Children*, Vol. 60, 154–62; here 159.

72. T. Ayllon, D. Layman, and H. J. Kandel (1975). A Behavioral-Educational Alternative to Drug Control of Hyperactive Children. *Journal of Applied Behavior Analysis*, Vol. 8, 137; See also M. D. Rapport, H. A. Murphy, and J. S. Bailey (1982). Ritalin vs. Response Cost in the Control of Hyperactive Children. *Journal of Applied Behavior Analysis*, Vol. 15, 205–16.

73. J. W. McKearney (Autumn 1977). Asking Questions about Behavior. *Perspectives in Biology and Medicine*, 110–20; here 116.
74. Swanson, op.cit., 159.
75. L. Hancock (March 18, 1996). Mother's Little Helper. *Newsweek*; 51–56.
76. From M. Fumento (June 1996). Sick of It All. *Reason*; 20–26, here 21.
77. These long-term consequences were summarized in a *Hastings Center Report* on Ritalin, in which the author writes:

> It is the family members and teachers who more often notice the child performing suboptimally and ask, "Did you take your pill today?" The question expresses an underlying message to the child about the drug's important contribution to performance and behavior, and, ultimately, this message may undermine the child's confidence. This sense of dependency is highlighted when the medication is used "as necessary," in the event-driven dosing, for example, when studying for an exam or attending a weekend family gathering. It is even possible that event-driven dosing may promote or exacerbate the often disorganized ADHD lifestyle by allowing the procrastinating individual to "catch up" at the last minute. The teenager and adult may also be tempted to stretch the normal wake-sleep cycle in order to achieve even greater performance, which could ultimately lead to an abuse pattern. The long-term consequences of self-administered stimulant by teenagers and adults for ADHD have not been studied to determine the likelihood of such a pattern developing. Thus, while achievement made under the influence of stimulants can enhance a sense of competence, self-esteem, and independence, the specter of psychological dependence, altered self-image, and potential abuse remains, especially in a society that paradoxically continues to be somewhat critical of psychotropic drugs while demanding greater performance.

Diller, op.cit.
78. See M. Conway and M. Ross (1984). Getting What You Want by Revising What You Had. *Journal of Personality and Social Psychology*, Vol. 47, 738–48.
79. Ibid., 747; italics added.
80. An early review of the literature is S. Zentall (1975). Optimal Stimulation as Theoretical Basis of Hyperactivity. *American Journal of Orthopsychiatry*, Vol. 45, 549–62.
81. N. Cohen (1970). Physiological Concomitants of Attention in Hyperactive Children. Unpublished Ph.D. dissertation, McGill University. Cited in J. M. Healy (1990). *Endangered Minds: Why Our*

Children Don't Think. New York: Simon & Schuster.

82. R. Schachar, G. Logan, R. Wachsmuth, and D. Chajczyk (1988). *Journal of Abnormal Child Psychology,* Vol. 16, 361–78.

83. J. van der Meere and J. Sergeant (1988). Focused Attention in Pervasively Hyperactive Children. *Journal of Abnormal Child Psychology,* Vol.16, 627–39; 637.

84. R. G. Jacob, K. D. O'Leary, and C. Rosenblad (1978). Formal and Informal Classroom Settings: Effects on Hyperactivity. *Journal of Abnormal Child Psychology,* Vol. 6, 47–59; 47.

85. This study was conducted by M. A. Roberts. Cited in M. Gordon (1991). *ADHD/Hyperactivity: A Consumer's Guide.* DeWitt, NY: GSI Publications.

86. See, for example, E. K. Sleator, and R. K. Ullmann (1981). Can the Physician Diagnose Hyperactivity in the Office? *Pediatrics,* Vol. 67, 13–17.

87. S. Landau, E. P. Lorch, and R. Milich (1992). Visual Attention to the Comprehension of Television in Attention-Deficit Hyperactivity Disordered and Normal Boys. *Child Development,* Vol. 63, 928–37; 928.

88. S. S. Zentall (1980). Behavioral Comparisons of Hyperactive and Normally Active Children in Natural Settings. *Journal of Abnormal Child Psychology,* Vol. 8, 93–109; 107.

89. American Psychiatric Association (1994). *Diagnostic and Statistical Manual of Mental Disorders,* 4th ed. Washington, D.C.: American Psychiatric Association.

90. As noted in Chapter 1, there are other reasons why a child might act out in class, including attention-seeking behaviors that result from emotional problems and problems of self-esteem. The classic signs of sensory addictions are those behaviors, such as fidgeting and restlessness, that will occur independent of any prevailing social reinforcement.

91. Zentall, op.cit.

92. D. V. Gauvin and F. A. Holloway (1991). Cross-Generalization between an Ecologically Relevant Stimulus and Pentyleneterazole-Discriminative Cue.

CHAPTER 6. DELIBERATE LIVING: BECAUSE PATIENCE COMES TO THOSE WHO WAIT.

1. Cited in J. Krakauer (1997). *Into the Wild.* New York: Anchor Books; 168.

2. Cited in K. A. Ericsson and N. Charness (1994). Expert Performance: Its Structure and Acquisition. *American Psychologist,* Vol. 49, 725–47.

3   B. Hart and T. Risley (1995). *Meaningful Differences in the Everyday Experiences of Young American Children.* Baltimore, MD: Paul H. Brookes Pub. Co.; 46.

4.   See R. Plomin and G. E. McClearn (1993). *Nature, Nuture, and Psychology.* Washington, D.C.: American Psychological Association.

5.   (March 9, 1998). Too, Too Much; 33–38, here 33. *Barron's.*

6.   B. McGrane (1998). The Zen Experiment. Article found on the Web at Adbusters: http://adbusters.org/Articles.

7.   N. Oxenhandler (June 16, 1997). Fall from Grace: How Modern Life Has made Waiting a Desperate Act. *The New Yorker;* 65–78.

8.   D. Blankenhorn, S. Bayme, and J. B. Elshtain (1991). *Rebuilding the Nest: A New Commitment to the American Family.* Milwaukee: Family Service America, 35.

9.   L. Shapiro (May 12, 1997). The Myth of Quality Time. *Newsweek;* 62–70.

10.   S. Hays (1996). The Cultural Contradictions of Motherhood. New Haven: Yale University Press.

11.   B. D. Whitehead (1997). *The Divorce Culture.* New York: Alfred A. Knopf.

12.   Ibid., 66–67.

13.   R. T. Krampe and K. Ericsson (1996). Maintaining Excellence: Deliberate Practice and Elite Performance in Young and Older Pianists. *Journal of Experimental Psychology: General,* Vol. 125, 331–59.

14.   Ericsson and Charness, Vol. 49, 725.

15.   Ibid., 738. See also K. A. Ericsson, R. Th. Krampe, and C. Tesch-Römer (1993). The Role of Deliberate Practice in the Acquisition of Expert Performance. *Psychological Review,* Vol. 100, 363–406.

16.   B. Guerin (1992). Behavior Analysis and the Social Construction of Knowledge. *American Psychologist,* Vol. 47, 1423–32; here 1428.

17.   T. Armstrong (1995). *The Myth of the ADD Child.* New York: Dutton; 77.

18.   Details of production costs for *Titanic* came from N. Griffin (December 1997). James Cameron Is The Scariest Man in Hollywood. *Esquire;* 98; and K. Masters (December 8, 1997). Trying to Stay Afloat. *Time;* 86.

19.   Griffin, op.cit., 98.

20.   Interview on the millennium with S. J. Gould (New Year's Eve, 1998). C-SPAN.

21.   P. Gay (1969). *The Enlightenment: An Interpretation.* New York: Norton; 543, 544.

22.   Cited ibid., 544.

23.   P. Goodman (1977). *Liberation,* Vol. 20, 9–14; here 9.

24. D. J. Morrow (September 2, 1997). Attention Disorder is Found in Growing Number of Adults. *New York Times;* D4.

25. C. Willis (July 18, 1994). Life in Overdrive. *Time,* 43–48, here 45.

26. R. M. Yando and J. Kagan (1968). The Effects of Teacher Tempo on the Child. *Child Development,* Vol. 39, 27–34.

27. J. W. McKearney (Autumn 1977). Asking Questions about Behavior. *Perspectives in Biology and Medicine,* 110–120.

28. B. Spock and M. B. Rothenberg (1992). *Dr. Spock's Baby and Child Care,* 6th ed. New York: Pocket Books.

Index